AF593979

COLLINS CHEERFUL COOKING

PARTY FARE

© Wm. Collins Sons & Co. Ltd. 1973
First published 1973
Latest reprint 1977
ISBN 0 00 435273 4

Devised, edited and designed by Youé & Spooner Ltd.

Printed in Great Britain by Collins Clear-Type Press

The Publishers gratefully acknowledge the help given by Allders of Croydon in supplying china and hardware for use in the colour pictures

COLLINS CHEERFUL COOKING

PARTY FARE

JANET WARREN

COLLINS
GLASGOW & LONDON

Useful weights and measures

WEIGHT EQUIVALENTS

Avoirdupois		*Metric*
1 ounce	=	28·35 grammes
1 pound	=	453·6 grammes
2·3 pounds	=	1 kilogram

LIQUID MEASUREMENTS

$\frac{1}{4}$ pint	=	$1\frac{1}{2}$ decilitres
$\frac{1}{2}$ pint	=	$\frac{1}{4}$ litre
scant 1 pint	=	$\frac{1}{2}$ litre
$1\frac{3}{4}$ pints	=	1 litre
1 gallon	=	4·5 litres

HANDY LIQUID MEASURES

1 pint	=	20 fluid ounces	=	32 tablespoons
$\frac{1}{2}$ pint	=	10 fluid ounces	=	16 tablespoons
$\frac{1}{4}$ pint	=	5 fluid ounces	=	8 tablespoons
$\frac{1}{8}$ pint	=	$2\frac{1}{2}$ fluid ounces	=	4 tablespoons
$\frac{1}{16}$ pint	=	$1\frac{1}{4}$ fluid ounces	=	2 tablespoons

HANDY SOLID MEASURES

			Approximate
Almonds, ground	1 oz.	=	$3\frac{3}{4}$ level tablespoons
Arrowroot	1 oz.	=	4 level tablespoons
Breadcrumbs fresh	1 oz.	=	7 level tablespoons
dried	1 oz.	=	$3\frac{1}{4}$ level tablespoons
Butter and Lard	1 oz.	=	2 level tablespoons
Cheese, grated	1 oz.	=	$3\frac{1}{2}$ level tablespoons
Chocolate, grated	1 oz.	=	3 level tablespoons
Cocoa	1 oz.	=	$2\frac{3}{4}$ level tablespoons
Desiccated Coconut	1 oz.	=	$4\frac{1}{2}$ tablespoons
Coffee—Instant	1 oz.	=	4 level tablespoons
Ground	1 oz.	=	4 tablespoons
Cornflour	1 oz.	=	$2\frac{1}{2}$ tablespoons
Custard powder	1 oz.	=	$2\frac{1}{2}$ tablespoons
Curry Powder and Spices	1 oz.	=	5 tablespoons
Flour	1 oz.	=	2 level tablespoons
Gelatine, powdered	1 oz.	=	$2\frac{1}{2}$ tablespoons
Rice, uncooked	1 oz.	=	$1\frac{1}{2}$ tablespoons
Sugar, caster and granulated	1 oz.	=	2 tablespoons
Icing sugar	1 oz.	=	$2\frac{1}{2}$ tablespoons
Syrup	1 oz.	=	1 tablespoon
Yeast, granulated	1 oz.	=	1 level tablespoon

AMERICAN MEASURES

16 fluid ounces	=	1 American pint
8 fluid ounces	=	1 American standard cup
0·50 fluid ounces	=	1 American tablespoon *(slightly smaller than British Standards Institute tablespoon)*
0·16 fluid ounces	=	1 American teaspoon

AUSTRALIAN MEASURES
(Cup, Spoon and Liquid Measures)

These are the measures in everyday use in the Australian family kitchen. The spoon measures listed below are from the ordinary household cutlery set.

CUP MEASURES

(Using the 8-liquid-ounce cup measure)

1 cup flour	4 oz.
1 cup sugar *(crystal or caster)*	8 oz.
1 cup icing sugar *(free from lumps)*	5 oz.
1 cup shortening *(butter, margarine, etc.)*	8 oz.
1 cup honey, golden syrup, treacle	10 oz.
1 cup brown sugar *(lightly packed)*	4 oz.
1 cup brown sugar *(tightly packed)*	5 oz.
1 cup soft breadcrumbs	2 oz.
1 cup dry breadcrumbs *(made from fresh breadcrumbs)*	3 oz.
1 cup packet dry breadcrumbs	4 oz.
1 cup rice *(uncooked)*	6 oz.
1 cup rice *(cooked)*	5 oz.
1 cup mixed fruit or individual fruit such as sultanas, etc.	4 oz.
1 cup grated cheese	4 oz.
1 cup nuts *(chopped)*	4 oz.
1 cup coconut	$2\frac{1}{2}$ oz.

SPOON MEASURES

	Level Tablespoon
1 oz. flour	2
1 oz. sugar *(crystal or caster)*	$1\frac{1}{2}$
1 oz. icing sugar *(free from lumps)*	2
1 oz. shortening	1
1 oz. honey	1
1 oz. gelatine	2
1 oz. cocoa	3
1 oz. cornflour	$2\frac{1}{2}$
1 oz. custard powder	$2\frac{1}{2}$

LIQUID MEASURES

(Using 8-liquid-ounce cup)

1 cup liquid	8 oz
$2\frac{1}{2}$ cups liquid	20 oz. (1 pint)
2 tablespoons liquid	1 oz.
1 gill liquid	5 oz. ($\frac{1}{4}$ pint)

Metric equivalents and oven temperatures are not listed here as they are included in all the recipes throughout the book.

When using the metric measures, in some cases it may be neeessary to cut down the amount of liquid used. This is in order to achieve a balanced recipe and the correct consistency, as 1oz equals, in fact, 28·35gm.

Introduction

Parties should be fun and, in fact usually are, for it is always pleasant to see people enjoying themselves, especially at a party you have organized.

There are many ways of entertaining people and my particular favourite is to hold a dinner party, as this gives me time to enjoy the company of my guests. However, in this book I deal not only with dinner parties, but also children's and teenagers' parties, food for socials, whist drives and harvest suppers; recipes for finger and fork buffets suitable for occasions such as wedding receptions, barbecues, housewarming parties, Chinese parties, curry parties and even ideas for entertaining at Christmas time.

I have had great fun and tremendous pleasure compiling this book, not only from all the parties I have given to test the various recipes, but from talking to people about the types of parties they most enjoy.

The key to all forms of entertaining, however large or small, is organization. If you, as the hostess, feel anxious about something concerned with the party, it is amazing how quickly this feeling transfers to your guests, giving the party a rather dampening effect.

Plan a menu that you feel you can cope with; a simple but successful meal is much more rewarding than an elaborate feast that does not quite live up to expectations. A word of warning here – it is never advisable to try a dish for the first time when guests are coming. Have a run-through prior to the party. Prepare as much of the food as possible in advance to give you more time for last-minute arrangements and do not forget to check on china, cutlery, glasses and so on. If it is a children's party you are planning, paper cups, plates and tablecloths are a very good idea as they do save the washing up, and the pretty designs on the market make a table most attractive.

Finally, all that is left for me to say is happy cooking and have a good party.

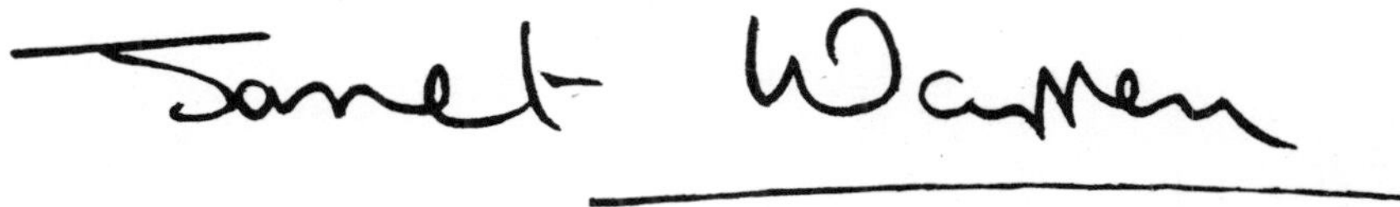

Dinner parties and suppers

Dinner parties at home are becoming more and more popular, so here are some ideas for large and small parties, including an impressive menu for entertaining the boss.

TWO'S COMPANY

MENU

Minted grapefruit

Pork and apple kebabs
Mushroom pilaff
Tomato and chicory salad

Ginger coffee cream

Irish coffee

Suggested wine: ½ bottle Anjou Rosé, a French medium dry wine.

MINTED GRAPEFRUIT
Serves 2

1 grapefruit
2 teaspoons caster sugar
2 peppermint creams
2 sprigs fresh mint

1. Cut the grapefruit in half and remove the membranes between the segments.
2. Sprinkle with the caster sugar.
3. Crush the peppermint creams and divide them between the two grapefruit halves in dishes.
4. Chill for 30 minutes and decorate with a sprig of mint just before serving.

PORK AND APPLE KEBABS
(Illustrated on page 17)
Serves 2

12oz (300gm) pork fillet or 2 pork chops
1 cooking apple
4 streaky bacon rashers
6 bayleaves
1oz (25gm) butter, melted

1. Light the grill.
2. Remove the meat from the bones if using chops then cut the meat into 16 pieces.
3. Peel, core and cut the apple in eight.
4. De-rind the bacon and stretch the rashers with the back of a knife, then cut each one in half.
5. Wrap a piece of bacon around each piece of apple.
6. Thread the pieces on to two kebab skewers in the order of pork, apple, pork, bayleaf, until all pieces are used.
7. Brush the kebabs with butter and grill for 3 minutes on either side then turn the grill down and continue to cook for 20 minutes, turning them again half way through the cooking.
8. Serve with mushroom pilaff.

MUSHROOM PILAFF
(Illustrated on page 17)
Serves 2

1 medium onion
2oz (50gm) mushrooms
1oz (25gm) margarine
4oz (100gm) long-grain rice
½ pint (250ml) stock
salt and pepper

1. Peel and finely slice the onion.
2. Trim the mushrooms, then slice them finely.
3. Melt the margarine, add the onion and cook for 5 minutes until soft but not coloured.
4. Add the rice and fry until opaque.
5. Stir in the mushrooms with the stock.
6. Bring to the boil, reduce the heat, cover and simmer for 20–25 minutes, until the rice is tender.
7. Check for seasoning.

TOMATO AND CHICORY SALAD
Serves 2

1 head chicory
4 tomatoes
French dressing using 4 tablespoons oil (see Basic recipes, page 100)
few chopped chives to garnish

1. Discard any damaged leaves from the chicory then cut the head into thin slices.
2. Plunge the tomatoes into boiling water for 20 seconds, transfer them to cold water and peel off the skins.
3. Slice the tomatoes thinly.
4. Arrange the tomatoes and the chicory in a dish.
5. Sprinkle over the French dressing at the last minute and garnish with chopped chives.

GINGER COFFEE CREAM
Serves 2

1 egg white
scant ¼ pint (approximately 125ml) double cream
1 level dessertspoon coffee powder
1 level dessertspoon caster sugar
1 tablespoon hot water
6 gingernuts
2 pieces preserved ginger, chopped

1. Whip the egg white until stiff.
2. Whisk the double cream until just stiff.
3. Dissolve the coffee and sugar in the water.
4. Crush four of the biscuits.
5. Stir the crushed biscuits and the ginger into the coffee.
6. Add it to the whipped cream with the egg white and mix the ingredients lightly together.
7. Turn into two dishes and leave in a cool place for 30 minutes.
8. Serve each with a gingernut.

IRISH COFFEE
Serves 2

3 tablespoons whiskey
2 dessertspoons brown sugar
freshly-made strong black coffee
double cream

1. Warm two stemmed goblets or medium coffee cups in hot water. Wipe dry.
2. Pour in the whiskey, add the sugar and fill with coffee to within 1 inch of rim.
3. Stir until the sugar dissolves.
4. Pour the cream on top of the coffee, over the back of a teaspoon which has the tip in the coffee.
5. Serve immediately. Sip the coffee through the cream.

To make the other special coffees substitute the whiskey for:
Rum (Jamaican coffee)
Brandy (French coffee)
Vodka (Russian coffee)

THE BOSS COMES TO DINNER

MENU
Serves 4

Liver sausage pâté

Duck in orange sauce
Duchesse potatoes
Orange salad
Garden peas (see page 10)

Chocolate mousse

Almond petits fours
Coffee

Suggested wines: 1 bottle Châteauneuf-du-Pape, a French, full-bodied, red wine or 1 bottle Pouilly Fuissé, a French, dry, white wine.

LIVER SAUSAGE PATE
Serves 4

4oz (100gm) liver sausage
1 packet (3oz or 75gm) cream cheese
2 streaky bacon rashers
1 tablespoon sherry
few drops Worcestershire sauce
1oz (25gm) butter, melted

1. Remove the skin from the liver sausage and put the liver sausage in a basin.
2. Add the cream cheese and beat together until blended.
3. De-rind the bacon and finely chop the rashers.
4. Fry over a high heat until brown and cooked and beat into the liver sausage mixture.
5. Add the sherry and Worcestershire sauce and check the seasoning.
6. Turn into a dish, smooth the surface and pour over the butter.
7. Leave in a cool place for the butter to set.
8. Serve with toast.

DUCK IN ORANGE SAUCE
Serves 4

1 roasting duck (4lb or 2 kilo, trussed weight)
salt and pepper
2 oranges
1oz (25gm) dripping or lard
1 medium onion, peeled and sliced
1 garlic clove, crushed
1 level tablespoon plain flour
1 can condensed consommé soup
1 level tablespoon honey
1 tablespoon red wine
watercress to garnish

1. Preheat oven to moderate to moderately hot, 375 deg F or gas 5 (190 deg C).
2. Season the inside of the duck with salt and pepper. Place in a roasting tin.
3. Roast in the centre of the oven for 30 minutes then reduce the heat to moderate, 350 deg F or gas 4 (180 deg C) for a further 1 hour, or until the duck is tender.
4. Meanwhile make the sauce. Thinly peel the rind from 1 orange, using a potato peeler, and shred it finely.
5. Bring the peel to the boil in a pan of water and drain at once.
6. Melt the fat in a pan, add the onion and fry until tender and golden brown.
7. Add the crushed garlic and fry a few more minutes.
8. Stir in the flour and brown it over a high heat, stirring all the time.
9. Remove the pan from the heat, gradually blend in the soup plus half a can of water, then return the pan to the heat and, stirring all the time, bring to the boil.
10. Add the orange juice from the 2 oranges, the honey, wine and most of the shredded peel.
11. Boil the sauce for 1 minute to combine the flavours; check seasoning.
12. When the duck is cooked, take it out of the tin and cut it into quarters.
13. Place the duck pieces on a serving dish and pour over the sauce. Keep warm.
14. Serve the duck garnished with the remaining pieces of peel and sprigs of watercress.

DUCHESSE POTATOES
Serves 4

1½lb (¾ kilo) potatoes, peeled
1oz (25gm) butter
1 large egg, beaten
salt and pepper
pinch of nutmeg

1. Boil the potatoes in salted water, drain then toss over the heat for 1 minute to dry.
2. Sieve the potatoes then beat in the butter and almost all the beaten egg, reserving a little to glaze.
3. Place the potatoes in a large piping bag with a large star pipe attached.
4. Pipe swirls of the mixture on to greased baking sheets.
5. Leave to cool and set, then brush with the remaining egg.
6. Place in the oven on the shelf above the duck and cook for 15–20 minutes, until tinged golden brown.

To freeze: duchesse potatoes are excellent for freezing. Place the unglazed, piped potatoes, on their baking sheets, in the freezer and, when they are frozen, remove from the sheets to polythene bags. Seal and label.
To serve: there is no need to thaw. Place on greased baking sheets, egg glaze them and cook for slightly longer than normal, or until golden brown.

ORANGE SALAD
Serves 4

5 oranges
French dressing (see Basic recipes, page 100)

1. Finely grate the rind from 1 of the oranges and mix it into the French dressing.
2. Using a very sharp knife cut the peel and pith from the oranges. The easiest way to do this is to cut the top from the orange then to work spirally around the orange cutting just below the pith and above the flesh.
3. Slice the oranges thinly and arrange on a plate.
4. Just before serving pour over the French dressing.

CHOCOLATE MOUSSE
Serves 4

6oz (150gm) plain chocolate
4 tablespoons water
½oz (12gm) butter
1 tablespoon rum
3 large eggs
¼ pint (125ml) double cream
chocolate vermicelli to decorate

1. Break the chocolate into pieces and put them into a pan with the water.
2. Melt over a very low heat.
3. Remove from the heat and beat in the butter and rum.
4. Separate the eggs and beat the yolks into the chocolate.
5. Whisk the cream until it just holds its shape.
6. Whisk the egg whites until they are stiff.
7. Fold half the cream and all the egg whites into the chocolate.
8. Divide the mousse between four dishes and leave in a cool place to set.
9. Decorate with the rest of the cream and the chocolate vermicelli.

ALMOND PETITS FOURS
Makes about 20

4oz (100gm) ground almonds
2oz (50gm) caster sugar
few drops almond essence
1 large egg white
glacé cherries
angelica diamonds

1. Preheat oven to moderate, 350 deg F or gas 4 (180 deg C).
2. Mix the ground almonds with the caster sugar and almond essence.
3. Whisk the egg white until stiff.
4. Using a metal spoon, carefully fold it into the ground almond mixture to make a fairly stiff dough.
5. Spoon the mixture into a large piping bag with a large star pipe (No. 8) attached.
6. Place rice paper on baking sheets, with the shiny side down.
7. Pipe the almond mixture on to the paper in small shapes.
8. Decorate each with a piece of cherry or angelica.
9. Bake in the centre of the oven for 10–15 minutes, or until a light golden brown colour.

AFTER THEATRE SUPPER

So often one goes out for the evening, perhaps to the theatre, and then has some friends back for supper. It is always a problem to know what to serve as time is so short, but there are really three ways of tackling the problem. The first way, which does not appeal to me very much, is to cook when you get home. The other two suggestions, which I think are more feasible, are to serve either a cold main course or a hot casserole. The hot casserole takes a long time to cook, so it can be put in the oven as you leave and will be ready on your return. The last two ideas I have incorporated into the following menu for you to make the choice.

MENU
Serves 4

Tomato cocktail with Peanut finger biscuits

Osso buco or
Veal and ham pie
French bread
Mixed salad (see page 38)

Grape crunch

TOMATO COCKTAIL
Serves 4

1½lb (¾ kilo) tomatoes
¼ pint (125ml) water
1 small onion, peeled and sliced
1 stick celery, chopped
1 small bayleaf
2 sprigs parsley
juice of half a lemon
few drops Worcestershire sauce
pinch of caster sugar
pinch of salt
freshly ground black pepper
4 lemon slices

1. Cut the tomato into pieces and put it into a pan with the water, onion, celery, bayleaf and parsley.
2. Cover and simmer for 30 minutes, until tender.
3. Strain, stir in the lemon juice, Worcestershire sauce, caster sugar and season to taste.
4. Chill the juice well then turn into four glasses and garnish each one with a slice of lemon.
5. Serve with peanut finger biscuits.

PEANUT FINGER BISCUITS
Makes 21

6oz (150gm) plain flour
4oz (100gm) margarine
3oz (75gm) cheese, grated
2oz (50gm) salted peanuts, chopped

1. Preheat oven to moderate to moderately hot, 375 deg F or gas 5 (190 deg C).
2. Sift the flour into a mixing bowl, add the margarine and rub in until the mixture resembles fine breadcrumbs.
3. Stir in the grated cheese and knead the ingredients together to form a dough.
4. On a lightly floured working surface, roll the dough into a rectangle 9 inches by 7 inches.
5. Scatter the nuts over the top and lightly roll them in.
6. Cut the dough into 21 fingers each 3 inches by 1 inch and place on a baking sheet.
7. Bake in the centre of the oven for 15 minutes, or until light brown in colour. Cool on a wire tray.
8. These biscuits store well in an airtight tin, or they can be stored, for up to 1 month, in the freezer.

OSSO BUCO
Serves 4

2oz (50gm) dripping
8oz (200gm) onions, peeled and chopped
$2\frac{1}{2}$lb ($1\frac{1}{4}$ kilo) shin of veal, cut into 5 pieces (ask the butcher to do this)
2oz (50gm) plain flour, seasoned with salt and pepper
2 carrots, peeled and sliced
1 bayleaf
pinch of mixed herbs
1 level dessertspoon tomato purée
$\frac{3}{4}$ pint (375ml) stock
4 tablespoons red wine or cider

1. Preheat oven to very moderate, 325 deg F or gas 3 (170 deg C).
2. Melt the dripping in a frying pan, add the onions and cook until tender and just starting to colour.
3. Coat the pieces of meat in seasoned flour.
4. Add them to the pan and cook quickly until brown all over.
5. Put the onions and meat into a large casserole dish with the carrots, bayleaf and mixed herbs.
6. Stir the rest of the seasoned flour into the fat in the pan then blend in the tomato purée and gradually stir in the stock until the sauce is smooth.
7. Return the pan to the heat and, stirring all the time, bring it to the boil.
8. Boil for a few minutes then stir in the wine or cider.
9. Pour into the casserole dish, cover and cook in the centre of the oven for at least 4 hours, or until the meat literally falls off the bone.

VEAL AND HAM PIE
Serves 4–5

8oz (200gm) gammon rashers
flaky pastry made with 8oz (200gm) flour (see Basic recipes, page 100)
1lb ($\frac{1}{2}$ kilo) pie veal
2 hard-boiled eggs, shelled
1 level tablespoon chopped parsley
pepper
$\frac{1}{4}$ pint (125ml) stock
little beaten egg to glaze

1. Preheat oven to moderate to moderately hot, 400 deg F or gas 6 (200 deg C).
2. Soak the gammon rashers in cold water for 1 hour.
3. Make the pastry and leave it in a cool place to rest.
4. Cut the veal into 1-inch pieces, removing any excess fat.
5. Chop the eggs and add them to the veal with the parsley and pepper (no salt is required).
6. Cut the rind and fat from the bacon, then cut the rashers into small pieces and add to the other ingredients.
7. Turn the filling into a $1\frac{1}{2}$-pint (approximately $\frac{3}{4}$-litre) pie dish and pour over the stock.
8. Roll the pastry into an oval at least $1\frac{1}{2}$ inches bigger all the way round than the pie dish.
9. Cut a 1-inch strip from around the edge of the pastry and stick it to the rim of the dish with a little water.
10. Moisten the rim of pastry and lift the main piece of pastry into position; press the edges firmly together.
11. Trim and knock the edges up with the back of the knife then flute them into large scallops.
12. Mark the top of the pie into diamonds and make a hole in the centre. Brush with beaten egg.
13. Bake in the centre of the oven for 25 minutes, then cover the pie with a piece of brown or greaseproof paper and reduce the heat to moderate, 350 deg F or gas 4 (180 deg C) for a further 1 hour.
14. Leave the pie to cool completely and serve cold.

GRAPE CRUNCH
Serves 4

3oz (75gm) digestive biscuits
8oz (200gm) black or green grapes
$\frac{1}{2}$ pint (250ml) double cream
3oz (75gm) demerara sugar

1. Crush the biscuits and put the crumbs in the bottom of a $1\frac{1}{2}$-pint (approximately $\frac{3}{4}$-litre) pie dish.
2. Wash, halve and pip the grapes and arrange them on top of the biscuit crumbs.
3. Whip the cream until it just holds its shape and spread it over the grapes so they are completely covered.
4. Leave the pudding, preferably overnight, in a cool place.
5. Just before serving, preheat the grill.
6. Sprinkle the sugar on top of the cream so it forms a thick coating.
7. Place the dish under the grill and very quickly caramelize the sugar.
8. As it starts to melt, keep the dish turning so the heat is evenly distributed.
9. Serve immediately – the sugar will be hard and crunchy and the cream underneath warm and melted.

FOUR TO DINNER

MENU

Kipper pâté

Cheesy pork chops
Garden peas
Sunset potatoes

Mocha melody

Suggested wines: 1 bottle Soave Bolla, an Italian, dry and light white wine or 1 bottle Mateus Rosé, a Portuguese, slightly sparkling, medium dry wine.

KIPPER PATE
Serves 4

This pâté is best made in a liquidizer. However, the smallest disc on a mincer can be used as long as the pâté is then beaten smooth with a wooden spoon.

12oz (300gm) kipper fillets
1 level teaspoon anchovy essence
4oz (100gm) butter, melted
1 tablespoon single cream (optional)
½ level teaspoon ground nutmeg
pepper

1. Cook the kippers until tender.
2. Put the fillets into a liquidizer with the anchovy essence, 3oz (75gm) melted butter, the cream, nutmeg and pepper.
3. Blend all the ingredients together until the mixture is smooth. Check the seasoning.
4. Turn the pâté into a small dish, smooth the surface and pour over the rest of the butter.
5. Leave in a cool place for the butter to set.
6. Serve with hot toast.

CHEESY PORK CHOPS
Serves 4

4 pork chops
salt and pepper
2oz (50gm) butter
2 tablespoons milk
1 level dessertspoon made mustard
8oz (200gm) Cheddar cheese, grated
4 tomatoes
watercress to garnish

1. Preheat the grill.
2. Sprinkle the chops with salt and pepper and place them under the preheated grill.
3. Cook them for about 10 minutes on one side until brown.
4. Meanwhile, melt the butter.
5. Remove the pan from the heat and stir in the milk, mustard and cheese.
6. Beat together to form a thick mixture.
7. Turn the chops over and cook for 5 minutes on the other side.
8. Spread the cheese mixture over each chop. Halve and season tomatoes; place on the grill pan.
9. Replace under the grill and continue to cook until the chops are tender and the cheese is golden and bubbling.
10. Serve the chops on a platter with the cooked tomatoes and garnish with watercress.

GARDEN PEAS
Serves 4

1lb (½ kilo) fresh peas
salt
½ level teaspoon caster sugar
little mint

1. Shell the peas and wash them.
2. Put the salt, sugar and mint into a pan of boiling water, add the peas.
3. Cook for 10–15 minutes, or until tender.
4. Drain well, remove the mint and serve immediately.

SUNSET POTATOES
Serves 4

1½lb (¾ kilo) new potatoes
1½oz (37gm) margarine
1 onion, peeled and sliced
1 level tablespoon tomato purée
1 level teaspoon dried herbs
1 pint (approximately ½ litre) chicken stock
salt
1 level teaspoon paprika pepper

1. Scrape the potatoes and cut into fairly thick slices.
2. Melt the margarine in a pan, add the onion and fry lightly for about 3 minutes.
3. Stir in the purée, herbs, stock and salt.
4. Cook over a low heat for a few minutes.
5. Add the sliced potatoes and the paprika pepper.
6. Simmer the potatoes, uncovered, for 20 minutes, until the potatoes are tender and the stock reduced.
7. Check the potatoes again for seasoning before turning them into a dish for serving.

MOCHA MELODY
Serves 4

4oz (100gm) fresh brown breadcrumbs
5oz (125gm) demerara sugar
1½oz (37gm) drinking chocolate powder
2 level tablespoons coffee powder
¼ pint (125ml) single cream
½ pint (250ml) double cream
2oz (50gm) plain chocolate, grated

1. Mix the breadcrumbs with the sugar, drinking chocolate powder and coffee.
2. Lightly whip the creams together and spread one-third over the bottom of a shallow dish.
3. Sprinkle half the dry mixture on top.
4. Spread a little more cream over the crumbs.
5. Then sprinkle on the rest of the dry mixture and spread it level.
6. Cover the surface completely with the rest of the cream.
7. Leave the pudding in a cool place, preferably overnight or for at least 3 hours for the layers to combine.
8. Sprinkle over the grated chocolate and serve.

ENTERTAINING THE COMMITTEE LADIES

A slightly impressive but easy to serve meal, ideal for six ladies.

MENU
Serves 6

Prawn cocktail

Cheddar chicken
Minted potatoes
Ratatouille

Pears in red wine

PRAWN COCKTAIL
Serves 6

1 pint (approximately ½ litre) fresh prawns or 8oz (200gm) canned or frozen prawns
1 lettuce
½ pint (250ml) mayonnaise (see Basic recipes, page 100)
3 level tablespoons tomato ketchup
little Worcestershire sauce
1 dessertspoon sherry (optional)
salt and pepper
6 lemon slices

1. Wash and peel all but six of the prawns.
2. Wash, dry and shred the lettuce.
3. Divide the lettuce between six glasses.
4. Mix the mayonnaise with the tomato ketchup, Worcestershire sauce and sherry, if used. Season if required.
5. Divide the prawns between the glasses.
6. At the last minute, spoon the sauce over the prawns and garnish each glass with a lemon slice and a whole prawn.
7. Serve with thin brown bread and butter.

CHEDDAR CHICKEN
Serves 6

1 roasting chicken (3½lb or 1¾ kilo, trussed weight)
salt and pepper
small sprig rosemary
4oz (100gm) margarine or butter
about ½ pint (250ml) chicken stock
½ pint (250ml) milk
1 small onion, sliced
2 small carrots, sliced
1 bayleaf
3 peppercorns
2oz (50gm) plain flour
5oz (125gm) Cheddar cheese
salt and pepper
watercress to garnish

1. Preheat oven to moderate to moderately hot, 375 deg F or gas 5 (190 deg C).
2. Sprinkle the inside of the chicken with salt and pepper and put in the rosemary.
3. Rub half the margarine or butter over the breast of the chicken.
4. Put the bird into a roasting tin and pour over half the stock.
5. Roast for 1½ hours, or until golden brown and tender.
6. Meanwhile put the milk into a pan with the onion, carrots, bayleaf and peppercorns and, very slowly, bring the milk to the boil.
7. Leave on one side to infuse.
8. Cut the chicken into joints and place on a serving dish and keep warm.
9. Melt the remaining margarine, remove the pan from the heat and stir in the flour.
10. Make the juices from the roasting tin to ½ pint (250ml) with remaining chicken stock.
11. Blend the stock into the pan with the strained milk.
12. When the sauce is smooth return the pan to the heat and, stirring continuously, bring to the boil to thicken.
13. Stir in most of the cheese and check the seasoning.
14. Pour the cheese sauce over the chicken in the dish.
15. Sprinkle over the rest of the cheese and brown under a preheated grill for 7–10 minutes.
16. Garnish with watercress just before serving.

MINTED POTATOES
Serves 6

1½lb (¾ kilo) new potatoes
2oz (50gm) butter
salt and pepper
3 mint sprigs

1. Preheat oven to moderate to moderately hot, 375 deg F or gas 5 (190 deg C).
2. Spread a doubled sheet of greaseproof paper in a roasting tin.
3. Turn the prepared potatoes into it and dot with butter.
4. Sprinkle with salt and pepper and add the mint.
5. Fold the paper around the potatoes, fastening it as a parcel, so they are completely covered.
6. Cook with the chicken for about 1 hour, or until they are soft.
7. To serve, tip the potatoes into a serving dish and garnish with fresh mint.

RATATOUILLE
Serves 6

Ratatouille also makes an ideal first course, served either hot or cold, with French bread.

1 large aubergine
1lb (½ kilo) tomatoes
1 green pepper
1 red pepper
4 tablespoons cooking oil
2 large onions, peeled and sliced
1 garlic clove, crushed
salt and pepper

1. Preheat oven to moderate to moderately hot, 375 deg F or gas 5 (190 deg C).
2. Wipe the aubergine, trim off the ends, then cut into 1-inch cubes.
3. Plunge the tomatoes into boiling water for 20 seconds, then transfer them to cold water and peel off the skins.
4. Cut the tomatoes into quarters.
5. Cut the peppers in half, remove the core and seeds and slice the flesh into strips.
6. Heat the oil in a large frying pan, add the prepared vegetables and cook for about 8 minutes.
7. Transfer to a casserole dish and add plenty of salt and pepper.
8. Cover and cook in the bottom of oven for 1½–2 hours, until tender.
9. Serve piping hot.

PEARS IN RED WINE

Serves 6

5oz (125gm) caster sugar
¼ pint (125ml) red wine
¼ pint (125ml) water
strip lemon peel
small piece cinnamon stick
little grated nutmeg
6 dessert pears
2 level teaspoons arrowroot
¼ pint (125ml) double cream
1oz (25gm) flaked almonds, browned

1. Preheat oven to moderate, 350 deg F or gas 4 (180 deg C).
2. Put the sugar, wine, water, lemon peel, cinnamon and nutmeg into a pan.
3. Over a very low heat, dissolve the sugar then, when every grain has melted, bring to the boil and cook it for 1 minute.
4. Peel the pears, leaving the stalk in but removing the eye.
5. Stand the pears in a small casserole, pour over the syrup and cover the dish.
6. Cook in the centre of the oven for 30–40 minutes, until tender.
7. Remove the pears from the dish and place them in individual dishes.
8. Strain the syrup, check the quantity and reduce to ½ pint (250ml), if necessary, by boiling.
9. Mix the arrowroot to a smooth paste with a little water.
10. Stir it into the syrup and continue to stir until it boils and clears; leave to cool slightly, then pour over the pears.
11. When the pears are cold, pipe a swirl of whipped cream around the stalk end like a cap, and scatter the almonds over the top.

SUMMER SUPPER FOR SIX

MENU

Salad niçoise

Eastern gammon steaks
Cheesy potatoes
Onion and pepper bake

Coffee meringue gâteau

Hazelnut petits fours
Coffee

Suggested wines: Piesporter, a German, dry and light-bodied, white wine or Côtes du Rhône, a French, dry and light-bodied, red wine. Serve either 1 bottle of each or 2 bottles of one of the wines.

SALAD NIÇOISE

(Illustrated on page 17)
Serves 6

1 can (7oz or 175gm) tuna fish
1 large packet frozen sliced beans
1lb (½ kilo) tomatoes
½ cucumber
1 level tablespoon chopped fresh herbs
French dressing (see Basic recipes, page 100)
1 can (2oz or 50gm) anchovy fillets
8 black olives

1. Drain the fish, flake it then place the pieces in the bottom of a shallow dish.
2. Cook the beans as directed on the packet, drain and scatter them over the fish.
3. Plunge the tomatoes into boiling water for 20 seconds. Immediately transfer them to cold water and peel off the skins.
4. Slice the tomatoes and arrange them on top of the beans.
5. Slice the cucumber thinly and arrange the slices, overlapping, on top of the tomatoes.
6. Mix the herbs with the French dressing, then sprinkle the dressing over the cucumber.
7. Lattice the top with the anchovy fillets and place a halved olive in the spaces formed by the lattice.
8. Serve chilled.

EASTERN GAMMON STEAKS

Serves 6

6 gammon rashers
2oz (50gm) margarine
1 large onion, peeled and finely chopped
3 oranges
½ level teaspoon mustard powder
6 tablespoons mincemeat
pepper
watercress to garnish (optional)

1. Preheat oven to moderate to moderately hot, 375 deg F or gas 5 (190 deg C).
2. Remove the rind from the rashers and snip the fat at ½-inch intervals to prevent it curling during cooking.
3. Rub the inside of a large roasting tin with half the margarine and lay the rashers in.
4. Melt the rest of the margarine, add the onion and fry until tender but not brown.
5. Remove the pan from the heat and stir in the grated rind and juice of 2 oranges, the mustard powder, mincemeat and plenty of pepper.
6. Pour this mixture over the rashers then bake them, uncovered, in the centre of the oven for 30–35 minutes, until tender.
7. Arrange on a large dish and use the other orange, sliced, to garnish. If liked, add a garnish of watercress.

CHEESY POTATOES

Serves 6

2lb (1 kilo) potatoes
2oz (50gm) margarine
8oz (200gm) Cheddar cheese, grated
salt and pepper

1. Preheat oven to moderate to moderately hot, 375 deg F or gas 5 (190 deg C).
2. Peel the potatoes and cut into chips.
3. Melt the margarine in a large pan over a low heat.
4. Stir in the cheese with plenty of salt and pepper.
5. Add the potatoes, cover the pan and shake it so the chips are well coated with the cheese mixture.
6. Turn the potatoes into an ovenproof dish and bake in the centre of the oven for about 1¼–1½ hours, until tender.

ONION AND PEPPER BAKE
Serves 6

2 large peppers
1oz (25gm) margarine
1½lb (¾ kilo) onions, peeled and sliced
salt and pepper
1 bayleaf

1. Preheat oven to moderate to moderately hot, 375 deg F or gas 5 (190 deg C).
2. Cut the peppers in half, remove the core and seeds then slice the flesh into ¼-inch strips.
3. Melt the margarine in a flameproof dish, add the peppers and onions and, over a high heat, fry them lightly until all the fat has been absorbed.
4. Season the mixture and put the bayleaf on top.
5. Cover and cook in the bottom of the oven for 1 hour, or until tender.

COFFEE MERINGUE GATEAU
(Illustrated on page 17)
Serves 6

The meringue part of this gâteau may be made several weeks before it is required and stored in an airtight tin. Complete the gâteau only 2 hours before it is to be eaten.

4 large egg whites
2 level tablespoons coffee essence
8oz (200gm) caster sugar
½ pint (250ml) double cream
¼ pint (125ml) single cream
3 bananas
juice of half a lemon
little extra icing sugar
few coffee sugar crystals

1. Preheat oven to cool, 300 deg F or gas 2 (150 deg C).
2. Put the egg whites, coffee essence and sugar into a bowl and place it over a pan of hot water.
3. Whisk for about 10 minutes, or until the mixture is stiff and shiny. (If you use an electric mixer there is no need to place the bowl over hot water.)
4. Remove from the heat and whisk for 2 more minutes.
5. Cover two baking sheets with bakewell paper.
6. Fill a piping bag with the mixture and pipe on to each tray an 8-inch circle.
7. Sprinkle the rounds with caster sugar then bake them for 1½–2 hours, until completely dry. Cool on a wire tray.
8. Whip the creams together until they hold their shape.
9. Place one round of meringue on a serving dish and spread over most of the cream.
10. Peel and slice the bananas, toss in lemon juice and arrange on top of the cream.
11. Place the other round on top.
12. Put the rest of the cream into a piping bag.
13. Sprinkle the surface of the gâteau with icing sugar, then pipe swirls of cream around the edge.
14. Sprinkle coffee sugar crystals on each swirl.

HAZELNUT PETITS FOURS
Makes 12

1oz (25gm) margarine
1oz (25gm) caster sugar
2oz (50gm) shelled hazelnuts, ground
1oz (25gm) plain chocolate
12 whole hazelnuts

1. Preheat oven to moderate, 350 deg F or gas 4 (180 deg C).
2. Cream the margarine and sugar together until soft and fluffy.
3. Mix in the ground hazelnuts.
4. Divide the mixture between 12 petit four tins.
5. Smooth the surface then make a fairly deep depression in the centre of each with the tip of a teaspoon.
6. Bake in the centre of the oven for 10–12 minutes.
7. Leave in the tins until quite cold, then run a knife around the inside edge and ease them out.
8. Melt the chocolate on a plate over a pan of hot water.
9. Run a little melted chocolate into the depression in each petit four.
10. Put the hazelnuts on to a baking sheet and toast them for a few minutes in a moderate oven, then rub the skins off between the folds of a teatowel.
11. Arrange a hazelnut in the centre of each petit four.

FONDUE BOURGUIGNONNE

Serves 6

This is a great way of giving a dinner party, especially if you are a working wife, as there is very little preparation.

Your guests help themselves to raw steak on a fondue skewer and proceed to fry the cubes in hot fat in a fondue pan. While the meat is cooking everyone helps themselves to all the pickles, sauces and accompaniments and then eats them with the steak when cooked to their taste.

Serve the meal with garlic bread and red wine and finish with fresh fruit and plenty of black coffee and cream.

STEAK

Allow 6–8oz (150–200gm) rump steak per person and cut it into 1-inch squares. Cook the meat in half lard and half oil which is best heated on the cooker before being placed on the fondue burner. (The pan should be only half full of fat when ready for use.)

SAUCES

All the sauces which accompany the meat are based on mayonnaise. You will require ¾ pint (375ml) (see Basic recipes, page 100). Divide the mayonnaise between four small dishes.

TOMATO

¼ of the mayonnaise
1 level dessertspoon tomato purée
few drops Worcestershire sauce

1. Mix all the ingredients together and check for seasoning.

HERB

¼ of the mayonnaise
1 level tablespoon chopped fresh herbs or 1 level dessertspoon dried herbs
1 level dessertspoon chopped parsley

1. Mix all the ingredients together and check for seasoning.

CURRY

½oz (12gm) margarine
1 small onion, finely chopped
1 level dessertspoon curry powder
1 level teaspoon apricot jam
¼ of the mayonnaise

1. Melt the margarine and fry the onion until tender.
2. Stir in the curry powder and fry it for 1 minute.
3. Mix the jam into the other ingredients in the pan and remove from the heat to cool.
4. Stir into the mayonnaise when cold.

MUSTARD

¼ of the mayonnaise
1 level dessertspoon made French mustard

1. Mix the ingredients together and check for seasoning.

OTHER ACCOMPANIMENTS

1. Stuffed olives, gherkins and pickled onions.
2. Bananas, sliced and sprinkled with lemon juice to prevent discoloration.
3. Home-made chutney.
4. Sliced tomatoes, dressed with French dressing.
5. A green salad, tossed in French dressing at the last minute.

Arrange all these accompaniments in separate bowls.

GARLIC BREAD

1 French loaf
4oz (100gm) butter
salt and pepper
2 garlic cloves, crushed

1. Preheat oven to moderate, 350 deg F or gas 4 (180 deg C).
2. Slice the bread almost through into 1-inch thick pieces.
3. Beat the butter to a soft cream and beat in the seasoning and garlic.
4. Spread the butter between the slices.
5. Wrap the loaf in foil and place in the centre of the oven for 15 minutes.
6. Cut through the slices and serve in a basket.

AN INFORMAL LUNCHEON PARTY

This menu, for 8–10 people, gives your guests a choice of a hot or cold first course and a hot or cold main course. All the food has been specially planned so it can easily be eaten with just a fork, standing up, if necessary. Serve a choice of red or white wine for the meal. I suggest 2 bottles of Liebfraumilch which is a German medium sweet wine, normally served chilled and 2 bottles of Beaujolais, a dry light-bodied red wine. Serve the red wine at room temperature. It is best to draw the cork an hour before the meal and leave the bottles on the table from where they are to be served.

MENU
Serves 8–10

Italian bake
Curried egg mayonnaise

Minted lamb cutlets
Coq au vin
Crispy potato salad
Carnival salad
Green salad

Summer spectacular
Finger meringues

ITALIAN BAKE
Serves 6–8

2lb (1 kilo) courgettes, sliced
salt
2 tablespoons corn oil
2oz (50gm) margarine
1lb (½ kilo) onions, sliced
1 garlic clove, crushed
6oz (150gm) sliced, cooked ham shoulder
6oz (150gm) Cheddar cheese, grated

1. Preheat oven to moderate to moderately hot, 375 deg F or gas 5 (190 deg C).
2. Place the courgettes on a large plate, sprinkle with salt and leave them on one side.
3. Heat the oil and margarine in a large frying pan, add the onions and fry gently.
4. Stir in the garlic and as soon as the onion starts to colour, turn the mixture into a 2½–3-pint (1¼–1½-litre) ovenproof dish.
5. Drain and dry the courgettes and fry in the pan with a little extra margarine and oil if necessary, until light brown.
6. Chop the ham, add it to the courgettes and fry for a few minutes.
7. Turn the mixture into the dish and mix them together with the onion and garlic.
8. Season, sprinkle the cheese over and bake for 30–40 minutes, on the shelf above the coq au vin, until the cheese has melted and is golden brown.
9. Serve with brown and white rolls.

CURRIED EGG MAYONNAISE
Serves 8

8 hard-boiled eggs
few lettuce leaves
2 level teaspoons curry paste
½ pint (250ml) mayonnaise (see Basic recipes, page 100)
salt and pepper
chopped parsley
paprika pepper

1. Shell the eggs and cut them in half lengthways.
2. Arrange the lettuce leaves on a large serving plate and put the eggs, cut side down, on top.
3. Blend the curry paste with the mayonnaise and check seasoning.
4. Just before the dish is to be served, spoon the curry mayonnaise over the eggs so they are completely coated.
5. Put the chopped parsley and the paprika pepper on to separate plates then, with the blade of a knife, dip it first in water, then into the parsley and place it on to the mayonnaise in a diagonal line so the parsley comes off.
6. Continue to dip the knife into the parsley and on to the curried egg mayonnaise so it makes a pattern of diagonal lines, each 2 inches apart.
7. Repeat this process with the paprika pepper putting the diagonal lines in between the ones of parsley.
8. Serve immediately.

MINTED LAMB CUTLETS
(Illustrated on page 17)
Serves 8–10

8–10 small lamb cutlets
salt and pepper
3 tablespoons corn oil
1 medium onion, peeled and diced
bunch of mint leaves
1 level teaspoon caster sugar
¾ pint (approximately ½ litre) aspic jelly (see Basic recipes, page 100)
3 tablespoons malt vinegar
watercress to garnish

1. Using a sharp knife trim any excess fat from the cutlets then trim the meat from the last ½ inch of the bone. Season.
2. Heat the oil in a frying pan, add the onion and the cutlets, six at a time, and fry on both sides for about 5 minutes.
3. Leave them to cool.
4. Chop the mint with the sugar and stir it into the aspic jelly with the vinegar. Check seasoning.
5. Leave on one side to cool, though not set.
6. Arrange the cutlets down either side of a serving dish with the bones pointing out.
7. Spoon a little aspic jelly over each so they are coated. Leave the rest to set, then chop it roughly with a wet knife.
8. Heap the aspic down the centre of the lines of chops and place watercress sprigs at either end.
9. Place a cutlet frill on the end of each cutlet.

COQ AU VIN
Serves 8–10

2 roasting chickens (3lb or 1½ kilo, trussed weight)
3oz (75gm) margarine
1 tablespoon cooking oil
4oz (100gm) gammon rashers
8oz (200gm) button onions
1 garlic clove, crushed
8oz (200gm) button mushrooms, trimmed
3 level dessertspoons plain flour
¾ pint (375ml) stock (see method)
4 tablespoons red wine
salt and pepper
bouquet garni

1. Preheat oven to very moderate, 325 deg F or gas 3 (170 deg C).
2. Cut the chickens into joints – a sharp knife and a pair of scissors are the tools required.
3. Cut off the legs, cutting through the thigh bones on each side of the bird.
4. Cut off the wings next, taking with each a little of the breast.
5. Cut the breast from the back bone by cutting through the ribs.
6. Remove all the skin and meat from the bones then cut the meat into convenient sized pieces. (The chicken bones, skin and giblets can all be boiled together for stock.)
7. Melt half the margarine and oil in a large frying pan and, adding the meat in batches, fry until golden brown. Transfer to a large casserole.
8. Cut the rind from the gammon rashers and cut them into ½-inch strips. Peel the onions.
9. Melt the rest of the margarine and oil and fry the gammon, garlic and onions quickly until starting to brown, then add the mushrooms and fry for a few more minutes.
10. Stir the flour into the fat in the pan.
11. Remove from the heat, then blend in the stock and wine and return the pan to the heat.
12. Stirring all the time, bring the sauce to the boil. Season then pour it into the casserole over the chicken.
13. Add the bouquet garni and cook in the centre of the oven for 1½–2 hours, or until the meat is tender.
14. Adjust the seasoning if necessary and remove the bouquet garni just before serving.

CRISPY POTATO SALAD
Serves 8–10

3lb (1½ kilo) new potatoes
French dressing made with 6 tablespoons olive oil (see Basic recipes, page 100)
3 tablespoons cooking oil
2 onions, peeled and cut into rings
little milk
1oz (25gm) plain flour
1 level dessertspoon chopped fresh thyme

1. Scrub the potatoes well but do not remove the skins.
2. Put into a large pan of boiling, salted water and cook for 20–25 minutes, until tender.
3. Drain well and, while they are still hot, cut into fairly large pieces.
4. Put into a bowl, pour over the French dressing and turn the potatoes for a few minutes to make sure they are well coated and the dressing is absorbed.
5. Leave the bowl on one side for the potatoes to cool.
6. Meanwhile, heat the oil in a frying pan.
7. Coat the onion rings with milk, sprinkle in flour then fry in the fat until golden and crispy.
8. Serve the salad in a large bowl with the onions and thyme sprinkled on top.

CARNIVAL SALAD
Serves 6

2 small green peppers
½ head celery
1lb (½ kilo) red-skinned apples
¼ pint mayonnaise (see Basic recipes, page 100)

1. Cut the peppers in half, remove the seeds and core them. Cut the flesh into thin strips.
2. Put the strips into a pan of water, bring the water to the boil, then drain the peppers and plunge them into cold water.
3. Scrub the celery, remove the ends and any leaves and cut the sticks into ½-inch chunks.
4. Quarter and core the apples and cut into thin slices.
5. Mix the peppers, celery and apples together, then dress immediately with the mayonnaise so the apples do not turn brown.
6. Turn into a bowl for serving.

GREEN SALAD
Serves 8–10

A green salad is basically shredded lettuce but any other green salad vegetable can be added such as cucumber, watercress, green pepper, etc.

1 lettuce
½ cucumber
1 bunch watercress
French dressing using 4 tablespoons olive oil (see Basic recipes, page 100)

1. Wash and dry the lettuce and tear it into convenient-sized pieces.
2. Wipe the cucumber and slice it thinly.
3. Wash the watercress, discarding any damaged leaves.
4. Put the French dressing into the serving bowl, add the green salad vegetables at the last minute and toss them so they are well coated.

SUMMER SPECTACULAR
Serves 8–10

This is a very attractive sweet, suitable for a party. It consists of a crème brûlée in the centre of a large round dish around which is arranged a selection of fresh summer fruits such as raspberries, strawberries, sliced peaches, sliced bananas, sliced oranges etc. Do not forget to toss the bananas in lemon juice before serving so they do not discolour. The pudding is also served with finger meringues.

½ pint (250ml) double cream
½ pint (250ml) single cream
4 large egg yolks (keep the whites for the finger meringues)
3 level tablespoons caster sugar
1 drop vanilla essence
2oz (50gm) caster sugar

1. Preheat oven to moderate, 350 deg F or gas 4 (180 deg C).
2. Put the single and double cream into a pan and bring slowly to boiling point.
3. Meanwhile beat the egg yolks and 3 tablespoons sugar together until smooth and light.
4. Beat the cream slowly into the egg yolks and sugar. Add the vanilla essence.
5. Strain the liquid into a 1½-pint (approximately ¾-litre) shallow ovenproof dish.
6. Stand it in a roasting pan and pour hot water around to a depth of 1 inch.
7. Cover the top loosely with a piece of greaseproof paper and cook the custard in the centre of the oven for 40–45 minutes, or until the cream custard is lightly set. Leave to cool, overnight if liked.
8. To finish the pudding, when it is quite cold, sprinkle the top thickly with caster sugar.
9. Place the dish under a preheated grill for a few seconds so that the sugar melts and caramelizes.
10. Place the crème brûlée in the centre and surround with fresh fruit.

FINGER MERINGUES
Makes 16–20

4 egg whites
8oz (200gm) caster sugar
1 level tablespoon cocoa powder
chocolate spread

1. Preheat oven to very cool, 225 deg F or gas ¼ (110 deg C).
2. Oil two baking sheets and dust with flour.
3. Whisk the egg whites in a bowl until really stiff.
4. Add 4 level tablespoons of the sugar then rewhisk the whites until they return to their original stiffness.
5. Fold in the rest of the sugar with a metal spoon and place half of the meringue into a large piping bag with a pipe (No. 8) attached.
6. Pipe 16–20, 4-inch length meringues on to a baking sheet.
7. Fold the sifted cocoa powder into the rest of the meringue, refill the bag and pipe out as for white meringues.
8. Cook the meringues in the centre and lower part of the oven for 3 hours, or until they lift straight off the trays.
9. Leave to cool, then store in an airtight tin until required.
10. Sandwich together with chocolate spread and arrange in a pretty basket for serving.

DINNER FOR TWELVE

MENU

Potato and leek soup or
Sunshine cocktail

Chicken royale
Savoury potatoes
Vichy carrots
Garden peas (see page 10)

Suggested wines: Chablis, a French, dry and light-bodied, white wine or Volnay, a French, dry and full-bodied, red wine. Two bottles of each will be sufficient for the meal.

POTATO AND LEEK SOUP
(Illustrated on page 18)
Serves 12

3lb (1½ kilo) leeks
4oz (100gm) butter
1lb (½ kilo) potatoes, peeled and chopped
2 medium onions, peeled and chopped
3 pints (approximately 1½ litres) chicken stock
1 pint (approximately ½ litre) milk
salt and pepper
¼ pint (125ml) single cream
chopped chives to garnish

1. Trim the leeks removing the root and outer leaves, then slit them to the root and wash under running water. Chop into small pieces.
2. Melt the butter and cook the leeks over a low heat for 10–15 minutes, stirring occasionally.
3. Add the potatoes and onions and cook for a few minutes.
4. Add the stock, cover and simmer for about 30 minutes, until the vegetables are tender.
5. Sieve the soup (or blend in a liquidizer) then return it to the pan, add the milk and check the seasoning.
6. Bring to the boil and if liked, sieve it again to give a really smooth texture.
7. Serve with a swirl of cream in the centre and garnished with a few chopped chives.

Pork and apple kebabs with mushroom pilaff (see page 6)

Salad niçoise (see page 12)

Coffee meringue gâteau (see page 13)

Minted lamb cutlets (see page 15)

Macaroni cheese (see page 20)

Potato and leek soup (see page 16)

Sunrise sausages and croissants (see pages 23 and 24)

Surprise savoury loaf (see page 28)

SUNSHINE COCKTAIL
Serves 8–10

1lb (½ kilo) tomatoes
1 green-skinned melon
3 bananas
2 tablespoons orange juice
1oz (25gm) caster sugar
mint sprigs

1. Plunge the tomatoes in boiling water for 20 seconds, then transfer them to cold water and peel off the skins.
2. Cut the tomatoes into eighths and put them into a bowl.
3. Cut the melon in half then remove the seeds.
4. Using a melon baller or teaspoon, cut the fruit from the skin in balls and place them in the bowl with the tomatoes.
5. Peel and slice the bananas and sprinkle with orange juice.
6. Mix all the ingredients together.
7. Put a little cold water on to a plate so it is about a ¼ inch deep.
8. Put the sugar on to another plate.
9. Take the glasses in which the cocktail is to be served and dip the rim first in the water and then in the sugar so the rim of each glass is frosted.
10. Divide the sunshine cocktail between the glasses and before serving decorate each with a sprig of mint.

CHICKEN ROYALE
Serves 12

12 chicken joints
2 cans condensed mushroom soup
1 level tablespoon curry powder
1 can (6½oz or 162gm) pimentos
2oz (50gm) flaked almonds, browned

1. Preheat oven to moderate, 350 deg F or gas 4 (180 deg C).
2. Cut the chicken joints into smaller pieces, if necessary, and place them in a large casserole dish.
3. Mix the undiluted soup with the curry powder.
4. Drain and chop the pimentos then stir them into the soup.
5. Pour this over the chicken and put the lid on the casserole.
6. Cook in the centre of the oven for 1½–2 hours.
7. Just before serving, sprinkle over the nuts.

SAVOURY POTATOES
Serves 12

2oz (50gm) butter
4lb (2 kilo) potatoes, peeled and sliced
1lb (½ kilo) onions, peeled and sliced
salt and pepper
½ pint (250ml) milk
½ pint (250ml) chicken stock

1. Preheat oven to moderate, 350 deg F or gas 4 (180 deg C).
2. Grease a large ovenproof dish with some of the butter.
3. Layer the potatoes and onions into the dish, adding plenty of seasoning between each layer.
4. Pour over the milk and stock.
5. Dot the surface with the rest of the butter.
6. Cover the dish and bake above the chicken royale for 2 hours, removing the cover for the last 15 minutes.

VICHY CARROTS
Serves 12

3lb (1½ kilo) young carrots
¾ pint (375ml) water
3oz (75gm) butter or margarine
1 level teaspoon demerara sugar
salt and pepper
1 level tablespoon chopped parsley

1. Scrub the carrots and cut into rings (there is no need to peel them).
2. Put into a pan with the water, butter or margarine, sugar, salt and pepper.
3. Cover with a piece of greased greaseproof paper.
4. Put the lid on the pan and cook the carrots gently until tender – about 10 minutes. When cooked, all the liquid should have been absorbed and only the butter left.
5. Increase the heat to brown the carrots.
6. Stir in the parsley and turn into a dish for serving.

BRANDIED PEACHES
Serves 12

2 cans (1lb 13oz or 725gm) sliced peaches
6 whole cloves
2-inch cinnamon stick
few drops vanilla essence
rind and juice of 2 oranges
3 tablespoons brandy

1. Put the peaches and their juice into a pan.
2. Add the cloves, cinnamon and vanilla essence.
3. Using a potato peeler, remove the peel from the oranges being careful not to take any white pith.
4. Cut the peel into thin strips and add it to the pan with the juice from the oranges.
5. Bring to the boil then reduce the heat, cover and simmer the peaches for 20–25 minutes, until the flavours are well combined.
6. Remove the pan from the heat, stir in the brandy, then leave in a cool place.
7. Spoon into a serving dish and serve chilled, with single cream.

PINEAPPLE CHEESECAKE
Serves 12

9oz (225gm) digestive biscuits
4oz (100gm) butter
6oz (150gm) caster sugar
1lb (½ kilo) cottage cheese
few drops vanilla essence
½oz (12gm) powdered gelatine
1 can (15oz or 375gm) pineapple rings
½ pint (250ml) double cream
4 egg whites
7 glacé cherries

1. Brush a 9½-inch (24-cm) spring form tin (or loose-bottomed tin) with oil and line the base with a circle of greaseproof paper.
2. Crush the biscuits with a rolling pin.
3. Melt the butter in a pan over a low heat then stir in the crumbs and 2oz (50gm) sugar off the heat.
4. Turn half this mixture into the tin and flatten it with the back of a wooden spoon.
5. Sieve the cottage cheese, add the remaining sugar and beat in the vanilla essence.
6. Dissolve the gelatine in 3 tablespoons of pineapple juice and stir it into the cheese mixture.
7. Whip the cream until it holds its shape.
8. Whisk the egg whites until stiff.
9. Using a metal spoon fold the egg whites and the cream lightly into the cheese mixture.
10. Turn it into the tin and level the top.
11. Sprinkle over the rest of the crumb mixture and leave in a cool place overnight.
12. Turn on to a serving dish and arrange the drained slices of pineapple around the top of the cheesecake and place a glacé cherry in the centre of each.
13. Serve with single cream.

HARVEST SUPPER

Simple food is what is required for a harvest supper, as the village hall kitchens are so often very sparsely equipped. Macaroni cheese is my choice for the main course as it is so easy to make. It can, in fact, be prepared the day before and left ready to reheat in a large roasting pan or dish. You will require two macaroni cheeses for a Harvest Supper for 25 people, followed by two hedgerow tarts and a honey cake – your meal is complete. I have also included a recipe for ginger beer which would be ideal to serve during the meal and, for interest, a bread platter signifying the loaves and fishes parable.

MENU
Serves 25

Macaroni cheese
Hedgerow tart
Honey cake
Ginger beer
Loaves and fishes

MACARONI CHEESE
(Illustrated on page 18)
Serves 12–13

2oz (50gm) margarine
1lb (½ kilo) onions, peeled and sliced
1 can (14oz or 350gm) tomatoes
6oz (150gm) short-cut macaroni

Sauce:
3oz (75gm) margarine
3oz (75gm) plain flour
1½ pints (approximately ¾ litre) milk
½ pint (250ml) macaroni liquid (see method)
12oz (300gm) Cheddar cheese, grated
2 level teaspoons made English mustard
salt and cayenne pepper

Topping:
4oz (100gm) Cheddar cheese, grated
4oz (100gm) fresh white breadcrumbs
8oz (200gm) tomatoes, sliced
8oz (200gm) streaky bacon rashers, de-rinded
½oz (12gm) margarine, melted

1. Preheat oven to moderate to moderately hot, 375 deg F or gas 5 (190 deg C) (if the macaroni cheese is to be cooked the same day).
2. Melt the margarine in a large pan, add the onions and cook gently until tender then stir in the tomatoes and turn the mixture

into a roasting tin or large ovenproof dish.
3. Cook the macaroni in boiling, salted water for about 15 minutes, or until a piece feels tender.
4. Drain it, reserving ½ pint (250ml) liquid for the sauce.
5. Melt the margarine for the sauce in a large pan, remove the pan from the heat and stir in the flour.
6. Gradually blend in the cold milk then stir in the macaroni liquid.
7. Return the pan to the heat and stirring all the time, bring to the boil.
8. Simmer for a few minutes to thicken.
9. Take the pan off the heat and stir in the grated cheese, with the mustard, salt and cayenne pepper to season.
10. Stir in the macaroni then turn it into the dish on top of the tomato and onion mixture.
11. Mix the grated cheese and breadcrumbs together for the top and sprinkle them thickly over the macaroni mixture.
12. Arrange the tomato slices and bacon rashers on the surface of the macaroni cheese and brush the tomato slices with the melted margarine.
13. At this stage it can be left in a cool place overnight.
14. Cook in the centre of the oven for 40–45 minutes until the surface is golden brown and bubbling.
15. Serve with hot crusty bread and butter and a salad, if liked.

HEDGEROW TART

Serves 12–13

9oz (225gm) plain flour
6oz (150gm) caster sugar
2oz (50gm) lard, softened
2oz (50gm) margarine, softened
2 egg yolks
1 tablespoon cold water
1 drop vanilla essence
2 large eggs
¼ pint (125ml) plus 4 tablespoons milk
1lb (½ kilo) cooking apples
2oz (50gm) butter
8oz (200gm) blackberries
2oz (50gm) granulated sugar

1. Preheat oven to moderate, 350 deg F or gas 4 (180 deg C).
2. Sift 8oz (200gm) flour on to a clean working surface and form it into a ring.
3. Put 4oz (100gm) of the sugar, lard, margarine, egg yolks, water and vanilla essence into the centre and squeeze them together with the tips of the fingers until they are evenly mixed.
4. Then, holding a palette knife in the other hand, flick the flour into the ingredients in the centre and knead well in to form a dough.
5. Wrap the pastry in greaseproof paper and leave in a cool place to rest for 15 minutes.
6. Roll out the pastry to line an 11-inch (28-cm) flan ring placed on a baking sheet (or use a deep pie plate).
7. For the filling, beat the remaining flour with the remaining caster sugar and the eggs, then gradually beat in the milk and keep this mixture on one side.
8. Peel, core and thickly slice the apples.
9. Melt the butter in a frying pan, add the apples and blackberries and simmer for a few minutes, shaking the pan occasionally.
10. When the colour from the blackberries starts to flow into the apples, sprinkle the granulated sugar over and turn mixture into the prepared flan case.
11. Pour in the egg mixture, then bake the tart in the centre of the oven for 45 minutes.
12. Serve hot or cold.

HONEY CAKE

Gives 50–60 slices

6oz (150gm) clear honey
4oz (100gm) granulated sugar
4oz (100gm) margarine
8oz (200gm) plain flour
1 level teaspoon ground ginger
1 level teaspoon bicarbonate of soda
2oz (50gm) ground almonds
2oz (50gm) crystallized ginger, chopped
1 large egg
4oz (100gm) icing sugar, sifted

1. Preheat oven to moderate to moderately hot, 400 deg F or gas 6 (200 deg C).
2. Brush a small roasting tin (10 inches, 25cm, by 8 inches, 20cm), with melted fat and line the base with a piece of greaseproof paper. Grease the lining.
3. Melt the honey, sugar and margarine in a pan over a low heat.
4. Sift the flour with the ground ginger and bicarbonate of soda into a mixing bowl.
5. Stir in the ground almonds and half the chopped ginger.
6. Beat the egg, make a hollow in the centre of the dry ingredients, add the egg and melted ingredients.
7. Stir the ingredients lightly but thoroughly together and turn it into the prepared tin.
8. Bake the cake in the centre of the oven for 20 minutes, then reduce heat to moderate, 350 deg F or gas 4 (180 deg C) for a further 45–50 minutes, or until the cake is cooked.
9. Turn on to a wire tray to cool and remove the paper.
10. When the cake is cold, sift the icing sugar into a mixing bowl and mix in a little cold water to make a coating consistency.
11. Pour the icing on top of the cake and allow the icing to trickle down the sides a little.
12. Scatter the remaining chopped ginger on top of the cake and cut into slices to serve.

To freeze: this cake is excellent for freezing. Place in a polythene bag, seal and label. Defrost and ice when required for serving.

GINGER BEER
Gives about 12 glasses

1 level dessertspoon caster sugar
1 pint (approximately ½ litre) warm water
½oz (12gm) dried yeast
1 level dessertspoon ground ginger

1. Melt the sugar in one-third of the water.
2. Whisk in the yeast and leave the liquid in a warm place for 10–15 minutes for the yeast to dissolve.
3. Add the rest of the water and the ground ginger and put the mixture into a jar.
4. Cover the jar loosely.
5. Each day for a week add 1 level dessertspoon ground ginger and 1 level dessertspoon caster sugar.
6. Stir into the mixture then re-cover the jar loosely.
7. To make the ginger beer, dissolve 12oz (300gm) granulated sugar in 1 pint (approximately ½ litre) boiling water. Add the juice of 2 small lemons, 2½ pints (approximately 1¼ litres) cold water and the liquid from the top of the mixture in the jar.
8. Put the ginger beer into bottles, cork them loosely and keep for a week before using.
9. The ginger beer will keep in a cool place for 3 weeks.

LOAVES AND FISHES

3lb (1½ kilo) strong plain flour
3 level teaspoons salt
1½ pints (approximately ¾ litre) warm water
½oz (12gm) dried yeast
1 level teaspoon caster sugar
2 currants
beaten egg to glaze
pinch of salt

1. Preheat oven to hot, 425 deg F or gas 7 (220 deg C).
2. Sift the flour and salt into a large mixing bowl.
3. Pour ½ pint (250ml) of the warm water on to the yeast and sugar and leave it to dissolve – about 10–15 minutes.
4. Pour the yeast liquid into the flour and, with your hand, beat it into a dough.
5. Turn the dough on to a floured working surface and knead it for about 5 minutes until it is smooth.
6. Put the dough into a large greased bowl; cover and leave in a warm place for about 1½ hours or until it doubles in bulk.
7. Knock the dough back gently to its original size then weigh off 2lb (1 kilo) for the platter.
8. Roll it into an oval approximately 12 inches by 10 inches and prick it all over with a fork.
9. Lift this on to a large greased baking sheet (use two placed together if one is not big enough).
10. From the remaining dough cut off a 5-oz (125-gm) piece for two fishes and a 1¼-lb (⅝-kilo) piece for five loaves.
11. Cut the remaining dough in half, then each half in half again and twist the pieces together for the border. Stick them round the edge of the platter with a little water, joining the ends together.
12. Cut the small piece of dough for the fishes in half and roll each into an oval, tapering slightly at one end.
13. Make a slit in the widest end for the mouth and one in the other end for the fork tail.
14. Make the fins by snipping the top of each fish like a fringe, mark the back with scales and place a currant on each for an eye.
15. Divide the remaining dough for the loaves into five equal parts.
16. Roll each into a sausage shape and make three diagonal slits across the top.
17. Position the fishes and the loaves on to the platter and stick them in position with water.
18. Beat the egg with the salt and glaze the whole platter.
19. Bake in the centre of the oven for 45–50 minutes, or until golden brown.

To freeze: place in a polythene bag, seal, label and freeze for about 1 month.

Parties for fun

The recipes in this chapter are not for any special celebration. They are just for those parties arranged for the sheer enjoyment of entertaining.

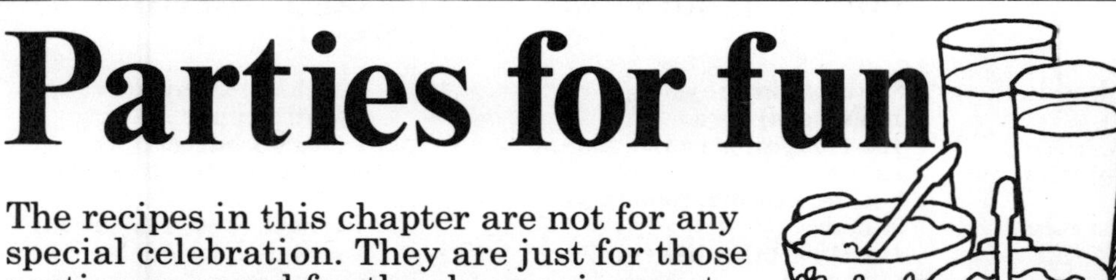

BRUNCH PARTY

Neither breakfast nor lunch, a brunch party is normally served around midday. It is ideal after an energetic morning playing tennis, swimming or riding. The party is for 12 people.

MENU
Serves 12

Fresh orange juice
Muesli

Sunrise sausages
Kedgeree
Kidney ragout
Baked tomatoes

Croissants
Brown rolls
Toast and marmalade
Coffee or tea

FRESH ORANGE JUICE
Serves 12

6 oranges
3 lemons
2¼ pints (approximately 1¼ litres) water
sugar to taste

1. Wash the oranges and lemons.
2. Chop roughly and put into the goblet of a liquidizer.
3. Add the water then switch the motor on for about 10 seconds.
4. The fruit should then still be in pieces but all the flesh should have been stripped. The juice will taste of pith if the machine is running too long.
5. Strain the juice through a sieve into a jug and stir in sufficient sugar to taste.
6. Add a few ice cubes just before serving.

MUESLI
Serves 10–12

Although muesli can be bought ready-made, it is far less expensive to make it yourself, especially when catering for a large party. It can be stored in a polythene or airtight container. Serve it with apples and bananas, milk and yogurt.

1lb (½ kilo) porridge oats
6oz (150gm) wholewheat flakes
12oz (300gm) seedless raisins
2oz (100gm) soft light brown sugar
3 level tablespoons dried milk powder
1 level tablespoon extract of malt
pinch of salt
2oz (50gm) flaked almonds
2oz (50gm) walnuts, chopped
4oz (100gm) hazelnuts

1. Put the porridge oats, wheat flakes, seedless raisins, sugar, dried milk, malt extract and salt into a large bowl.
2. Mix them together thoroughly.
3. Chop the almonds roughly and add them with the walnuts to the other ingredients.
4. Brown the hazelnuts under a preheated grill to loosen the skins then rub the skins off completely, between a teatowel.
5. Chop the hazelnuts and stir them into the bowl.
6. Serve the muesli in one large bowl from which your guests can help themselves.

SUNRISE SAUSAGES
(Illustrated on page 18)
Makes 8

8 slices white bread
1oz (25gm) lard or dripping
2lb (1 kilo) pork sausages
1oz (25gm) butter or margarine
4 tablespoons milk
6 large eggs
salt and pepper
2 tomatoes
watercress to garnish

1. Preheat oven to moderate to moderately hot, 375 deg F or gas 5 (190 deg C).
2. Cut the largest circle possible from each slice of bread.
3. Spread the lard or dripping over the slices then place them, fat side down, in a roasting tin.
4. Cut the sausages into pairs.
5. Along one side only of each pair make slits in the skin about 1 inch apart and a ½ inch deep.
6. Curve the sausages into a circle with the slits on the outer side and place each ring on to a circle of bread.
7. Bake the sausage circles in the centre of the oven for 40–45 minutes, until they are golden brown.
8. Meanwhile, melt the butter or margarine and add the milk.
9. Beat the eggs together, add them to the pan with the salt and pepper.
10. Scramble the eggs over a low heat.
11. When the sausage circles are cooked, transfer them to a serving dish.
12. Divide the scrambled egg between the sausages, placing it in the hole in the centre.
13. Top the egg with a slice of tomato and garnish with watercress sprigs.

KEDGEREE
Serves 6–8

12oz (300gm) smoked haddock
4 tablespoons milk
4 tablespoons water
2oz (50gm) butter or margarine
salt and pepper
6oz (150gm) long-grain rice
3 hard-boiled eggs
2 level tablespoons chopped parsley
parsley sprigs

1. Put the haddock in a shallow pan, pour over the milk and water and add the butter or margarine and pepper.
2. Cover the pan with a lid or foil and simmer the fish for 10–15 minutes over a low heat until tender.
3. Cook the rice in boiling, salted water for 12–15 minutes; drain and run hot water through the grains to separate them.
4. Remove the cooked fish from the pan, reserving the liquor for later. Remove the skin and bones, then flake the flesh into pieces.
5. Mix the rice with the fish and fish liquor.
6. Shell and chop all but 1 egg.
7. Stir the chopped eggs into the kedgeree with the parsley.
8. Check the mixture for seasoning then turn it into a serving dish and garnish with the other hard-boiled egg, shelled and sliced, and a few parsley sprigs.

KIDNEY RAGOUT
Serves 6–8

8 lambs' kidneys
1oz (25gm) lard
4oz (100gm) streaky bacon rashers
2 large onions, peeled and sliced
4oz (100gm) mushrooms, trimmed
1 level tablespoon plain flour
1 can (14oz or 350gm) tomatoes
¼ pint (125ml) stock
salt and pepper
toast

1. Remove the skin from the kidneys. Cut each one in half and, using a sharp knife, remove the cores then cut each half in half again.
2. Melt the lard in a frying pan.
3. Cut the rind and any small bones from the bacon then cut the rashers into 1-inch pieces.
4. Fry the bacon in the fat for 2 minutes, then add the onions and fry for a further 2 minutes; add the kidneys.
5. Over a medium heat fry the kidneys for 3–4 minutes, until they are sealed.
6. Stir in the mushrooms with the flour.
7. Cook the mixture for 1 minute stirring, then add the tomatoes and stock.
8. Stir the mixture until it boils then reduce the heat and cover the pan.
9. Cook, stirring occasionally, for about 15 minutes, until the kidneys are tender.
10. Check the mixture for seasoning then turn it into a serving dish.
11. Garnish with triangles of toast.

BAKED TOMATOES
Serves 12

1½lb (¾ kilo) tomatoes
salt and pepper
2oz (50gm) butter
few chopped fresh herbs

1. Preheat oven to moderate to moderately hot, 375 deg F or gas 5 (190 deg C).
2. Cut the tomatoes in half and arrange them in an ovenproof dish.
3. Sprinkle with salt and pepper and dot with butter then sprinkle with herbs if available.
4. Bake in the centre of the oven for 30 minutes, or until tender. (They can be cooked below the sunrise sausages, but they will take a few minutes longer.)

CROISSANTS
(Illustrated on page 18)
Makes 12

1 level tablespoon dried yeast
1 level teaspoon caster sugar
¼ pint (125ml) plus 4 tablespoons water
1lb (½ kilo) strong plain flour
pinch of salt
1oz (25gm) lard
1 large egg
5oz (125gm) margarine
beaten egg to glaze

1. Preheat oven to hot, 425 deg F or gas 7 (220 deg C).
2. Put the yeast and sugar into a small bowl.
3. Heat the water to blood heat, whisk it into the yeast then leave the bowl in a warm place for the yeast to dissolve.
4. Sift the flour and salt into a bowl and rub in the lard.
5. Add the lightly beaten egg, pour in the yeast mixture and work it into the flour to form a dough.
6. Turn the dough on to a floured working surface and knead it for about 10 minutes, until it is smooth.
7. Roll the dough into an oblong 18 inches by 8 inches.
8. Soften the margarine and divide it into four portions.
9. Dot the top two-thirds of the dough with one portion of margarine, leaving a 1-inch border.
10. Fold the bottom third up over

the middle and the top third down over the centre.
11. Firmly seal the edges and turn the dough a quarter turn, anti-clockwise.
12. Roll out to an oblong again, add another portion of margarine; fold and turn. Repeat this process, folding and turning until all the margarine is used.
13. Slip the dough in a polythene bag and leave it in a cool place to rest for 30 minutes.
14. Then roll, fold and turn the dough four more times, this time without any fat.
15. Rest it for another 30 minutes.
16. To shape the croissants, roll the dough into an oblong about 22 inches by 13 inches.
17. Trim the edges to make it 12 inches by 21 inches and cut it in half lengthways.
18. Cut each strip into six triangles, each 6 inches wide at the base. You will be left with half triangles at the ends. They can be made into small rolls.
19. Brush the surface of all the triangles with egg beaten with a little salt.
20. Roll each one from the wide end to the point and curve it into a crescent.
21. Put the croissants on to baking sheets, brush with egg then leave in a warm place for about 30 minutes to prove, until they have risen in size.
22. Bake on the second and third shelves from the top of the oven for 15–20 minutes.
23. Serve warm with butter and black cherry jam.

BROWN ROLLS
Makes 12

½oz (12gm) dried yeast
1 level tablespoon soft brown sugar
¾ pint (375ml) water
1 level teaspoon salt
1½lb (¾ kilo) wholewheat flour
½oz (12gm) lard
1 large egg
salt

1. Preheat oven to hot, 450 deg F or gas 8 (230 deg C).
2. Put the yeast into a bowl with a little of the sugar.
3. Heat the water to blood heat and whisk half of it into the yeast and sugar with a fork.
4. Leave the yeast in a warm place for about 15 minutes to dissolve.
5. Add the salt and remaining sugar to the water.
6. Tip the flour into a large bowl and rub in the lard.
7. Make a well in the centre and pour in the water and dissolved yeast.
8. Working from the centre mix the flour into the liquid so it forms a dough.
9. Turn the dough on to a floured working surface and knead it for at least 5 minutes until it is smooth.
10. Lightly grease a bowl, add the dough, cover it with a damp cloth or a sheet of greased polythene and leave the dough in a warm place, for about 45 minutes, to rise and double in bulk.
11. Turn on to the working surface and knead it very lightly until it is back to its original size.
12. Brush two 7½-inch (19-cm) sandwich tins with melted fat.
13. Divide the dough in half then each half into six even pieces.
14. Knead each piece into a ball and place six in a tin, five around the edge and one in the centre.
15. Brush the roll clusters with the egg lightly beaten with a pinch of salt.
16. Leave in a warm place to prove for about 15 minutes.
17. Bake in the centre of the oven for 20 minutes, then reduce the heat to moderately to moderately hot, 400 deg F or gas 6 (200 deg C) for a further 15–20 minutes, or until the base sounds hollow if tapped with the knuckles.
18. Cool on a wire tray then divide into rolls for serving.

To freeze: bread stores excellently in the freezer – pack in polythene bags, seal and label. Store for up to 2 months. Thaw at room temperature overnight and heat in the oven for a few minutes before serving.

A HOUSEWARMING PARTY

The move is over, the new house almost straight, so a housewarming party is next on the agenda to meet new neighbours and renew old acquaintances. With so many other tasks to tackle in a new house, the food for the party should be fairly simple.
This is why I have chosen to serve a fork buffet. There is a hot or cold dish from which your guests can select their main course, with various salads for accompaniments. Two cold dishes form the dessert. They can both be made the day before with only the assembling and decoration left for the day of the party. Serve a red wine punch for your guests to drink with a choice of beer, if preferred. The party caters for 12 people, but double or treble any recipe to suit the number of guests you have coming.

MENU
Serves 12

Moussaka
Savoury pork parcel
Rainbow rice salad
Mushroom salad
Green salad (see page 16)
Crispy rolls

Pineapple dream
Banana chocolate crunch

Red wine punch

see overleaf for recipes

MOUSSAKA
Serves 8

1lb (½ kilo) aubergines
salt and pepper
1¼lb (¾ kilo) raw minced beef
pinch of herbs
2oz (50gm) lard
1lb (½ kilo) onions, peeled and sliced
8oz (200gm) tomatoes, sliced
6 tablespoons cooking oil
1lb (½ kilo) potatoes, peeled, cooked and sliced
2oz (50gm) margarine
2oz (50gm) plain flour
¾ pint (375ml) milk
1 large egg
2oz (50gm) strong cheese, grated
pinch of nutmeg

1. Preheat oven to moderate, 350 deg F or gas 4 (180 deg C).
2. Wipe the aubergines, trim the ends, then cut into ½-inch slices.
3. Lay the slices on a plate and sprinkle them liberally with salt.
4. Leave the aubergines in a cool place for at least 15 minutes to remove some excess moisture.
5. Fry the minced beef in a pan (no extra fat is required) until it has separated and is starting to brown.
6. Stir in the herbs with salt and pepper and transfer the mince to a 6-pint (approximately 3-litre) casserole dish.
7. Melt half the lard and fry the onions until golden brown and tender. Place on top of the mince.
8. Cover the onions with a layer of tomatoes.
9. Melt the rest of the lard in a pan and add a little oil.
10. Dry the aubergine slices on absorbent kitchen paper then fry them in the fat until golden brown on both sides. Add more oil when required.
11. Place the aubergines on top of the tomatoes and cover with the sliced cooked potatoes.
12. Melt the margarine in a pan over a gentle heat.
13. Remove from the heat, stir in the flour then gradually blend in the milk.
14. Return to the heat and, stirring all the time, bring the sauce to the boil.
15. Separate the egg and mix a little sauce into the yolk.
16. Return this to the main bulk of the sauce, with the cheese and nutmeg and stir it in well. (Do not allow to boil.)
17. Finally, whisk the egg white until it is stiff and stands in straight peaks.
18. Fold it carefully into the sauce then pour it over the moussaka.
19. Spread it to the sides.
20. Bake in the centre of oven for 50 minutes–1 hour, or until the top is golden brown and puffy.
21. Serve piping hot.

SAVOURY PORK PARCEL
Serves 4–6

flaky pastry made with 8oz (200gm) flour (see Basic recipes, page 100)
12–14oz (300–350gm) pork fillet (in 1 piece)
1 onion, peeled and chopped
1 level tablespoon sage and onion stuffing mix
salt and pepper
little beaten egg to glaze

1. Preheat oven to hot, 425 deg F or gas 7 (220 deg C).
2. Roll the pastry into a rectangle wide enough to completely encase the pork fillet plus 2 inches.
3. Place the fillet on the centre of the pastry.
4. Mix the onion with the stuffing mix and salt and pepper and sprinkle the mixture over the meat.
5. Moisten the pastry edges with water and wrap the fillet in the pastry, overlapping the sides and folding the ends up to keep in all the juices.
6. Turn the roll over so all the joins are underneath and transfer it to a baking sheet.
7. Brush the pastry with egg glaze and score it lightly with the back of a knife.
8. Make a small hole at each end to allow steam to escape.
9. Leave the roll to rest for 30 minutes in a cool place.
10. Bake in the centre of the oven for 10 minutes, then reduce the heat to moderate to moderately hot, 375 deg F or gas 5 (190 deg C) for a further 30–35 minutes, until the roll is cooked.
11. If the pastry becomes too brown, cover it with greaseproof paper.

To freeze: wrap in foil or polythene, seal and label. Store for up to 3 months. Thaw in the refrigerator overnight.

RAINBOW RICE SALAD
Serves 12–15

1lb (½ kilo) long-grain rice
8oz (200gm) carrots, peeled and chopped
1 packet (8oz or 200gm) frozen sliced beans
1 packet (8oz or 200gm) frozen peas
1 small onion, peeled and grated
1 level tablespoon chopped parsley
French dressing (see Basic recipes, page 100)
1lb (½ kilo) tomatoes

1. Cook the rice in a large pan of boiling, salted water for 12–15 minutes, until tender. Drain and run cold water through the grains to keep them separate.
2. Boil the carrots in salted water for 5–10 minutes, adding the beans and peas for the last 3 minutes' cooking time.
3. Drain, then stir the vegetables into the rice with the onion and parsley. Allow to cool.
4. Moisten the salad with French dressing and turn it into a large dish for serving.
5. Slice the tomatoes and arrange them all around the edge of the dish as a garnish.

MUSHROOM SALAD
Serves 8

1lb (½ kilo) button mushrooms
juice of 1 lemon
8 tablespoons oil
salt and pepper
chopped chives
chopped parsley

1. Trim the mushrooms and slice them very thinly; put into a salad bowl.
2. Mix the lemon juice and oil together and add plenty of seasoning.
3. Pour the dressing over the mushrooms and toss them well so they are completely coated.
4. Place the bowl in a cool place for at least 30 minutes for the flavours to combine.
5. Sprinkle the chives and parsley over the top before serving.

CRISPY ROLLS
Makes 16

1lb (½ kilo) plain flour
good pinch of salt
1½ level teaspoons bicarbonate of soda
2 level teaspoons cream of tartar
1oz (25gm) margarine
about ½ pint (250ml) milk
little beaten egg to glaze

1. Preheat oven to moderate, 350 deg F or gas 4 (180 deg C).
2. Sift the flour, salt, bicarbonate of soda and cream of tartar into a bowl.
3. Rub in the margarine until it is evenly distributed.
4. Bind the dry ingredients together with sufficient milk to make a fairly stiff consistency.
5. Knead the dough lightly then divide it into 16 even pieces.
6. Knead each piece into a round and place them on greased baking sheets.
7. Brush each roll with egg glaze then bake in the centre of the oven for 20 minutes, or until golden brown and cooked. Cool on a wire tray.

To freeze: place the rolls in a polythene bag, seal and label; they will keep for 6 weeks. Thaw at room temperature for 3 hours, or heat, from frozen, in a moderate oven, 350 deg F or gas 4 (180 deg C) for 15 minutes.

PINEAPPLE DREAM
Serves 6

1 can (1lb 15oz or approximately 1 kilo) pineapple chunks
2 large eggs
4oz (100gm) caster sugar
juice of half an orange
4 tablespoons single cream
¼ pint (125ml) double cream
½oz (12gm) powdered gelatine
2 tablespoons water
1 tablespoon sieved redcurrant jelly

1. Drain the juice from the pineapple.
2. Separate the eggs and put the yolks into a bowl with the caster sugar and orange juice.
3. Place the bowl over a pan of hot water and whisk the mixture until it starts to thicken, then add the pineapple juice and whisk for a few more minutes.
4. Stir the pineapple into the mixture.
5. Whip the creams together until they are stiff and hold their own shape and fold half into the pineapple mixture.
6. Put the gelatine into a pan with the water and, over a very low heat, dissolve the granules.
7. Stir the liquid gelatine into the pineapple mixture, then put the bowl on ice or in very cold water and leave it, stirring occasionally, until it starts to set.
8. Quickly whisk the egg whites until they are really stiff, then fold them lightly and carefully into the mixture.
9. Turn it into a dish to set.
10. When the pineapple dream is set, carefully spread the surface with the rest of the cream.
11. Put the redcurrant jelly into a piping bag and pipe lines across the dessert 1-inch apart.
12. Take a skewer and draw it across the piped lines first one way and then the other, about 1-inch apart, until a feather design has formed on the surface.
13. Serve with single cream if liked.

BANANA CHOCOLATE CRUNCH
Serves 6–8

4oz (100gm) margarine or butter
4oz (100gm) icing sugar, sifted
4 level tablespoons golden syrup
4 level tablespoons cocoa powder
6oz (150gm) cornflakes
¼ pint (125ml) double cream
4 tablespoons single cream
3 bananas
little lemon juice
2 glacé cherries

1. Cut two circles of greaseproof paper to fit the base of an 8-inch (20-cm) cake tin.
2. Brush the tin with a little oil and place one round of paper in the base. Brush the paper lining.
3. Melt the margarine or butter in a large saucepan over a low heat.
4. Remove the pan from the heat and stir in the icing sugar and golden syrup.
5. When they are thoroughly mixed stir in the sifted cocoa powder with the cornflakes.
6. Turn half the mixture into the prepared tin and press it down firmly.
7. Cover with the second layer of greaseproof paper and, with the back of a wooden spoon, level the surface.
8. Leave the two layers in a cool place – preferably the refrigerator – overnight to harden.
9. Next day, run a knife around the inside of the tin and turn the cake out.
10. Separate the two layers and remove the greaseproof paper.
11. Whip the two creams together and place some in a piping bag.
12. Pipe eight stars around the top of one layer.
13. Spread all the rest of the cream on top of the other layer.
14. Peel and slice the bananas and toss them in lemon juice to prevent them discoloring. Reserve eight pieces for decoration and place the remainder over the cream filling.
15. Carefully sandwich the two layers together and put the cake on a plate for serving.
16. Cut the cherries into quarters and put a slice of banana and a piece of cherry on each star of cream before serving.

RED WINE PUNCH
Gives 20 glasses

1 bottle inexpensive red wine
2 bottles damson fruit wine
1 pint cold water
apple, orange and lemon slices to decorate
ice cubes

1. Just before the party starts, stir the red wine, fruit wine and water together in a large bowl.
2. Add the sliced fruit for decoration and ice cubes, if available, to cool the drink.

A BEACH PARTY FOR SIX

MENU

Individual pork pies
Surprise savoury loaf
Summer pudding
Almond slices
Cherry cake

Summer drink

INDIVIDUAL PORK PIES
Makes 6

1½lb (¾ kilo) thick end belly of pork
salt and pepper
pinch of dried sage
1½lb (¾ kilo) plain flour
7oz (175gm) lard
2 level teaspoons salt
¼ pint (125ml) plus 4 tablespoons warm water
little beaten egg to glaze
¼ pint (125ml) plus 4 tablespoons stock
1½ level teaspoons powdered gelatine

1. Preheat oven to hot, 425 deg F or gas 7 (220 deg C).
2. Cut all the bone, fat and skin from the meat then chop the meat finely.
3. Mix in the salt and pepper with the sage and leave the filling on one side while making the pastry.
4. Sift the flour and salt into a mixing bowl.
5. Melt the lard slowly, add the water and bring the mixture to the boil.
6. Pour it immediately into the flour and salt and, with a palette knife, combine the ingredients.
7. As it cools knead the dough with you hands until it is smooth.
8. The pastry will start to set as it cools, so to keep it soft and pliable cover any pieces not in use with a bowl.
9. Divide the dough into four and use a quarter at a time.
10. Cut the dough in half then mould each piece to a pie shape over an upturned 1-lb (½-kilo) jam jar.
11. Turn the jars the right way up and gently ease off the pie shape.
12. Work it back into shape with the fingers if damaged.
13. Divide a third of the meat between the two pies.
14. Divide another quarter of dough into six pieces for the lid and shape two only to fit the tops of the pies ready (keep the rest covered until required).
15. Moisten the edges and place the lid in position pressing the joins firmly together.
16. Put the pies on to a baking sheet and trim the tops with a pair of scissors to neaten them.
17. Make two holes in each pie with a skewer.
18. Make the other four pies in exactly the same way using the rest of the dough.
19. Brush the pies with beaten egg then bake them in the centre of the oven for 30 minutes, then reduce the heat to very moderate, 325 deg F or gas 3 (170 deg C) for a further hour.
20. When the pies are cooked and cold melt the gelatine in the stock over a low heat.
21. Leave it to cool but not set.
22. Insert a pointed knife into one of the holes on top of one of the pies and run some stock down it to fill the pie.
23. Fill the others in the same way, then leave to cool and set.

SURPRISE SAVOURY LOAF
(Illustrated on page 18)
Serves 8

1 small French loaf
3oz (75gm) butter
1 tablespoon salad cream
4 hard-boiled eggs
3 tomatoes
few lettuce leaves
salt and pepper

1. Split the loaf in half lengthways and remove enough of the bread from both pieces to hold the eggs and tomatoes.
2. Beat the butter and salad cream together and spread it over the inside of both pieces.
3. Shell and slice the eggs. Plunge the tomatoes into boiling water for 20 seconds, then transfer to cold water and peel off the skins; cut in slices.
4. Arrange the lettuce leaves in the bottom half of the loaf, place the egg and tomato slices down the centre and sprinkle with salt and pepper.
5. Replace the top of the loaf.
6. Wrap the loaf in foil and carry it to the beach uncut.
7. To serve, cut the loaf into thick slices.

SUMMER PUDDING
Serves 6–8

8oz (200gm) blackcurrants
2½lb (1¼ kilo) rhubarb
¼ pint (125ml) water
4–6oz (100–150gm) demerara sugar
1 large thinly-sliced white loaf

1. Strip the blackcurrants from their stalks by running a fork down each one. Wash the fruit.
2. Trim off the ends from the rhubarb and cut the stalks into short lengths.
3. Put the blackcurrants and rhubarb into a saucepan with the water and cook gently until the fruits are tender.
4. Stir in the sugar and leave the fruit on one side for the sugar to dissolve.
5. Brush a 2-pint (approximately 1-litre) basin with a little oil.
6. Cut the crusts from the slices of bread then cut all but one slice in half.
7. Cut a circle from the remaining slice to fit the bottom of the basin and place it in position.
8. Line the basin with some of the pieces of bread, overlapping.
9. Layer the fruit and bread into the basin ending with a complete layer of bread, neatly cut to fit.
10. Put a saucer over the pudding and weigh it down with kitchen weights or full cans of fruit.
11. Leave the pudding in a cool place overnight.
12. Remove the weights, cover the basin and take it on the picnic in a large polythene bag. (Do not forget to pack bowls and spoons for serving the pudding.)

ALMOND SLICES
Makes 16

shortcrust pastry made with 8oz (200gm) flour (see Basic recipes, page 100)
4oz (100gm) raspberry jam
2 large egg whites
4oz (100gm) ground almonds
2oz (50gm) ground rice
6oz (150gm) caster sugar
few drops almond essence
2oz (50gm) flaked almonds

1. Preheat oven to moderate to moderately hot, 375 deg F or gas 5 (190 deg C).
2. Roll the pastry into a rectangle and use to line a Swiss roll tin.
3. Trim off any surplus pastry from around the edges.
4. Spread the jam over the base of the pastry.
5. Put the egg whites into a bowl and break them up lightly with a fork.
6. Mix in the ground almonds, ground rice, sugar and almond essence to make a stiff paste.
7. Spread this paste over the jam. It does not matter if a little jam shows through the mixture as it will spread during cooking.
8. Sprinkle flaked almonds over the top.
9. Bake in the centre of the oven for 20–25 minutes, or until the top is golden brown and the pastry cooked.
10. Leave to cool in the tin, cut into 16 pieces then wrap in foil or a polythene bag ready for the picnic.

To freeze: this freezes well. Wrap in a polythene bag or foil and store for 3–6 months. Thaw out at room temperature.

CHERRY CAKE
Gives 8–10 slices

4oz (100gm) margarine
4oz (100gm) caster sugar
2 large eggs
7oz (175gm) plain flour
1½ level teaspoons baking powder
pinch of salt
6oz (150gm) glacé cherries, washed and dried
1 dessertspoon milk

1. Preheat oven to moderate, 350 deg F or gas 4 (180 deg C).
2. Brush a 6-inch (15-cm) cake tin with melted fat and cut two circles of greaseproof paper the size of the base.
3. Place one in position and brush it with melted fat.
4. Cut a doubled strip of greaseproof paper 2 inches wider than the depth of the tin and 1 inch longer all the way round.
5. Make a 1-inch fold along one of the longer sides, then make slanting cuts to the fold.
6. Place this piece of paper around the inside of the tin with the cut edge fitting round the inside over the base.
7. Place the other round of paper on top and brush the entire lining with melted fat.
8. Beat the margarine until it is soft and creamy.
9. Add the caster sugar and beat the two ingredients together until the mixture is light and fluffy in both colour and texture.
10. Beat the eggs then add them gradually to the creamed mixture, beating well between each addition.
11. Sift the flour, baking powder and salt together.
12. Cut the cherries in half and stir 1 tablespoon of the flour through them so they are coated.
13. Carefully fold the dry ingredients, milk and cherries into the creamed mixture.
14. Turn it into the prepared cake tin, smooth over the surface and slightly hollow out the centre.
15. Bake in the centre of the oven for 1 hour 40 minutes.
16. To test if it is cooked, push a warmed skewer into the centre. If it comes out clean the cake is cooked but if any mixture adheres to the skewer cook the cake for a little longer.
17. Turn the cake on to a wire tray to cool.
18. Remove the greaseproof paper and store the cooled cake in a tin, ready for the picnic.

SUMMER DRINK
Gives 6 long drinks

1 pint (approximately ½ litre) pineapple juice
1 pint (approximately ½ litre) water
2 tablespoons orange squash
2 tablespoons lime squash
ice cubes

1. Mix the pineapple juice with the water, orange squash and lime squash.
2. Crush the ice cubes, in a teatowel, with a rolling pin.
3. Place the crushed ice into vacuum flasks and pour on the drink.
4. Do not fill the flask right to the top so as to allow for the ice melting.
5. If the flasks are sealed properly you should have an ice-cold drink for your beach party.

A CURRY PARTY

More and more people are becoming enthusiastic about this spicy dish with its accompaniments, so to have it as the centrepiece for a party would, I feel sure, prove very popular. It is quite an easy party to organize as the curry sauce is best made the day before – the flavour improves with keeping and all that is required after the meal is fresh fruit. This party is sufficient for 16 people.

MEATBALL CURRY

(Illustrated on page 35)
Serves 16

6oz (150gm) margarine
3lb (1½ kilo) onions, peeled and sliced
2 level tablespoons turmeric
½ level teaspoon ground ginger
½ level teaspoon ground cinnamon
2 level tablespoons curry powder
1 level teaspoon curry paste
½ level teaspoon red chilli powder
2 level teaspoons salt
4 bayleaves
1 can (14oz or 350gm) tomatoes
2½ pints (approximately 1¼ litres) stock
½ pint (125ml) coconut milk (obtained either from a fresh coconut or from 2 level tablespoons desiccated coconut infused for 30 minutes in boiling water and strained)
4lb (2 kilo) raw minced beef
8oz (200gm) fresh breadcrumbs
1 level dessertspoon dried mixed herbs
3 large eggs
salt and pepper
2oz (50gm) plain flour, seasoned with salt and pepper
2oz (50gm) lard
2 dessert apples
1 cauliflower

1. Make the sauce the day before it is required.
2. Melt the margarine in a large pan and fry the onions until they start to soften.
3. Stir in the turmeric, ground ginger, ground cinnamon, curry powder and paste, chilli powder, salt and bayleaves.
4. Allow these ingredients to fry for about 10 minutes.
5. Pour in the can of tomatoes with the stock and coconut liquid and stir the curry sauce until it comes to the boil.
6. Reduce the heat, cover the pan and simmer the sauce for about 1 hour.
7. When the sauce has cooked transfer it to a bowl and leave it in a cool place for the next day.
8. Mix the minced beef with the breadcrumbs and herbs.
9. Beat the eggs and work them into the meat with the seasoning.
10. Divide the mixture into 36 pieces and roll each into a ball.
11. Toss them in the seasoned flour so they are well coated.
12. Melt the lard in a frying pan and fry the balls until they are evenly brown.
13. Transfer them to the curry sauce and cook gently for about 1 hour.
14. Peel, quarter, core and dice the apples and cut the cauliflower into small sprigs.
15. Add the apple and the cauliflower to the curry 20 minutes before the end of the cooking time.
16. Serve the curry in a large dish.

THE ACCOMPANIMENTS

PAPPADOMS

1. These are normally bought in cans – allow 1 pappadom per person.
2. Fry one at a time in hot fat; they puff up during cooking.
3. Keep warm in the oven.

BOILED RICE

(Illustrated on page 35)
Serves 16

Rice can be kept warm, for up to 1 hour, if spread in a greased ovenproof dish; dot with butter and cover with foil. Place in a very moderate oven, 325 deg F or gas 3 (170 deg C).

2lb (1 kilo) long-grain rice
4 level teaspoons salt
small piece of lemon

1. Put the rice in a large pan of boiling water with the salt and lemon.
2. When it comes back to the boil simmer the rice for about 12 minutes.
3. To test if it is cooked, take a grain and rub it between thumb and first finger. If the rice still has a hard core cook it for a little longer.
4. Drain the rice well then run hot water through the grains to separate them and remove excess starch.
5. Turn the rice into a large bowl for serving and remove the lemon.

DAHL
(Illustrated on page 35)
Serves 16

An accompaniment to curry very similar to a highly seasoned pease pudding.

2oz (50gm) margarine
2 large onions, peeled and chopped
3 level teaspoons curry powder
2 level teaspoons salt
1lb (½ kilo) red lentils
2 pints (approximately 1 litre) stock
4oz (100gm) butter

1. Melt the margarine and fry the onions slowly until soft.
2. Add the curry powder and salt and fry for a few more minutes.
3. Wash the lentils and stir them into the pan with the stock.
4. Cover and simmer for about 35 minutes, until the lentils are soft and all the liquid has been absorbed.
5. Beat in the butter before serving hot in an ovenproof dish. (Dahl can also be kept warm, covered with foil, at the same oven temperature as the rice.)

CUCUMBER AND YOGURT
(Illustrated on page 35)

1. Cut a cucumber into fairly small dice – leave the skin on as it looks more attractive.
2. Put it into a bowl and just before serving spoon over a carton of natural yogurt.

HARD-BOILED EGGS
(Illustrated on page 35)

1. Hard boil 4 large eggs then leave them in cold water to cool.
2. Separate the yolks from the whites and sieve them.
3. Arrange them in a bowl with the whites on the outside and the sieved yolk in the centre.

COCONUT
(Illustrated on page 35)

1. Saw a fresh coconut in half.
2. Scoop out the flesh and cut off any dark skin.
3. Grate the coconut and serve it in small bowls. (Desiccated coconut can be used if fresh is not available.)

MANGO CHUTNEY
(Illustrated on page 35)

Mango is the usual chutney to serve with a curry. However, if you would prefer to serve one of your own as long as it is a sweet one, it will be delicious.

1. Turn it into a small dish for serving.

TOMATO AND ONION
(Illustrated on page 35)

1. Plunge 1½lb (¾ kilo) tomatoes into boiling water for 20 seconds.
2. Transfer them to cold water and peel off the skins.
3. Slice the tomatoes and arrange them, overlapping, in a dish.
4. Peel and grate 1 onion and scatter it over the top of the tomatoes.

BANANA

1. Slice 6 bananas and place in a dish.
2. Sprinkle with lemon juice to prevent discoloration.

SALTED ALMONDS
(Illustrated on page 35)

1. Melt 2oz (50gm) butter in a pan.
2. Add 4oz (100gm) halved, blanched almonds.
3. Fry nuts, turning frequently until they are evenly brown.
4. Drain on absorbent paper and sprinkle with salt before serving in a small bowl.

A BARBECUE

The barbecue itself can either be bought or home-made. If the latter, build two staggered rows of bricks, two bricks high and suspend two cake cooling trays between them to form the grid.

A barbecue 2 feet long will provide sufficient fire to cook for 12 people. If you have invited more, either extend the barbecue or build another one in a different part of the garden.

Light the fire about an hour before your guests arrive so you can be sure of not leaving them too long without food. The open air is a great stimulator of appetites.

A good plan is to start the food with a warming soup – this is a good opener while the first round of food is being cooked. Follow it with food that is simple to cook and also easy to eat in the fingers, then round the meal off with treacle tarts, again easy to eat in the fingers, cheese and biscuits and fresh fruit. Lastly serve piping hot coffee.

A good choice for drink is beer and cider, but do position the bar away from the cooking to encourage people to move about.

CARROT SOUP
Serves 14–16

2oz (50gm) margarine
3lb (1½ kilo) carrots, peeled and sliced
2 onions, peeled and sliced
8oz (200gm) red lentils
3 pints (approximately 1½ litres) chicken stock
1 bayleaf
salt and pepper
1¾ pints (scant 1 litre) milk

1. Melt the margarine, add the carrots, onions and lentils.
2. When the fat is absorbed, stir in the stock, bayleaf and salt and pepper.
3. Bring the soup to the boil, cover the pan, reduce the heat and simmer for 1½ hours.
4. Sieve the soup. Check for flavour, stir in the milk, then reheat when necessary.
5. The easiest way to serve the soup is in mugs.

BARBECUE CHOPS AND SAUSAGES

(Illustrated on page 35)

For the main course allow 1 chop and 2 sausages per person with corn cogs, a good supply of fried onions and a fresh green salad with whole tomatoes. Serve soft rolls and French bread to eat with the meat and, of course, have some barbecue sauce to lavishly coat the food while cooking.

sausages
lamb cutlets
cooking oil
onions, peeled and sliced
soft rolls

1. Thread the sausages on to a pair of long skewers so they are easier to turn. Have no more than 6 sausages per pair of skewers.
2. Brush the cutlets and the sausages with cooking oil.
3. Place them over the fire and cook them, brushing the food with barbecue sauce occasionally, until the food is brown all over and tender.
4. Fry the onions in a little oil in a pan over the fire, turning them frequently.
5. Serve the chops in serviettes and the sausages in rolls with fried onions.

BARBECUE SAUCE

Makes about ½ pint (250ml)

1 can (14oz or 350gm) tomatoes
1 tablespoon tomato ketchup
1 dessertspoon vinegar
2 level tablespoons sweet chutney
1 level dessertspoon horseradish sauce
3 teaspoons Worcestershire sauce
salt and pepper

1. Sieve the tomatoes and their juice into a bowl.
2. Stir in the other ingredients to make a spicy sauce and season with salt and pepper.
3. The sauce can be made the day before it is required and stored in a covered glass bowl.

CORN COGS

Make 12

3 large sweetcorn cobs (fresh or frozen)
8oz (200gm) thinly cut streaky bacon rashers

1. If using fresh cobs take off all the outer leaves and silky strands inside.
2. Cook the cobs in boiling water – do not add any salt until the last 5 minutes – for 10–20 minutes, until the kernels are tender.
3. Drain then cut each cob into 4 rounds.
4. Remove the rind and any small bones from the bacon, then wrap a rasher around each piece of sweetcorn, covering the kernels.
5. Secure in place with a wooden cocktail stick.
6. Brush with barbecue sauce and cook over the heat, turning frequently until the bacon is cooked.
7. Serve in serviettes.

TREACLE TART

Serves 6

shortcrust pastry made with 8oz (200gm) flour (see Basic recipes, page 100)
8 level tablespoons golden syrup
1 dessertspoon lemon juice
pinch of ground cinnamon
2oz (50gm) fresh breadcrumbs

1. Preheat oven to moderate to moderately hot, 400 deg F or gas 6 (200 deg C).
2. Cut off a little of the pastry for the trellis and roll the rest into a circle slightly larger than a 9-inch (23-cm) ovenproof plate.
3. Lift it on to the plate, press it it into the base and trim off the excess pastry with a knife.
4. Add the trimming to the other piece of pastry.
5. Warm the syrup in a pan over a low heat, stir in the lemon juice and cinnamon.
6. Remove from the heat and mix in the breadcrumbs.
7. Turn the mixture on to the lined plate and spread it to within 1 inch of the edge.
8. Roll the piece of pastry left into a strip and cut from it 8 thin strips, long enough to go across the pie.
9. Moisten the edge of the tart and arrange the strips, trellis fashion, on top.
10. Decorate the edge with the prongs of a fork.
11. Bake in the centre of the oven for about 30 minutes, until golden brown.
12. Serve hot or cold with single cream if liked.

CHINESE PARTY FOR TWENTY

With the taste for Chinese food growing all the time I thought it would be fun to have a party and serve only Chinese dishes. Even the simplest of Chinese meals has two or three main courses and with a soup to start and a Chinese fruit salad to end, your meal is complete.

Just one word of warning though, before you rush into the party. To serve three hot main dishes entails a considerable amount of hard work and so I do suggest you enrol the help of a friend. Incidentally, borrow her large saucepans as well, as I can assure you they will be needed.

The art of Chinese cookery is that all the vegetables should still be crisp so, although the initial preparation is lengthy, the actual cooking time is quick. This does though raise another problem in that everything is last minute. However, with two of you cooking it will all fall into place.

MENU

Ham and sweetcorn soup

Barbecued spare ribs
Chicken chow mein
Sweet and sour pork
Shrimp crackers
Special fried rice
Boiled rice (see page 30)

Chinese fruit salad
Raisin biscuits

Jasmine tea
White wine cup

HAM AND SWEETCORN SOUP

Serves 20

6 pints (approximately 3 litres) chicken stock
1lb (½ kilo) frozen sweetcorn kernels
3 level tablespoons cornflour
1 level teaspoon monosodium glutamate (obtainable from most leading grocers)
3 level tablespoons water
1 bunch spring onions
1lb (½ kilo) ham, minced

1. Bring the stock to the boil, add the sweetcorn kernels and cook for a few minutes until tender.
2. Blend the cornflour and monosodium glutamate together to a paste with the water.
3. Mix a little of the hot stock with the cornflour, then pour it all into the main bulk of the soup and, stirring all the time, bring it to the boil.
4. Trim the roots and top leaves from the spring onions, remove any damaged leaves then cut the onions into small rings.
5. Stir the onions and minced ham into the soup and continue to boil the soup for 3 more minutes.
6. Serve the soup hot with French and brown bread.

BARBECUED SPARE RIBS

(Illustrated on page 35)

Serves 20 for a party or 12 people for a main meal

It is perfectly all right to leave the chops marinating in the sauce all day before they are roasted. Make sure they are in a china dish and are left in a cool place.

6lb (3 kilo) belly of pork
3 pints (approximately 1½ litres) water
7 tablespoons vinegar
6 tablespoons soya sauce
6 tablespoons clear honey
6 tablespoons plum or apricot jam
1 tablespoon Worcestershire sauce
1 tablespoon made mustard
juice of half a lemon
1 tablespoon tomato ketchup

1. Preheat oven to moderate, 350 deg F or gas 4 (180 deg C).
2. Remove the rind and any excess fat from the meat then cut it into chops between the bones.
3. Cut each chop in half for ease of eating.
4. Put the meat into a large pan with the water and 4 tablespoons of the vinegar.
5. Bring to the boil then reduce the heat and simmer the chops for 15 minutes.
6. Drain the chops and place them in a roasting tin.
7. In a pan, mix the soya sauce with the honey, the remaining vinegar, the jam, Worcestershire sauce, mustard, lemon juice and tomato ketchup.
8. Place over a gentle heat until the ingredients are well blended.
9. Pour the sauce over the chops then cook in the centre of the oven for 40 minutes, basting them occasionally.
10. Increase the oven heat to moderate to moderately hot, 400 deg F or gas 6 (200 deg C), for 15 minutes to brown the chops. Serve in a large dish.

CHICKEN CHOW MEIN

Serves 20 people at a party or 10–12 people as a main meal

1 boiling chicken (about 4½lb or 2¼ kilo)
6 peppercorns
1 bayleaf
4 tablespoons corn oil
2 large onions, peeled and chopped
½ small head celery, chopped
8oz (200gm) mushrooms
2½ pints (approximately 1¼ litres) chicken stock (see method)
12oz (300gm) Chinese noodles
1 can (1lb 2oz or 450gm) bean sprouts
1 can (1lb 4oz or 500gm) water chestnuts
6 level tablespoons cornflour
6 tablespoons soya sauce
1 level teaspoon monosodium glutamate
salt and pepper

1. On the day before the party put the chicken, with its giblets, into a large pan.
2. Almost cover the chicken with water, add the peppercorns and bayleaf and bring slowly to the boil.
3. Reduce the heat, cover the pan and simmer for 2 hours, or until chicken is tender.
4. Leave to cool in the water for 1 hour then drain off the stock into a bowl and put the chicken on to a plate to cool.
5. Next day, remove the chicken meat from the bones and shred it into fork-size pieces.
6. Heat the oil in a large pan, add the onions and celery and, over a low heat, cook them for 5 minutes.
7. Trim and slice the mushrooms.
8. Add the mushrooms and the chicken stock and bring the mixture to the boil.
9. Simmer for 10 minutes.
10. Meanwhile, cook the noodles in a large pan of boiling, salted water until they are tender, about 10 minutes.
11. When cooked, drain and run hot water through the strands to separate them and turn them into a serving dish. Keep hot.
12. Drain the bean sprouts and water chestnuts and cut the latter into slices.
13. Blend the cornflour with the soya sauce to make a smooth paste.
14. Mix in about 3 tablespoons of the hot stock then stir it all into the main bulk.
15. Stirring all the time, bring the mixture to the boil.
16. Add the bean sprouts, water chestnuts and chicken with the monosodium glutamate and cook for 2–3 minutes to heat the ingredients through.
17. Check the mixture for flavour and season if necessary, then spoon it on top of the noodles. Serve immediately.

SWEET AND SOUR PORK
Serves 20 people for a party or 12 people for a main meal

3lb (1½ kilo) forehock or spare rib of pork
1 level tablespoon soft brown sugar
5 tablespoons soya sauce
1 level teaspoon salt
1 level teaspoon monosodium glutamate
1 dessertspoon sherry (optional)

Batter:
9oz (225gm) self-raising flour
pinch of salt
3 large eggs, separated
2 tablespoons corn oil
½ pint (250ml) water

Sauce:
1 green pepper
3 onions, peeled and sliced
3 carrots, peeled and sliced
¾ pint (375ml) malt vinegar
8oz (200gm) soft brown sugar
1 level teaspoon salt
¼ pint (125ml) tomato ketchup
1 can (15½oz or 387gm) pineapple pieces
1 pint (approximately ½ litre) pineapple juice
3 level tablespoons cornflour
¼ pint (125ml) stock

1. Cut the skin and any fat from the meat, remove the bone then cut the meat into 1-inch pieces.
2. Put the pieces into a bowl, add the sugar, soya sauce, salt, monosodium glutamate and the sherry; stir together then cover the meat and leave it for at least 1 hour in a cool place to marinate.
3. To make the batter, sieve the flour and salt into a mixing bowl.
4. Make a well in the centre and add the egg yolks and oil.
5. Using a wooden spoon, gradually work the flour into the liquid then, little by little, add the water until a smooth batter is formed.
6. Heat a deep fat fryer two-thirds full of cooking oil. (You do not require the fat basket.)
7. Whisk the egg whites and, using a metal spoon, fold them into the batter.
8. Coat the meat with the batter and fry it in batches for about 5–7 minutes.
9. Drain each batch on kitchen paper then keep the cooked pieces in a warm oven while cooking the other batches. Reheat the fat between each batch.
10. For the sauce, cut the pepper in half, remove the core and cut the flesh into strips.
11. Boil the pepper with the onions and carrots in salted water for 5 minutes then drain immediately.
12. Put the vinegar, sugar, salt, tomato ketchup, pineapple pieces, with their syrup, and the pineapple juice into a pan.
13. Blend the cornflour with a little of the stock to a smooth paste.
14. Add the rest of the stock to the main bulk of ingredients and bring the mixture to the boil.
15. Stir 3 tablespoons into the cornflour then return the paste to the pan and, stirring all the time, bring the sauce to the boil.
16. Boil for 3 minutes then stir in the vegetables and pour the sauce over the fried pork and serve.

SHRIMP CRACKERS

Shrimp crackers are bought in packets ready for cooking from Chinese grocers. For a party of 20 people you will require 4oz (100gm). Heat a deep fat fryer, half full of cooking oil, until it is really hot, then add 6 or 7 crackers and cook them for only about 10 seconds. You will be amazed how quickly they swell to about three times their size. They will keep crisp for several hours, so they can be cooked at least 1 hour before your guests arrive.

SPECIAL FRIED RICE
Serves 20

It is advisable to serve both plain and fried rice. For plain boiled rice you will require 12oz (300gm). See page 30 for instructions on cooking boiled rice.

12oz (300gm) long-grain rice
1 can (1lb 3oz or 475gm) bamboo shoots
2oz (50gm) margarine
3 large eggs
pinch of salt
3 tablespoons soya sauce
2 level teaspoons monosodium glutamate
1 can (6oz or 150gm) peeled shrimps, drained

1. Cook the rice in boiling, salted water for 12–15 minutes, until the grains are tender.
2. Drain the rice thoroughly and leave it to cool. (The rice can be cooked earlier in the day.)
3. Drain the bamboo shoots and cut them into small pieces.
4. Melt the margarine in a large frying pan.
5. Beat the eggs with the salt, add to the pan and start to scramble the mixture.
6. While the egg is still half liquid, add the rice and, stirring quickly, coat the grains with the egg.
7. Keep stirring the rice so it heats up.
8. Mix in the soya sauce with the monosodium glutamate, the shrimps and the bamboo shoots and when the fried rice is really hot, turn it into a serving dish.

Meatball curry with accompaniments (see page 30)

Barbecue chops and sausages (see page 32)

Barbecued spare ribs (see page 33)

Sangria (see page 38)

Fish pools (see page 41)

Noughts and crosses savoury (see page 43)

Fort cake (see page 46)

Toffee apples (see page 48)

CHINESE FRUIT SALAD
Serves 20

½ pint (250ml) water
8oz (200gm) granulated sugar
1 large fresh pineapple or
2 cans (1lb 3oz or 475gm) pineapple pieces
2 cans (1lb 4oz or 500gm) lychees in syrup
1 can (11oz or 275gm) mandarin oranges
4oz (100gm) glacé cherries, chopped
4oz (100gm) preserved stem ginger, sliced
2oz (50gm) flaked almonds, browned

1. Put the water and sugar into a pan and, over a gentle heat, dissolve the sugar.
2. When every grain has dissolved, increase the heat, bring to the boil and boil for 3 minutes.
3. Leave the syrup on one side to cool.
4. Meanwhile, peel the fresh pineapple and cut the top and bottom from the fruit.
5. Using a sharp knife and following the lines between the eyes, make slanting cuts behind them so the cut slants towards the centre of each line.
6. Remove the eyes with the skin – this piece should be wedge shaped.
7. Continue round the pineapple until all the skin is removed.
8. Cut the flesh into thin slices and remove the core. Cut each slice into four.
9. Place the fresh or canned pineapple pieces in a serving dish with the lychees and their syrup and the mandarin oranges.
10. Finally stir in the cherries, ginger and the cooled syrup.
11. Sprinkle the top with the flaked almonds and serve with raisin biscuits and single cream. 1 pint (approximately ½ litre) cream is sufficient for 20 people.

RAISIN BISCUITS
Makes about 36

4oz (100gm) margarine
8oz (200gm) granulated sugar
1 large egg
1 teaspoon vanilla essence
12oz (300gm) plain flour
2 level teaspoons baking powder
pinch of salt
seedless raisins to decorate

1. Preheat oven to moderate, 350 deg F or gas 4 (180 deg C).
2. Cream the margarine and sugar together until light and fluffy.
3. Beat in the egg and vanilla essence.
4. Sift the flour, baking powder and salt and knead it into the creamed mixture to make a fairly stiff dough.
5. Roll the mixture into small balls about the size of an unshelled walnut.
6. Place on greased baking sheets and put a raisin on each.
7. Press flat with the back of a fork.
8. Bake in the centre of the oven for about 20 minutes, until golden brown.
9. Cool on a wire tray then store in an airtight tin until required.

JASMINE TEA

Allow 1 level tablespoon of jasmine tea for every 1 pint (approximately ½ litre) of boiling water. Always make the tea in a china teapot and leave it to brew for 2–3 minutes. It is very pale in colour and is not normally served with milk or sugar.

WHITE WINE CUP
Gives 60 glasses

It saves a lot of time and effort if only one drink is served throughout the party. My suggestion is a white wine cup, which is very easy to drink and appreciated by almost everybody. The quantities given in this recipe should be sufficient for the whole evening. It is perfectly all right to make the punch up in half or even quarter quantities if you do not have a very large punch bowl.

1 gallon (4½ litres) inexpensive white wine
½ pint (250ml) vodka
1 pint (approximately ½ litre) orange squash
4 large bottles lemonade (each bottle contains 2 pints or approximately 1 litre)
ice cubes
1 orange, sliced
1 lemon, sliced

1. At the last minute mix the wine with the vodka, orange squash and lemonade in the punch bowl.
2. Stir in the ice cubes with the sliced orange and lemon and ladle the punch into glasses for serving.

A SPANISH EVENING

With paella as the centrepiece and sangria as the drink, the Spanish atmosphere is set for a very enjoyable party. This party is for 8–10 people.

MENU
Serves 8–10

Paella
Mixed salad

Caramel oranges

Sangria

see overleaf for recipes

PAELLA
Serves 10

4 chicken joints
8oz (200gm) gammon rashers
1 packet (8oz or 200gm) frozen French beans
1 small red pepper
2 small green peppers
¼ pint (125ml) unpeeled prawns
1 jar (4oz or 100gm) mussels in brine
2oz (50gm) margarine
4 tablespoons corn oil
8oz (200gm) onions, peeled and chopped
1 garlic clove, crushed
1lb (½ kilo) long-grain rice
1 packet saffron powder
1¾ pints (generous ¾ litre) chicken stock
3 tomatoes, peeled and chopped
salt and pepper
1 lemon

1. Cut the chicken into small pieces.
2. De-rind the gammon and cut it into 1-inch pieces.
3. Bring the beans to the boil, drain then cut into 1-inch pieces.
4. Cut the peppers in half, remove the core then slice the flesh into thin strips.
5. Peel all but four of the prawns.
6. Drain the mussels.
7. Heat half the margarine and oil in a paella pan or frying pan.
8. Fry the chicken for 10 minutes until the pieces are browned.
9. Add the gammon and cook for a further 5 minutes.
10. Remove to a plate and keep warm.
11. Gently fry the onions and garlic until tender but not brown.
12. Add the rest of the oil and margarine and when it has melted stir in the rice.
13. Fry it gently until the grains are opaque.
14. Sprinkle in the saffron powder and pour in the stock.
15. Add the beans, tomatoes and peppers with the chicken and gammon.
16. Cover the pan with foil and simmer for 15 minutes, until all the stock has been absorbed and the rice is tender.
17. Finally stir in the mussels and the peeled prawns then cook for a further 3 minutes.
18. Check for seasoning. Cut the lemon into 8 slices and arrange them around the dish and place the reserved prawns on top.

MIXED SALAD

Choose four or five ingredients from the list below and mix them together in a salad bowl. Toss in French dressing (see Basic recipes, page 100) before serving.

1. **Lettuce:** break the leaves apart, wash them well then pat them dry in a teatowel.
2. **Spring onions:** trim the root and top leaves, then remove any damaged leaves and wash the onions. Pat them dry.
3. **Radishes:** trim the root and leaves from the radishes, wash them and slice into rings.
4. **Celery:** trim off the root and leaves, wash the sticks thoroughly, then cut them into thin strips.
5. **Cucumber:** can be peeled although the skin is attractive. Cut into slices or cubes.
6. **Chicory:** remove any damaged leaves then slice the chicory into thin rings.
7. **Tomatoes:** plunge into boiling water for 20 seconds, transfer to cold water then peel off the skins; slice or quarter the tomatoes.
8. **Hard-boiled eggs:** remove the shell and serve either sliced or quartered.
9. **Cooked beetroot:** trim off the stalks and root, peel off the skin then cut into cubes. Add beetroot to the salad at the very last minute.

CARAMEL ORANGES
Serves 8–10

12 small oranges
1lb (½ kilo) granulated sugar
1 pint (approximately ½ litre) water
1 tablespoon sherry (optional)

1. Using a potato peeler, peel the rind from 1 orange and cut it into very thin shreds.
2. Put the pieces into a pan of cold water and bring to the boil, drain immediately and run under cold water.
3. Peel the oranges. Do this using a sharp knife and work spirally around the orange cutting between the pith and flesh.
4. Cut the oranges into thin slices and leave them in a cool place.
5. Put the sugar and half the water into a pan and, over a very low heat, dissolve the sugar.
6. When it has melted, bring the syrup to the boil and boil rapidly without a lid until it starts to change to a light caramel colour.
7. Remove from the heat – it will continue to darken all the time.
8. Cover the hand holding the pan, as the mixture is likely to spit, then pour in the rest of the water.
9. Return the pan to the heat and slowly dissolve the caramel again.
10. Leave to cool slightly then pour over the oranges.
11. Stir in the sherry (if used) and leave the caramel oranges in a cool place for the flavours to blend.
12. Just before serving, sprinkle the shredded peel over the surface and serve cream separately.

SANGRIA
(Illustrated on page 35)

A deliciously cooling Spanish drink, sufficient for 12 glasses.

8oz (200gm) caster sugar
1½ pints (approximately ¾ litre) water
2 oranges, sliced
2 lemons, sliced
3-inch cinnamon stick
2 pints (approximately 1 litre) inexpensive red wine
4 tablespoons brandy
1 pint (approximately ½ litre) soda water
ice cubes

1. Put the sugar and water into a pan and, over a very low heat, dissolve the sugar.
2. When every grain has dissolved bring the syrup to the boil and boil rapidly for 2 minutes.
3. Remove from the heat and add the orange and lemon slices and the cinnamon stick.
4. Leave in a cool place for at least 6 hours for the flavours to blend.
5. Just before serving, add the wine, brandy, soda water and plenty of ice.
6. Pour into a large jug.

Parties for the young-set

A collection of birthday party ideas for children from one year old to teenage, as well as suggestions for a Guy Fawkes party and a picnic party.

YOU'RE ONE TODAY

The first birthday party is a very special occasion. The grandparents will be there as well as a few friends of the birthday child, with their respective mothers. The food for the party must be suitable for both the old and young alike and here is my suggestion for a tea party for 12 people.

MENU
Serves 12

Candle cake
Sandwiches: Thunder and lightning
Egg
Fish tartlets
Drop scones
Chocolate fudge swirls
Madeleines
Fish pools

Tea or orange squash

CANDLE CAKE
Serves 12

10oz (250gm) soft margarine
4oz (100gm) caster sugar
2 large eggs
4oz (100gm) self-raising flour
1 level tablespoon coffee powder
pinch of salt
1 tablespoon milk
12oz (300gm) icing sugar, sifted
little coffee powder
chocolate drops

1. Preheat oven to moderate to moderately hot, 375 deg F or gas 5 (190 deg C).
2. Brush two 15-oz (375-gm) cans with melted fat and line the base of each with a circle of greaseproof paper. Brush the greaseproof paper.
3. Put 4oz (100gm) of the margarine, the sugar, eggs, sifted flour, coffee powder and salt into a bowl with the milk.
4. Mix the ingredients together with a wooden spoon then beat them for 1 minute so they are all well combined.
5. Divide the mixture between the cans and hollow out the centres slightly.
6. Bake in the centre of the oven for 40 minutes, or until well risen and springy to the touch.
7. Leave in the tins to cool for 15 minutes then run a knife between the can and the cake and turn on to a wire tray.
8. Beat the remaining margarine, for the icing, until soft then beat in the sifted icing sugar.
9. Dissolve the coffee powder in hot water, making it very concentrated and beat sufficient into the icing to give it a good coffee colour and flavour.
10. Trim off the top of one of the cakes so it is level then cut each cake into three rounds.
11. Spread the rounds with most of the butter cream then pile them one on top of the other to form a large candle with the remaining domed top the last round in place.
12. Put the candle cake on a serving plate and very carefully cover the sides and the top with the remaining butter cream.
13. Mark the sides with a fork then encircle them in a spiral with a row of chocolate buttons working from bottom to top.
14. Cut some buttons in half and place them around the top edge, cuts towards the centre, so they give the candle a frilled top effect.
15. Lastly, place a real candle in the centre of the cake.
16. Any remaining chocolate buttons may be placed around the base of the dish.

To freeze: place in heavy duty polythene bags, seal and label. Store for up to 3 months. Thaw out at room temperature for about 3 hours before decorating.

SANDWICHES
Makes 32 sandwiches

1 small sliced brown loaf
1 small sliced white loaf
6oz (150gm) butter

Thunder and lightning filling:
golden syrup
2oz (50gm) clotted cream

Egg filling:
½oz (12gm) butter
2 tablespoons milk
4 large eggs
salt and pepper
little mustard and cress

1. Spread the slices of bread thinly with butter.
2. For the thunder and lightning sandwiches use the brown bread. Spread half the slices with golden syrup and the other half with clotted cream.
3. Sandwich the slices together, cut off the crusts then cut each sandwich into half, diagonally.
4. For the egg filling, melt the butter in a pan over a low heat.
5. Remove from the heat, add the milk then beat in the eggs with plenty of seasoning.
6. Over a very low heat and stirring all the time, scramble the eggs.
7. Turn into a basin to cool and mix in some of the mustard and cress.
8. Spread the filling between half the slices of white bread.
9. Make into sandwiches then cut off the crusts and cut each sandwich in half.
10. Arrange the sandwiches on plates and garnish the egg ones with the remaining mustard and cress.

FISH TARTLETS
Makes 24

shortcrust pastry made with 8oz (200gm) flour (see Basic recipes, page 100)
1 can (8oz or 200gm) pilchards in tomato sauce
2 level tablespoons salad cream
2oz (50gm) frozen sweetcorn
squeeze of lemon juice
salt and pepper
1 tomato

1. Preheat oven to moderate to moderately hot, 400 deg F or gas 6 (200 deg C).
2. Roll the pastry out to just under an ⅛-inch thickness.
3. Using a 2½-inch (6·3-cm) fluted cutter, cut out rounds, then gather up the scraps and re-roll the pastry to cut out more rounds.
4. Line patty tins with the rounds and prick the base of each with a fork.
5. Bake in the centre of the oven for 15–20 minutes, until golden brown. Cool the cases on a wire tray.
6. Mix the pilchards with the salad cream.
7. Mash the ingredients together until they are smooth and creamy.
8. Cook the sweetcorn in boiling, salted water for 5 minutes.
9. Drain and run under cold water, then add to the filling with the lemon juice and seasoning.
10. Just before serving, divide the filling between the cases.
11. Cut the tomato into six slices, divide each slice into four and garnish each tartlet with a piece of tomato.

DROP SCONES
Makes about 15

8oz (200gm) self-raising flour
good pinch of salt
1 level tablespoon caster sugar
1 large egg
¼ pint (125ml) plus 4 tablespoons milk
small piece of lard

1. Sift the flour and salt into a mixing bowl.
2. Stir in the caster sugar and make a well in the centre.
3. Beat the egg and pour it into the centre with the milk.
4. Gradually work the flour from the sides of the bowl into the liquid.
5. Mix until the batter is smooth but do not beat at this stage. It should be quite thick when ready.
6. Rub a heated girdle with a small piece of lard held in a piece of paper.
7. Increase the heat under the girdle and drop spoonfuls of the mixture on to it – bubbles should start to rise to the surface almost immediately.
8. When the undersides are brown turn the scones over and cook them on the other side.
9. Transfer to a teatowel to keep warm while making the others.
10. Arrange the drop scones in a pretty napkin for serving and have plenty of butter and jam to eat with them.

CHOCOLATE FUDGE SWIRLS
Makes 16

5oz (125gm) plain flour
pinch of salt
8oz (200gm) margarine or butter
2oz (50gm) caster sugar
4oz (100gm) soft brown sugar
2 level tablespoons golden syrup
1 small can sweetened condensed milk
few drops vanilla essence
3oz (75gm) plain chocolate
2oz (50gm) white chocolate

1. Preheat oven to moderate, 350 deg F or gas 4 (180 deg C).
2. Brush a shallow 7-inch (18-cm) square tin with melted fat.
3. Sift the flour and salt into a mixing bowl.
4. Add half the fat and rub it in until the mixture resembles fine breadcrumbs.
5. Stir in the caster sugar then knead the ingredients into a ball.
6. Press the mixture into the tin, level it with a palette knife and bake in the centre of the oven for 25 minutes. Leave to cool in the tin.
7. Put the remaining margarine, the brown sugar, syrup and condensed milk into a pan and, over a gentle heat, dissolve the sugar.
8. When every grain has dissolved, bring the mixture to the boil and,

stirring continuously, boil gently for 7 minutes.
9. Remove from the heat, beat in the vanilla essence and continue to beat the mixture until it starts to thicken.
10. Pour it on to the base in the tin and leave in a cool place for the filling to set.
11. Cut the chocolate into pieces and, on separate plates over separate pans of hot water, melt the white and the dark chocolate until they are both liquid.
12. When the filling is quite cold and set, tip on the dark chocolate and spread it to the edges.
13. Tip on the white chocolate next and, with a palette knife, swirl the two chocolates together.
14. Leave to set completely then remove the mixture from the tin and cut it into 16 pieces. Arrange on a plate for serving.

MADELEINES
Makes 14

4oz (100gm) margarine
4oz (100gm) caster sugar
2 large eggs
4oz (100gm) self-raising flour
little milk
2oz (50gm) desiccated coconut
about 8oz (200gm) raspberry jam

1. Preheat oven to moderate to moderately hot, 375 deg F or gas 5 (190 deg C).
2. Brush 14 castle pudding moulds with melted fat.
3. Beat the margarine until it is soft, add the caster sugar and beat together until light and fluffy in colour and texture.
4. Beat the eggs then add them to the creamed mixture gradually, beating well between each addition.
5. Fold the sifted flour into the mixture with a little milk so it is of a soft dropping consistency.
6. Fill the tins about one-third full with the mixture and hollow out the centre so the cakes rise evenly during baking.
7. Put the moulds on to a baking sheet and cook in the centre of the oven for 12–15 minutes, or until golden brown and cooked.
8. Turn the cakes on to a wire tray to cool.
9. When they are completely cold level the base of each if slightly risen.
10. Put the coconut on to a piece of paper.
11. Spread the sides of each madeleine with jam and roll the sides in the coconut so they are coated.
12. Stand the cakes upright in paper cases and top each cake with a blob of jam.

To freeze: place, undecorated, in polythene bags or foil or plastic containers, seal and label. Store for up to 3 months. Thaw at room temperature for 3 hours, then decorate as above.

FISH POOLS
(Illustrated on page 36)
Serves 10

2 lime jellies
1 can (1lb 13oz or 725gm) peach halves
10 currants
10 Polo mints

1. Make the jellies according to the directions on the packets and leave to cool.
2. When the jelly starts to set, pour it evenly between 10 trifle cases and leave in a cool place to set completely.
3. To decorate the jellies, take a sliver from each side of the peach halves, then place a peach half on each jelly.
4. Take one sliver of peach and place it at the end with the curve going away to form the tail.
5. Cut the other sliver of peach into two and place a piece on either side for fins.
6. Position a currant for the eye and a Polo for an air bubble.
7. Serve with single cream.

OFF TO THE WOODS

With the weather set fine what could be nicer than to have a birthday party in the country? Picnics are always a favourite, and think of the advantages of having eight children to tea without the worry of the furniture and carpets being spoilt. Organize enough cars with other mums to get you to your destination and do not forget to pack flannels and towels for the inevitable sticky fingers.

MENU
Serves 8

Egg and meat roll
Sandwiches: Egg
Cheese and chutney
Banana and raspberry jam
Ring doughnuts
Chocolate fingers
Eskimo birthday cake
Jelly fruit tubs

Lemon and orange squash

EGG AND MEAT ROLL
Makes 12 slices

shortcrust pastry made with 8oz (200gm) flour (see Basic recipes, page 100)
8oz (200gm) pork sausagemeat
4oz (100gm) minced beef
1 onion, peeled and grated
salt and pepper
3 hard-boiled eggs
little beaten egg to glaze

1. Preheat oven to moderate to moderately hot, 400 deg F or gas 6 (200 deg C).
2. Roll the pastry to a rectangle 11 inches by 10 inches.
3. Mix the sausagemeat, minced beef and onion together with plenty of salt and pepper.
4. Spread the meat mixture over the pastry leaving a 1-inch border all the way round.
5. Shell the eggs and place them end to end down the centre.
6. Moisten the edges and bring the sides of the pastry up over the eggs then fold the ends up.
7. Turn the roll over and place on a baking sheet so the edges are all underneath.
8. Brush the pastry with the beaten egg and mark it with the back of a knife in a diamond design.
9. Bake just above the centre of the oven for 20 minutes then reduce the heat to moderate, 350 deg F or gas 4 (180 deg C) for a further hour, until the pastry is golden brown.
10. Leave the roll to cool completely.
11. Cut into 12 slices and wrap it in foil ready for the picnic.
12. Take some washed lettuce and tomatoes in a polythene bag to eat with the roll.

SANDWICHES

8oz (200gm) butter
1 thinly sliced white loaf

Egg filling:
2 hard-boiled eggs
4 level tablespoons salad cream
salt and pepper
½ punnet mustard and cress

Cheese and chutney filling:
2 level dessertspoons apple chutney
6oz (150gm) Cheddar cheese, grated

Banana and raspberry jam filling:
2 tablespoons raspberry jam
2 bananas
juice of half a lemon

1. Soften the butter and spread it over the slices of bread.
2. For the egg filling, shell the eggs and mash them with a potato masher into small pieces.
3. Bind together with the salad cream and season with salt and pepper.
4. Stir in the mustard and cress.
5. Spread the filling over 4 slices of bread.
6. Make into sandwiches, cut off the crusts and cut them into four.
7. Wrap in polythene to keep fresh.
8. For the cheese and chutney filling, spread the chutney over slices of bread.
9. Divide the grated cheese between them and make into sandwiches.
10. Cut off the crusts, cut into four and wrap in polythene.
11. For the banana and raspberry jam filling, spread the jam over 3 slices of bread.
12. Peel and slice the bananas and toss them in the lemon juice.
13. Divide the slices between the pieces of bread and make them into sandwiches using the last 3 slices of bread.
14. Cut the crusts off the rounds, cut them into four and wrap them in polythene ready for the picnic.

RING DOUGHNUTS
Makes 16

1lb (½ kilo) strong plain flour
pinch of salt
1½oz (37gm) margarine
½oz (12gm) dried yeast
5oz (125gm) caster sugar
¼ pint (125ml) milk
scant ¼ pint (125ml) water
oil for deep frying

1. Sift the flour and salt into a mixing bowl.
2. Rub in the margarine until it is evenly distributed.
3. Put the yeast and 1 teaspoon of the sugar into a small bowl.
4. Heat the milk and water in a pan to blood heat, then whisk half of it into the yeast.
5. Leave the small bowl on one side for the yeast to dissolve and form a good froth on top.
6. Reserving 4oz (100gm) sugar, add the rest to the liquid.
7. When the yeast is ready stir it into the flour with the other liquid.
8. Beat the dough until it is not sticky but very elastic.
9. Turn it on to a well floured working surface and knead the dough until it is smooth.
10. Brush a mixing bowl with a little melted fat, put in the dough and cover the bowl with a damp cloth or a sheet of polythene.
11. Leave the bowl in a warm place for about 1 hour or until the dough has risen to double its bulk.
12. Knock it back gently then divide the dough into 16 pieces.
13. Roll each piece into a ball and make a *large* hole in the centre of each with your finger.
14. Put the rings on a greased baking sheet and leave them in a warm place for about 30 minutes until they have doubled in size.
15. Half-fill a deep fat fryer with cooking oil and heat it to 350 deg F (180 deg C). To test, if you have no thermometer, a piece of bread in fat should turn brown in 20 seconds.
16. Put the remaining sugar on to a piece of paper.
17. When the fat is ready, lower 4 or 5 doughnuts into it and fry them for 2–3 minutes on each side. Repeat until all the doughnuts are fried, reheating the oil between each batch.
18. Lift on a draining spoon and tip on to the sugar.
19. Coat them with sugar. Cool and pack for the picnic.

CHOCOLATE FINGERS
Makes 24

2½oz (62gm) margarine
2½oz (62gm) lard
2oz (50gm) caster sugar
6oz (150gm) plain flour
1oz (25gm) cocoa powder
1½oz (37gm) digestive biscuit crumbs
12oz (300gm) icing sugar
1oz (25gm) cocoa powder

1. Preheat oven to moderate, 350 deg F or gas 4 (180 deg C).
2. Beat the margarine and lard together to a soft cream.
3. Add the caster sugar and beat again until the mixture is light in colour and texture.
4. Sift the flour and cocoa powder together and work it into the creamed mixture, with the biscuit crumbs.
5. Brush an 8-inch (20-cm) by 12-inch (30-cm) Swiss roll tin with melted fat and spread the mixture over the base, levelling the surface with a palette knife.
6. Bake in the centre of the oven for 25 minutes. Immediately the mixture is cooked, cut it into 24 fingers then leave in the tin to cool completely.
7. To make the icing, sift the sugar and cocoa powder into a mixing bowl and stir in enough water to make a thick coating consistency.
8. Ice the fingers in the tin and when the icing has nearly set, again divide the mixture into fingers.
9. Leave it in the tin for ease of carrying on the picnic.

ESKIMO BIRTHDAY CAKE

This cake keeps very well.

4oz (100gm) margarine, softened
4oz (100gm) caster sugar
2 large eggs
4oz (100gm) self-raising flour
2 tablespoons milk
2oz (50gm) ground almonds
few drops almond essence
3oz (75gm) butter
6oz (150gm) icing sugar, sifted
1oz (25gm) desiccated coconut

1. Preheat oven to moderate, 350 deg F or gas 4 (180 deg C).
2. Grease a 7½-inch (19-cm) sandwich tin and line the base with a circle of greaseproof paper

cut to fit. Grease the paper lining.
3. Put the margarine, sugar, eggs, sifted flour, milk, ground almonds and almond essence into a bowl.
4. With a wooden spoon, or an electric mixer, mix the ingredients together then beat for 1 minute.
5. Turn the mixture into the tin, smooth over the surface and hollow out the centre slightly.
6. Bake in the centre of the oven for 30–40 minutes, or until it feels springy to the touch. Cool on a wire tray.
7. Beat the butter to a soft consistency, then gradually beat in the sifted icing sugar.
8. When the cake is cold spread the icing over the top and sides and sprinkle with coconut.
9. Decorate the top with Eskimo candle holders, a polar bear and igloo cake decorations, if available.

JELLY FRUIT TUBS
Makes 10

3 trifle sponges
2 packets strawberry jelly
1 can (1lb 14oz or 750gm) fruit cocktail

1. Divide the sponges between 10 small empty cream or yogurt cartons.
2. Dissolve the jellies in ¾ pint (375ml) liquid, then make it up to 2 pints (approximately 1 litre) with juice from the drained fruit cocktail and water.
3. Divide the fruit between the containers.
4. Pour the jelly on top.
5. Leave in a cool place to set.
6. Place them in a tin to carry on the picnic and keep the tin upright. Do not forget to pack teaspoons.

LEMON AND ORANGE SQUASH
Makes 6–8 diluted pints

1lb (½ kilo) granulated sugar
¾ pint (375ml) water
finely grated rind and juice of 2 oranges and 1 lemon
2 level teaspoons tartaric acid

1. Put the sugar and water into a pan and, over a low heat, dissolve the sugar.
2. When it has dissolved bring the syrup to the boil and simmer for 10 minutes.
3. Pour the syrup over the lemon and orange rinds and the tartaric acid in a bowl.
4. Leave the mixture to cool overnight.
5. Stir in the fruit juices the next day and keep the concentrated mixture in corked bottles in a cool place. Dilute to taste.

A FUN AND GAMES PARTY

Planned for the 10–12-year olds, this party has fun and games as its theme. The food includes noughts and crosses savoury, domino biscuits and chequerboard trifle and is sufficient for 9 children.

MENU
Serves 9

Noughts and crosses savoury
Biteful kebabs
Lucky dip with tasty twists
Dice cakes
Domino biscuits
Chequerboard trifle
Mysterious quencher

NOUGHTS AND CROSSES SAVOURY
(Illustrated on page 36)
Serves 9

12oz (300gm) self-raising flour
pinch of salt
4oz (100gm) margarine
4oz (100gm) Cheddar cheese, grated
1 large egg
milk to mix
6 frankfurter sausages
4 streaky bacon rashers
5 flat mushrooms
3oz (75gm) butter
little yeast extract
parsley sprigs

1. Preheat oven to hot, 425 deg F or gas 7 (220 deg C).
2. Sift the flour and salt into a mixing bowl and rub in the margarine so it is evenly distributed.
3. Add the cheese and, when it is well mixed, stir in the egg and enough milk to make a soft but not sticky dough.
4. Turn the dough on to a lightly floured working surface and roll it into a 9-inch square.
5. Place on a baking sheet, trim the edges, then bake on the second shelf of the oven for 25 minutes, or until golden brown. Cool on a wire tray.
6. Cook the frankfurters following the instructions on the packet.
7. Remove the rind from the bacon and grill the rashers with the trimmed mushrooms.
8. To assemble the dish, cut the scone into nine 3-inch squares.
9. Slice the pieces in half, spread with butter and yeast extract, then sandwich them back together.
10. Reassemble the square on a serving plate.
11. Cut the frankfurters in half lengthways and lay then over the cuts to make two lines of 3 frankfurters, each way.
12. Put sprigs of parsley where the sausages connect.
13. Cut the rashers of bacon in half widthways and place the mushrooms for noughts and the bacon pieces, crossed, for crosses on the board to represent a game of noughts and crosses.

BITEFUL KEBABS
Makes 18

8oz (200gm) streaky bacon rashers
3oz (75gm) butter
squeeze of lemon juice
salt and pepper
6oz (150gm) button mushrooms
2 tomatoes
18 small pickled onions
9 bridge rolls

1. Preheat the grill.
2. Cut the rind and any small bones from the bacon.
3. With the back of a knife, stretch each rasher to almost double its size then cut into two.
4. Roll the pieces up and grill them until cooked. Leave to cool.
5. Melt a little of the butter in a small pan, add the lemon juice with a little salt and pepper. Cook the trimmed mushrooms for about 5 minutes or until tender. Drain and cool.
6. Cut each tomato into nine pieces.
7. Thread a roll of bacon, mushroom, onion and tomato on to 18 wooden cocktail sticks.
8. Split each bridge roll and spread with the remaining butter.
9. Place a kebab on each halved roll, then make a flag for each guest with their name on; place the flags on cocktail sticks and put one in the centre of each kebab.
10. Put them either on the table as place names or serve them on a large platter so everyone can help themselves to their own savoury.

LUCKY DIP
Serves 9

8oz (200gm) cottage cheese
4 tablespoons natural yogurt
1 can (8oz or 200gm) crushed pineapple
1oz (25gm) walnuts, chopped
salt and pepper
little cayenne pepper

1. Mix the cottage cheese with the yogurt.
2. Drain the pineapple and stir the pieces into the dip with the walnuts.
3. Check the dip for seasoning, then turn it into a serving bowl.
4. Sprinkle the centre with cayenne pepper and arrange the tasty twists around the bowl.

TASTY TWISTS
Makes 36

shortcrust pastry made with 4oz (100gm) flour (see Basic recipes, page 100)
1 small onion, peeled and grated
4oz (100gm) sausagemeat
little milk
salt and pepper

1. Preheat oven to moderate to moderately hot, 400 deg F or gas 6 (200 deg C).
2. On a lightly floured working surface, roll the pastry into a rectangle 9 inches by 8 inches. Trim the edges.
3. Mix the onion with the sausagemeat.
4. Brush the pastry with milk then very carefully spread the sausagemeat on top, making sure it goes right to the edges. Sprinkle with salt and pepper.
5. Cut the pastry into two strips each 9 inches by 4 inches, then cut each strip, widthways, into ½-inch pieces.
6. Twist each piece into a cork-screw shape and place on baking sheets.
7. Leave in a cool place to rest for 15 minutes.
8. Bake in the centre of the oven for about 20 minutes, or until golden brown.
9. Cool on a wire tray then serve around the lucky dip.

DICE CAKES
Makes 16

6oz (150gm) margarine
6oz (150gm) caster sugar
grated rind of 1 orange
3 large eggs
6oz (150gm) self-raising flour
pinch of salt
1lb (½ kilo) icing sugar, sifted
juice of 1 orange
few drops orange food colouring
Smarties

1. Preheat oven to moderate to moderately hot, 375 deg F or gas 5 (190 deg C).
2. Brush a 7-inch (18-cm) square cake tin with melted fat and line the base with a square of paper cut to fit. Brush the paper lining.
3. Cream the margarine, add the sugar and orange rind and beat the ingredients until light and fluffy.
4. Beat the eggs together then add them gradually to the creamed mixture, beating well between each addition.
5. Sift the flour and salt together then, using a metal spoon, fold the dry ingredients into the mixture and turn it into the prepared tin.
6. Smooth the mixture to the sides and hollow out the centre slightly so the cake rises evenly.
7. Bake in the centre of the oven for 1–1¼ hours, until it feels springy and starts to shrink away from the sides of the tin. Cool on a wire tray, then peel off the greaseproof paper.
8. When the cake is cold cut it into 16 small squares and space the cakes out on the wire tray.
9. Mix the icing sugar with the orange juice and sufficient water to make a fairly thick consistency.
10. Stir in a few drops of orange food colouring.
11. Coat the top and sides of the cakes with the icing using a palette knife to guide the icing on to the sides.
12. Leave the cakes to finish dripping and start to set.
13. Just before they are completely set press the Smarties on top and on to the sides of each cake so they resemble dice.
14. Leave to set completely before placing each cake in a paper case for serving.

DOMINO BISCUITS
Makes 20

Biscuits:
4oz (100gm) margarine
4oz (100gm) caster sugar
6oz (150gm) plain flour
2oz (50gm) custard powder
2 level tablespoons cocoa powder
½ level teaspoon baking powder
1 small egg

Filling:
2oz (50gm) margarine
2½oz (62gm) icing sugar, sifted
1 level tablespoon drinking chocolate powder
1 level teaspoon coffee powder

Icing:
2oz (50gm) icing sugar, sifted

1. Preheat oven to moderate, 350 deg F or gas 4 (180 deg C).
2. Cream the margarine then add the sugar and cream together until light and fluffy.
3. Sift the flour, custard powder, cocoa powder and baking powder together.
4. Beat the egg then add it to the creamed mixture with the dry ingredients.
5. Work the ingredients together to form a rather stiff dough.
6. Roll the dough out on a floured working surface to an ⅛-inch thickness.
7. Cut into fingers 3 inches by 1½ inches.
8. Gather up any scraps, re-roll and cut out more biscuits.
9. Prick the biscuits with a fork and place them on lightly greased baking sheets.
10. Bake in the centre and lower part of the oven for 15–20 minutes, then cool on a wire tray.
11. Beat the margarine for the filling to a soft cream then gradually beat in the icing sugar with the chocolate and coffee powder.
12. Sandwich the biscuits in pairs with the filling.
13. Mix the icing sugar for the decoration with a little water to make it of a piping consistency.
14. Put it into a small greaseproof icing bag and pipe each biscuit as a domino piece.
15. Serve on a flat board arranged, if possible, into a game.

CHEQUERBOARD TRIFLE
Serves 9

8 trifle sponges
6 level tablespoons raspberry jam
2 cans (1lb 3oz or 475gm) raspberries
1lb (½ kilo) marshmallows
1 large can unsweetened evaporated milk, chilled
1 dessertspoon lemon juice
9 rectangular chocolate biscuits

1. Split the trifle sponges and spread them with jam.
2. Place in a large shallow dish.
3. Strain the juice from the raspberries.
4. Leaving 6 pink and 6 white marshmallows on one side for later, cut the rest into pieces with scissors and put them into a bowl.
5. Heat 6 tablespoons of the raspberry juice to boiling point then pour it over the marshmallows and leave until dissolved.
6. Pour the rest of the juice over the sponges.
7. Put the evaporated milk into a bowl, add the lemon juice and whisk it until really stiff.
8. Sieve the raspberries and stir the raspberry purée into the milk with the melted marshmallows.
9. Pour the mixture over the sponges, then leave the trifle to set in a cool place.
10. Cut the biscuits in half and place them on the trifle to form a chequerboard.
11. Place the reserved pink marshmallows on the chocolate squares at one end and the white marshmallows on the trifle at the other end to complete the game.

MYSTERIOUS QUENCHER
Gives 10 glasses

2 pints (approximately 1 litre) Coca cola
5 tablespoons orange cordial
1 pint (approximately ½ litre) cold water
1 small can pineapple juice
orange slices
ice cubes

1. Mix the Coca cola, orange cordial, water and pineapple juice together in a jug.
2. Float orange slices on top and serve chilled with ice cubes.

A CHILDREN'S PARTY

First decide the theme of the party – I have chosen wagon trail – send out the invitations about 2 weeks before the appointed day and ask all those invited to come dressed for a wagon trail. The food must also obviously follow the theme of wagon trail and with that in mind I have arranged the party for 12 little guests.

MENU
Serves 12

Sausage centipede
Baked bean tartlets
Beefburgers
Coconut wigwams
Fire cakes
Fort cake

Lemon squash

SAUSAGE CENTIPEDE

1lb (½ kilo) pork chipolata sausages
1 French loaf (about 18 inches long)
2 green stuffed olives

1. Preheat the grill.
2. Keeping the sausages still in one string, twist each sausage in the centre to make two smaller ones.
3. Prick them with a fork then separate the sausages with a pair of scissors.
4. Place them under the grill and cook them, turning frequently, until they are brown all over. Leave to cool.
5. Turn the loaf upside down and press two rows of cocktail sticks into the base for legs.
6. Spear a cooked sausage on to each stick then turn the centipede over on to its feet.
7. Put the olives on to separate sticks and press them into the loaf at the head.
8. Put the centipede on to a board or long plate.

BAKED BEAN TARTLETS
Makes about 36

cheese pastry made with 8oz (200gm) flour (see Basic recipes, page 100)
1 can (15oz or 375gm) baked beans
4 rashers streaky bacon
5 tomatoes
2oz (50gm) cheese, grated

1. Preheat oven to moderate to moderately hot, 400 deg F or gas 6 (200 deg C).
2. Roll the pastry out to an $\frac{1}{8}$-inch thickness and with a 3-inch (7·5-cm) plain cutter cut about 36 rounds, gathering up and re-rolling the scraps if necessary.
3. Line patty tins with the rounds.
4. Divide the baked beans between the tartlets.
5. Cut the bacon into 16 pieces and place one piece on top of 16 tarts.
6. Cut each tomato into 4 slices, place one on each of the remaining tartlets, then sprinkle the slices with cheese.
7. Bake in the centre of the oven for 15–20 minutes.
8. Serve warm if possible.

BEEFBURGERS
Makes 16

8 frozen beefburgers
1oz (25gm) lard or dripping
2 medium onions, peeled and sliced
8 baps or soft rolls, split

1. Cook the beefburgers as instructed on the packet; keep them warm.
2. Melt the lard in a frying pan and fry the onions until cooked.
3. Place a burger and some onions in each bap.
4. Cut the baps in half and wrap each half in a check paper nakpin.
5. Keep warm until ready to serve with tomato ketchup.

COCONUT WIGWAMS
Makes 14

2 large egg whites
6oz (150gm) desiccated coconut
6oz (150gm) caster sugar
little vanilla essence

1. Preheat oven to very moderate, 325 deg F or gas 3 (170 deg C).
2. Whisk the egg whites until stiff.
3. Mix the coconut and sugar together and fold into the egg whites with the vanilla essence.
4. Lay rice paper on an ungreased baking sheet.
5. Divide the mixture into 14 pieces, shape each piece into a pyramid and place on the rice paper.
6. Bake in the centre of the oven for 25–30 minutes, until tinged golden brown.
7. Trim off the rice paper around the edge of each wigwam and place a feather in the top.
8. Leave to cool on a wire tray.

FIRE CAKES
Makes about 16

3oz (75gm) margarine
3 level tablespoons golden syrup
2oz (50gm) icing sugar, sifted
3 level tablespoons cocoa powder
4oz (100gm) cornflakes
8 glacé cherries, halved

1. Put the margarine, syrup and sifted icing sugar together with the cocoa powder into a fairly large saucepan.
2. Melt the ingredients over a low heat.
3. Remove from the heat and stir in the cornflakes.
4. Heap the mixture into paper cases and place a halved glacé cherry in the centre of each.
5. Leave the cakes on one side to set.

FORT CAKE
(Illustrated on page 36)

Cake:
6oz (150gm) softened margarine
6oz (150gm) caster sugar
3 large eggs
5oz (125gm) self-raising flour
1oz (25gm) cocoa powder
1 tablespoon milk

Icing:
6oz (150gm) margarine, softened
7oz (175gm) icing sugar, sifted
1½oz (37gm) cocoa powder

Decoration:
little brown and green food colouring
1oz (25gm) desiccated coconut
31 small chocolate flakes
4-inch square piece plain chocolate

1. Preheat oven to moderate to moderately hot, 375 deg F or gas 5 (190 deg C).
2. Brush a 7-inch (18-cm) square cake tin with melted fat and line the base with a piece of greaseproof paper cut to fit. Brush the paper lining.
3. For the cake, beat the margarine, sugar, eggs, sifted flour and cocoa powder together with the milk to make a soft dropping consistency.
4. Turn the mixture into the tin, spread it level then slightly hollow out the centre so the cake rises evenly during cooking.
5. Bake in the centre of the oven for 35–40 minutes, until it starts to shrink away from the sides of the tin and the cake feels springy to the touch.
6. Cool on a wire tray then remove the paper.
7. Beat the margarine for the icing, then gradually beat in the icing sugar and cocoa powder.
8. Work a little brown and green colouring into the coconut to make it look like grass.
9. Spread an 11-inch (28-cm) cake board with a thin layer of icing then sprinkle over the coloured coconut.
10. Leaving a $1\frac{1}{2}$-inch border, cut the centre from the cake then cut this piece into nine small squares.
11. Spread the frame of the cake with icing so it is covered, then very carefully lift it on to the centre of the board.
12. Spread eight small pieces of cake with icing (the ninth one is spare so can be eaten

immediately) and place a square at each corner and one in the centre of each wall so as to give the fort eight turrets.
13. Along three of the walls position the flakes, sticking them to the walls in the order of two whole flakes and two halves, ending with two whole flakes. This should work out so that the whole flakes cover the turrets.
14. The fourth side is for the door. Cover the sides in the same way but leave the centre turret. To this stick the piece of plain chocolate and then stick a flake across the top for the cross beam.
15. Finally arrange model soldiers and Red Indians around the cake so the fort is under attack.

LEMON SQUASH

This recipe makes 2¾ pints (approximately 1½ litres) concentrated lemon squash which, when diluted, will be sufficient for about 30 glasses.

1½lb (¾ kilo) granulated sugar
1½oz (37gm) tartaric acid
¼oz (6gm) Epsom salts (3 level teaspoons)
1½ pints (approximately ¾ litre) boiling water
finely grated rind and juice of 2 lemons

1. Put the sugar, tartaric acid and Epsom salts into a large bowl.
2. Pour over the boiling water and stir until the sugar has dissolved.
3. Leave the liquid to cool then stir in the grated lemon rind and juice.
4. Pour the squash, once it is quite cold, into bottles, cover and keep in a cool place.
5. It will keep for 2–3 weeks.

GUY FAWKES PARTY

Hot, warming but easy-to-eat food is called for at a bonfire party. I have devised recipes that are suitable more for children as fireworks are obviously mainly for them. It is advisable to have some adults about to supervise the actual firework display to prevent unnecessary accidents. Just one word of warning: please do not put the unlit fireworks either near the fire or the place from where they are to be set off. Not only can it be dangerous but to set all the fireworks off at once is such a waste. The other important point is to keep pets in the house. The noise of fireworks can distress them tremendously and again can lead to accidents.

MENU
Serves 8–10

Bean feast
Sausage candles
Toffee apples
Bomb cakes
Gingerbread men

Hot steaming cocoa

BEAN FEAST
Serves 8–10

1lb (½ kilo) haricot beans
1½lb (¾ kilo) belly of pork
1lb (½ kilo) breast of lamb
1lb (½ kilo) pork sausagemeat
1lb (½ kilo) onions, peeled and sliced
1lb (½ kilo) carrots, peeled and sliced
2 pints (approximately 1 litre) stock
good pinch of herbs
salt and pepper

1. Place the beans in a bowl, cover with cold water and leave to soak overnight.
2. Next day preheat oven to very moderate, 325 deg F or gas 3 (170 deg C).
3. Remove all the bones and excess fat, plus the skin, from the pork and lamb.
4. Cut the meat into 1½-inch pieces.
5. Fry the meat in a pan without any fat (sufficient should come out of the meat) until all the sides are brown and sealed.
6. Divide the sausagemeat into 12 pieces, then with floured hands roll each piece into a ball.
7. Fry the sausage balls in the pan so they are also sealed.
8. Drain the beans then, starting with them, layer all the ingredients in a casserole dish, ending with a layer of beans. (Do not forget to add the herbs and seasoning as you fill the dish.)
9. Cover and bake in the centre of the oven for about 4 hours, or until the meat is tender and the beans soft.
10. The easiest way to eat this recipe is in soup bowls. Hand crusty bread round with the bean feast, if liked.

SAUSAGE CANDLES
Serves 12

1½lb (¾ kilo) pork sausages
2oz (50gm) lard
1 French loaf, cut into 12 slices
2oz (50gm) butter
tomato ketchup or made mustard

1. As you have the oven on for the bean feast it is advisable to cook the sausages in the oven also. Put them into a roasting tin with the lard and place them on the top shelf of the oven.
2. Cook for 40–50 minutes, or until they are golden brown. (Turn them during cooking.)
3. Spread the bread with butter and make a hole in the centre of each slice with your finger.
4. When the sausages are cooked leave them to cool slightly then stand one up in each slice of bread.
5. Dot the top with tomato ketchup or mustard for the flame and serve on a large tray.

TOFFEE APPLES
(Illustrated on page 36)
Serves 12

12 small eating apples
1lb (½ kilo) granulated sugar
½ pint (250ml) water

1. Brush a baking sheet with oil.
2. Wipe the apples, remove the stalks and push a wooden meat skewer or lollipop stick in through the stalk end.
3. Put the sugar and water into a pan and, over a low heat, dissolve the sugar.
4. When all the grains have dissolved, bring to the boil and boil the syrup rapidly for 15–20 minutes, until it turns a light golden brown.
5. Take the pan off the heat. The syrup will continue to darken for a little while.
6. Tilt the pan to make a deep pool of toffee and carefully dip each apple in so it is completely coated.
7. Stand the coated apples on the oiled sheet and leave to cool and set before serving.

BOMB CAKES
Makes 12

10 digestive biscuits
5 level tablespoons drinking chocolate powder
5 level tablespoons desiccated coconut
2oz (50gm) margarine
1 small can sweetened condensed milk
extra desiccated coconut
1 liquorice strip

1. Using a rolling pin, crush the biscuits to crumbs.
2. Put into a bowl with the sifted chocolate powder and the desiccated coconut.
3. Melt the margarine and mix it into the dry ingredients with the condensed milk.
4. Divide the mixture into 12 even pieces and roll each into a small ball.
5. Put the extra desiccated coconut into a polythene bag and add two balls at a time.
6. Toss the balls until they are coated with coconut then put each into a paper case.
7. Cut the liquorice into 1-inch strips and push a piece into each ball to resemble the fuse.

GINGERBREAD MEN
Makes 12

8oz (200gm) margarine
4oz (100gm) caster sugar
12oz (300gm) plain flour
1 level teaspoon ground ginger
currants and glacé cherries

1. Preheat oven to very moderate, 325 deg F or gas 3 (170 deg C).
2. Beat the margarine to a soft cream.
3. Add the caster sugar and beat until light and fluffy in colour and texture.
4. Sift the flour and ginger together and stir into the creamed mixture.
5. Knead the mixture so it combines.
6. Roll it out to a ¼-inch thickness on a floured working surface and cut out shapes with a gingerbread man cutter.
7. Place on baking sheets.
8. Gather up the scraps, re-roll the mixture and cut out more men.
9. Make a face out of two currants for eyes and a slither of glacé cherry for a mouth.
10. Position three more currants down the centre of the gingerbread man for buttons.
11. Bake on the third and fourth shelves of the oven for 25 minutes, or until pale brown. Cool on a wire tray.

HOT STEAMING COCOA
Serves 8–10

3 pints (approximately 1½ litres) milk
1 pint (approximately ½ litre) water
4 level tablespoons cocoa powder
3oz (75gm) granulated sugar
12 marshmallows

1. Put the milk and water into a pan and stir in the cocoa powder.
2. Add the sugar then, over a low heat and stirring all the time, blend in the cocoa powder – it will mix in as the milk heats.
3. Bring to just below boiling, taking care to watch it all the time.
4. Divide the marshmallows between two jugs, then pour the cocoa over and let the marshmallows float to the surface.
5. Serve immediately.

A TEENAGE PARTY

A teenage party is always so easy to cater for as nothing must be too organized for the kids.

Clear a room of furniture, have a record player with plenty of discs which, no doubt, some of the guests will add to, and plenty of food.

It is always a good idea to serve the food and drink in the kitchen if it is large enough. This means people can come and go as they please without interrupting the dancing.

The pizzas can be left, completely prepared, with instructions for cooking and the potatoes are easily heated. In fact, the girls usually enjoy helping with the food. Put out plenty of bowls of potato crisps as they are always very popular.

MENU
Serves 30

Cheesy-baked potatoes
Pizza express
Sausage and baked bean pie
Savoury party dip
Sweet temptation
Apple and orange cake

Cool-it-man punch

CHEESY-BAKED POTATOES
(Illustrated on page 53)
Serves 40

20 medium potatoes
salt and pepper
4oz (100gm) margarine
8oz (200gm) mushrooms
8oz (200gm) Cheddar cheese

1. Preheat oven to moderate, 350 deg F or gas 4 (180 deg C).
2. Scrub the potatoes, prick them all over with a fork and rub a little salt into the skins.
3. Place on the shelves of the oven and cook for 1½–2 hours, or until they are soft.
4. Melt half the margarine in a small pan, add the trimmed and sliced mushrooms and fry until tender.
5. When the potatoes are cooked, remove them from the oven and cut each one in half.
6. Using a spoon, scoop out the potato into a bowl and mix in the

rest of the margarine with plenty of salt and pepper.
7. Put the potato skins on to baking sheets and divide the cooked mushrooms between them, reserving a few to garnish.
8. Spoon the potato mixture on top, spreading out where necessary, then top with a little grated cheese and the reserved mushroom slices.
9. Reheat the potatoes when required in a hot oven, 425 deg F or gas 7 (220 deg C) for about 15 minutes or until the cheese on top melts and is golden brown and crispy.
10. Serve the potatoes with potato crisps, and plenty of potato napkins for ease of eating.

PIZZA EXPRESS

(Illustrated on page 53)
Makes 30

15 baps or round soft rolls
1½lb (¾ kilo) Cheddar cheese
1 pint (approximately ½ litre) tomato ketchup
1 pint (approximately ½ litre) water
4 level tablespoons made English mustard
salt and pepper
2 cans anchovy fillets
1 can (15oz or 375gm) prunes
parsley

1. Preheat the grill.
2. Cut each bap in half.
3. Coarsely grate the cheese into a bowl.
4. Stir in the tomato ketchup, water, mustard and seasoning.
5. Divide this mixture between the baps.
6. Smooth it almost to the sides – it will spread during cooking.
7. Cut the anchovy fillets in half lengthways and the prunes into pieces, removing the stones.
8. Criss-cross the top of each pizza with the anchovies and garnish with pieces of prune.
9. Place under the grill until golden brown and bubbling.
10. Garnish with parsley sprigs and serve hot.

SAUSAGE AND BAKED BEAN PIE

Serves 24

flaky pastry made with 12oz (300gm) flour (see Basic recipes, page 100)
12oz (300gm) pork sausagemeat
1 small can curried baked beans
little beaten egg to glaze

1. Preheat oven to hot, 425 deg F or gas 7 (220 deg C).
2. Divide the pastry into two and roll one half out and use it to line the base and sides of a Swiss roll tin.
3. Spread the sausagemeat over the base and spoon the baked beans on top, spreading them evenly over the meat.
4. Roll the other piece of pastry out to fit the top of the tin.
5. Moisten the edges with a little water then lift the pastry on top and press the edges securely together.
6. Trim off the surplus pastry and pinch the edges together with the fingers.
7. Brush the pastry with egg glaze and mark it into 24 squares.
8. Leave the pie in a cool place to rest for 15 minutes.
9. Bake in the centre of the oven for 20 minutes, then reduce the heat to moderate to moderately hot, 375 deg F or gas 5 (190 deg C) and bake for a further 25–30 minutes.
10. Cut the pie into squares, using the marked lines as a guide and serve hot or cold.

SAVOURY PARTY DIP

Serves 30

2oz (50gm) margarine
8oz (200gm) onions, peeled and chopped
2oz (50gm) plain flour
¼ pint (125ml) milk
½ pint (250ml) stock
3 tomatoes
1 can (7oz or 175gm) sweetcorn niblets
1 level tablespoon chopped parsley
salt and paprika pepper
3 hard-boiled eggs
1 French loaf
3oz (75gm) butter

1. Melt the margarine, add the onions and cook slowly until tender but not coloured.
2. Remove from the heat and stir in the plain flour, then very gradually blend in the milk and stock.
3. Return to the heat and, stirring all the time, bring to the boil to thicken.
4. Chop the tomatoes roughly and stir into the sauce with the undrained sweetcorn niblets and the parsley.
5. Add seasoning then simmer the dip slowly for the flavours to blend. (Stir occasionally so it does not stick to the pan.)
6. Shell the eggs, cut in half and using a potato masher, mash them into small pieces.
7. Stir the egg into the dip and turn it into a bowl.
8. Slice and spread the bread with butter and hand round with the dip.

SWEET TEMPTATION
Makes 24

6oz (150gm) margarine
6oz (150gm) caster sugar
2 large eggs
1 egg yolk
6oz (150gm) self-raising flour
2 egg whites
4oz (100gm) caster sugar
2oz (50gm) glacé cherries, chopped
½oz (12gm) angelica, chopped

1. Preheat oven to moderate, 350 deg F or gas 4 (180 deg C).
2. Brush a 14-inch (35-cm) by 9-inch (23-cm) Swiss roll tin with melted fat.
3. Melt the margarine over a low heat.
4. Remove from the heat and stir in the sugar.
5. Beat the 2 eggs and 1 yolk together then mix into the pan.
6. Sift the flour and add to the ingredients in the pan. Mix well together.
7. Turn the mixture into the tin and spread it level with a palette knife.
8. Bake in the centre of the oven for about 40 minutes, until it feels springy to the touch and is shrinking away from the sides of the tin. Cool in the tin. Turn the oven heat to cool, 250 deg F or gas ½ (130 deg C).
9. Whisk the egg whites until stiff then add 2 level tablespoons of the sugar and re-whisk the mixture so it is as stiff as before.
10. Carefully fold in the rest of the sugar with the chopped cherries and angelica.
11. Spread the topping on to the cooked base, peaking the surface. Return to the oven for about 35 minutes, to brown the meringue.
12. Cool, then cut into 24 squares and arrange on pretty plates for the party.

APPLE AND ORANGE CAKE

Each cake will serve 12 people so make three for the party.

1 large egg
3oz (75gm) caster sugar
5oz (125gm) margarine
10oz (250gm) plain flour
pinch of salt
2lb (1 kilo) cooking apples
3 small oranges
4 level tablespoons sieved apricot jam

1. Preheat oven to moderate to moderately hot, 375 deg F or gas 5 (190 deg C).
2. Brush a shallow 10-inch (25-cm) tin with melted fat and line the base with a circle of greaseproof paper cut to fit. Brush the lining.
3. Beat the egg and sugar together with a rotary or electric beater until light and creamy.
4. Melt the margarine and stir it into the egg and sugar with the sifted flour and salt.
5. Mix the ingredients together to form a stiff paste and press it into the base of the tin, smoothing over the surface with a palette knife.
6. Peel, core and thinly slice the apples then, keeping enough good slices aside to form two rows for the top of the cake, arrange the rest neatly on top of the cake pressing them slightly into the base.
7. Using a sharp knife remove the peel and pith from the oranges and cut them into thin slices.
8. Arrange the orange slices and the remaining apple slices in rows on top of the cake. It should make three rows of oranges and two rows of apples.
9. Warm the apricot jam and brush some over the fruit.
10. Bake in the centre of the oven for about 1 hour 10 minutes.
11. Cool slightly, then run a knife around the edge and turn the cake on to a wire tray to finish cooling.
12. Remove the paper and turn the cake on to a serving plate.
13. Warm the rest of the jam and brush it liberally over the surface.
14. Serve the cake hot or cold with single cream.

COOL-IT-MAN PUNCH
Gives 35 glasses

3 bottles (1½ pints or approximately ¾ litre) apple juice
3 bottles (1½ pints or approximately ¾ litre) lemonade
12 tablespoons lime cordial
ice cubes
¼ cucumber, sliced
few mint sprigs

1. Tip the apple juice, lemonade and lime cordial into a large bowl.
2. Stir in the ice.
3. Float the cucumber slices and the mint on top.
4. Serve cold.

A TEENAGE PARTY FOR TWELVE

MENU

Cornish pasties
Sunrise, sunset flan
Bread and cheese circle
Pasta salad
Pickled red cabbage
Gaytime oranges
Chocolate velvet squares

CORNISH PASTIES
Makes 12

shortcrust pastry made with 1lb 12oz (700gm) flour (see Basic recipes, page 100)
4 medium potatoes
4 medium onions
1¼lb (¾ kilo) chuck steak
salt and pepper
3oz (75gm) margarine
little beaten egg to glaze
lettuce and watercress to garnish

1. Preheat oven to moderate to moderately hot, 400 deg F or gas 6 (200 deg C).
2. Cut the pastry into 12 even pieces and roll out each piece to a 6-inch circle, trimming the edges as necessary.
3. Peel the potatoes and onions and slice them very thinly – a potato peeler is useful for slicing potatoes really thinly.
4. Trim any fat from the meat then cut it into small pieces with a sharp knife.
5. Place a short line of potato across the centre of each pastry

circle and cover with sliced onions.
6. Arrange a layer of meat on top nestling it into the vegetables so that the filling is tightly packed.
7. Season with salt and pepper and place a small dot of margarine in the centre of each.
8. Brush the edges with water and draw the sides to the top of the filling, enclosing it completely.
9. Crimp the edges with the thumb and forefinger making sure they are really sealed.
10. Brush with egg glaze then place on baking sheets and bake on the top two shelves of the oven for 45 minutes to 1 hour, or until the pastry is golden brown and the filling tender. (Cover with foil if the pastry becomes too brown.)
11. Serve on a bed of lettuce and garnish with watercress.

To freeze: pasties freeze well. Place in a polythene bag, seal and label. Store for 2–3 months and thaw at room temperature. To serve hot, heat them in a moderate oven, 350 deg F or gas 4 (180 deg C) for 20–30 minutes.

SUNRISE, SUNSET FLAN
Serves 6–8

shortcrust pastry made with 6oz (150gm) flour (see Basic recipes, page 100)
2 eggs
¼ pint (125ml) milk
2 tablespoons tomato ketchup
6oz (150gm) cheese, grated
1 can (11oz or 275gm) sweetcorn kernels
1 onion, peeled and grated
salt and pepper
1 tomato, sliced

1. Preheat oven to moderate to moderately hot, 375 deg F or gas 5 (190 deg C).
2. Roll the pastry into a circle and use to line an 8-inch (20-cm) flan ring, placed on a baking sheet.
3. Trim the edge by running the rolling pin across the top in both directions.
4. Beat the eggs then stir in the milk, tomato ketchup and 4oz (100gm) of the cheese.
5. Drain the sweetcorn kernels and stir them into the mixture with the grated onion. Season.
6. Pour the filling into the flan case and bake in the centre of the oven for about 40 minutes, until the filling is set.
7. Cover the surface with the tomato slices, evenly arranged.
8. Sprinkle with the remaining cheese, then place the flan under a preheated grill and cook until golden brown.
9. Remove the flan ring, slide the flan on to a plate and serve hot.

BREAD AND CHEESE CIRCLE
Serves 10

1 long French loaf
2oz (50gm) butter
6oz (150gm) Cheddar cheese
chutney

1. Using a sharp knife, cut the bread from one side almost through to the other to make 10 even pieces.
2. Spread both sides of the cuts with butter.
3. Cut the cheese into 10 wedge-shaped pieces.
4. Put a wedge of cheese into each slit and, as you work, the bread automatically forms itself into a circle.
5. Put some chutney in a small bowl and place it in the centre of the circle, with a spoon, so your guests can help themselves.

PASTA SALAD
Serves 12

1lb (½ kilo) pasta shapes
1 bunch spring onions
8oz (200gm) carrots, peeled and grated
1oz (25gm) walnuts, chopped
1oz (25gm) sultanas
4oz (100gm) cottage cheese
mayonnaise (see Basic recipes, page 100)

1. Cook the pasta in plenty of boiling, salted water for 10–15 minutes, until the pieces are tender.
2. Drain well and run cold water through the shapes to remove the excess starch and keep them separate.
3. Put the pasta into a bowl.
4. Trim and wash the onions then cut them into rings.
5. Stir the onions into the pasta with the carrots, walnuts, sultanas and cottage cheese.
6. Bind the ingredients together with mayonnaise then turn the salad into a large bowl for serving.

PICKLED RED CABBAGE

Serves 12

Make this 10 days before it is required.

1 red cabbage
salt
1 pint (approximately ½ litre) vinegar
¼oz (6gm) allspice berries
¼oz (6gm) peppercorns
1 bayleaf

1. Remove any coarse leaves from the cabbage. Cut it into four then shred each quarter very finely with a sharp knife.
2. Put a layer of shredded cabbage in a bowl, sprinkle it with salt and continue layering the cabbage, ending with a layer of salt.
3. Leave the bowl on one side for 24 hours.
4. Put the vinegar into an enamel saucepan with the allspice berries, peppercorns and bayleaf.
5. Place the pan over a low heat and bring the vinegar slowly to the boil.
6. Boil it briskly for 1 minute, then leave to cool. Strain.
7. Next day, drain the cabbage to remove as much liquid as possible.
8. Pack it into jars filling them almost to the top.
9. Pour in sufficient spiced vinegar to clear the top of the cabbage by approximately ½ inch.
10. Cover the jars with polythene and secure with string.
11. Label and store in a cool place for at least 10 days.
12. Serve the cabbage for the party in a bowl.

GAYTIME ORANGES

Serves 12

12 medium oranges
1 can (15½oz or 387gm) apricots
3 level tablespoons custard powder
1 pint (approximately ½ litre) milk
2 egg yolks
sugar to taste
2 egg whites
4oz (100gm) caster sugar

1. Preheat oven to hot, 425 deg F or gas 7 (220 deg C).
2. Cut off the tops of the oranges and, using a teaspoon, scoop out the inside.
3. Keep the flesh and juice on one side for later.
4. Shave a very little off the base of each orange, if necessary so it stands level.
5. Strain the juice from the apricots and purée the fruit to make about ½ pint (250ml) purée.
6. Blend the custard powder in a pan with a little of the milk then stir in all the milk.
7. Put the pan over the heat and stirring all the time, bring the custard to the boil and cook for 2 minutes, stirring.
8. Beat the egg yolks together, then pour on a little of the hot custard and when the ingredients are blended, return them to the main bulk of the sauce.
9. Heat the custard again to cook the eggs. (Do not allow to boil.)
10. Remove from the heat, stir in the apricot purée with the flesh and juice from the oranges.
11. Sweeten the filling if necessary then divide it between the oranges placed on a baking sheet.
12. Whisk the egg whites until stiff, then add 2 level tablespoons of the sugar.
13. Whisk the mixture so it is as stiff as before.
14. Fold in the remaining sugar with a metal spoon.
15. Divide the meringue between the oranges making sure the filling is completely covered.
16. Leave the surfaces rough and flash-bake for 2–3 minutes, until golden brown.

CHOCOLATE VELVET SQUARES

Makes 16

4oz (100gm) butter or margarine
4oz (100gm) plain chocolate
2oz (50gm) sultanas
2oz (50gm) walnuts, chopped
1 small can sweetened condensed milk
8oz (200gm) digestive biscuits

1. Brush a 7-inch (18-cm) square cake tin with a little cooking oil.
2. Put the butter or margarine into a pan with the chocolate, broken into pieces.
3. Melt over a very low heat. Do not allow the mixture to boil.
4. Remove from the heat and stir in the sultanas, walnuts and condensed milk.
5. Put the biscuits into a polythene bag and, with a rolling pin, crush them slightly.
6. Stir the pieces into the pan.
7. Turn the mixture into the tin and level it with a knife.
8. Leave in a cool place until set.
9. Loosen the mixture around the edge, cut into 16 squares and remove the pieces from the tin with a palette knife.
10. Arrange on a plate for serving.

Cheesy-baked potatoes (see page 48)

Pizza express (see page 49)

Devils on horseback (see page 58)

Tuna and tomato pancakes (see page 59)

Walnut fudge cake (see page 65)

Easter bonnets (see page 69)

Savoury porcupine (see page 79)

Chocolate truffles (see page 73)

Social gatherings

If you want to give a cocktail party, a cheese and wine party or to help with the refreshments at a whist drive, then this is the chapter for you.

WELCOME HOME PARTY

Each dish at this party represents a foreign country, perhaps some of the places that the guest of honour has visited since he or she departed. The party caters for about 16 people.

MENU
Serves 16

Florida cocktail
Tomato ring

Terrine
Risotto
Russian salad
Green salad (see page 16)

Pavlova gâteau
Nuss torte

FLORIDA COCKTAIL (from America)
Serves 8–10

4 large oranges
4 grapefruit
sugar to taste
maraschino cherries

1. Using a sharp stainless steel knife, cut the ends off the oranges.
2. Working spirally around the fruit cut just below the pith and just above the flesh to remove the skin.
3. Cut the oranges into segments between the membranes and put the fruit into a large bowl.
4. Peel and segment the grapefruit in the same way.
5. Stir the fruit thoroughly together then divide it evenly between individual glass dishes.
6. Sprinkle with sugar if required and decorate the centre of each dish with a cherry.

TOMATO RING (from Spain)
Serves 8

¾ pint (375ml) tomato juice
½ pint (250ml) chicken stock
½ teaspoon Worcestershire sauce
¾oz (18gm) powdered gelatine
1 level tablespoon caster sugar
salt and pepper
watercress to garnish

1. Brush a 1½-pint (approximately ¾-litre) mould with a little oil.
2. Mix the tomato juice with the chicken stock and Worcestershire sauce.
3. Put the gelatine into a pan, add 3 tablespoons of liquid and, over a low heat, melt the gelatine.
4. Stir in the sugar and, when dissolved, stir both ingredients into the main bulk of liquid.
5. Add salt and pepper then pour into the ring mould.
6. Leave the mould in a cool place overnight to set.
7. To serve, loosen the mixture from the sides of the mould then turn it on to a plate.
8. Place a bunch of watercress in the centre and serve thinly sliced bread and butter as an accompaniment.

TERRINE (from France)
Serves 8–10

12oz (300gm) streaky bacon rashers
8oz (200gm) pig's liver
1 onion, peeled and chopped
1 garlic clove, peeled
8oz (200gm) sausagemeat
1lb (½ kilo) belly of pork, minced
salt and pepper
2 hard-boiled eggs, chopped
pinch of mixed herbs
1 large egg, beaten
1 bayleaf

1. Preheat oven to moderate, 350 deg F or gas 4 (180 deg C).
2. Cut the rind and any small bones from the bacon and use the rashers to line a 2-lb (1-kilo) loaf tin, widthways, across the bottom and up the sides.
3. Mince the liver with the onion and garlic clove.
4. Stir them into the sausagemeat and minced pork.
5. Season the mixture well and stir in the chopped eggs with the herbs.
6. Mix in the beaten egg then turn the mixture into the lined tin, spread it level and place the bayleaf on top.
7. Cover the tin with foil, place in a roasting pan, half filled with water, and cook in the centre of the oven for 1–1¼ hours, or until it feels firm.
8. When cooked, remove the foil and bayleaf and leave to cool overnight.
9. Turn on to a bed of lettuce for serving.

RISOTTO (from Italy)
Serves 10–12

4oz (100gm) margarine
1 dessertspoon cooking oil
4 onions, peeled and sliced
1lb (½ kilo) long-grain rice
1lb (½ kilo) cold cooked meat, chopped
4oz (100gm) sultanas
1lb (½ kilo) tomatoes
4oz (100gm) mushrooms
2½ pints (approximately 1¼ litres) stock
salt and pepper
grated Parmesan cheese

1. Preheat oven to moderate to moderately hot, 375 deg F or gas 5 (190 deg C).
2. Melt the margarine in a large pan, add the oil and when it is heated, fry the onions.
3. Add the rice and stir over a gentle heat for a few minutes.
4. Stir in the chopped meat with the sultanas.
5. Cut the tomatoes into eighths and add them with the trimmed and quartered mushrooms to the pan.
6. Stir in the stock with plenty of seasoning.
7. Turn the mixture into a large ovenproof dish and cook in the centre of the oven for 1–1¼ hours, until the liquid is absorbed and the rice tender.
8. Serve the risotto, from the casserole, with Parmesan cheese.

RUSSIAN SALAD
Serves 12–16

2lb (1 kilo) potatoes, peeled and cooked
8oz (200gm) peas, cooked
8oz (200gm) carrots, peeled and cooked
4 sticks celery
4 gherkins
French dressing (see Basic recipes, page 100)
mayonnaise (see Basic recipes, page 100)
capers

1. Cut the potatoes into small cubes and put them into a bowl with the peas.
2. Slice the carrots into rings.
3. Trim and slice the celery and dice the gherkins.
4. Mix the carrots, celery and gherkins with the potatoes and peas.
5. Toss the vegetables in French dressing so they are well coated.
6. Turn them on to a serving plate and, at the last minute, spoon over mayonnaise and sprinkle the top with capers.

PAVLOVA GATEAU (from Australia)
Serves 8

2 egg whites
4oz (100gm) caster sugar
few drops vanilla essence
1½ level teaspoons cornflour
½ teaspoon white vinegar
¼ pint (125ml) double cream
1 can (14oz or 350gm) cherry pie filling

1. Preheat oven to very cool, 225 deg F or gas ¼ (110 deg C).
2. Brush a baking sheet with melted fat and cover the surface with either foil or bakewell paper.
3. Mark out on the covering an 8-inch (20-cm) circle then brush the foil or paper with melted fat.
4. Whisk the egg whites until stiff.
5. Add the sugar very gradually whisking well between each addition.
6. Fold in the vanilla essence, cornflour and vinegar, very lightly, with a metal spoon.
7. Turn the mixture on to the marked baking sheet and spread it to fill the marked-out circle; flick the sides with a palette knife.
8. Bake in the lower part of the oven for 3 hours, or until firm to touch.
9. Turn it upside down when cooked and peel off the foil or paper – the centre of the gâteau should still be soft. Cool on a wire tray.
10. Whip the cream until it holds its shape.
11. Spread the cream over the base which reverts to the top for serving, then carefully spoon on the pie filling.
12. Serve at once.

NUSS TORTE (from Austria)
Serves 8–10

6oz (150gm) margarine
6oz (150gm) caster sugar
3 large eggs
4oz (100gm) hazelnuts, ground
5oz (125gm) self-raising flour
1oz (25gm) cocoa powder
1 can (15oz or 375gm) apple purée
4oz (100gm) plain chocolate
1 teaspoon cooking oil
2 tablespoons cold water
1oz (25gm) caster sugar

1. Preheat oven to moderate to moderately hot, 375 deg F or gas 5 (190 deg C).
2. Brush a 7-inch (18-cm) cake tin with melted fat and line the base with a circle of greaseproof paper, cut to fit. Brush the paper lining.
3. Beat the margarine to a soft cream, add the caster sugar and beat again until the mixture is light and fluffy.
4. Beat the eggs together then add them gradually to the creamed mixture beating well between each addition.
5. Stir in the ground nuts.
6. Sift the flour and cocoa powder together and, using a metal spoon, carefully and lightly fold them into the mixture.
7. Turn the mixture into the prepared tin, hollow out the centre and bake in the centre of the oven for 40–45 minutes.
8. To test if it is cooked insert a warmed skewer into the centre of the cake. If it comes out clean the cake is ready, but if any mixture adheres to the skewer, cook the cake for a little longer.
9. Turn the cooked cake on to a wire tray to cool and remove the greaseproof paper.
10. Split the cake in half and place one half on a serving plate.
11. Cover this layer with the apple purée and put the other layer on top.
12. Break the chocolate into pieces and put them into a pan with the oil, water and sugar.
13. Over a very low heat, melt the ingredients (do not allow them to boil), stirring them occasionally to combine.
14. Pour on to the surface of the cake and smooth it with a palette knife to the edges, allowing it to trickle down the sides in places.
15. Leave the chocolate to set then cut the cake in slices to serve.

COCKTAIL PARTY

A cocktail party should be great fun for both the guests and the hostess if it is planned properly. Invite the number of people that fit comfortably into your room, allowing for a few refusals. Make sure you have plenty of ash trays around the room and remove any vases or ornaments that could be knocked over.

It is advisable to serve a small selection of drinks, as too many bottles and glasses just create confusion. A good choice I think is sherry, gin and whisky with additions such as tonic water, dry ginger and bitter lemon, plus non-alcoholic drinks such as fruit or tomato juice. Allow 3–4 short drinks or two long drinks per person. From a bottle of spirit you should get 20–25 glasses using about 10 splits of tonic, bitter lemon or ginger ale, and from a bottle of sherry 16 glasses.

There are two drinks I have not mentioned; one is beer, which I do suggest you serve if the party is large, as there is sure to be a proportion of beer drinkers, and the other drink is champagne. If you really want to make the catering and serving simple on the drinks side, champagne is the answer, and it also gives the party a very luxurious air. A bottle of champagne will serve 6 glasses.

For the food serve a choice of hot and cold bite-size foods that give different textures and attractive colours. The party I have catered for is sufficient for 25 people. Do not forget to have bowls of nuts, crisps and olives around the room.

MENU
Serves 25

Cheese delights
Celery boats
Tasty bitefuls
Portugese fish rolls
Party parcels
Devils on horseback
Onion dip

CHEESE DELIGHTS
Makes 25

cheese pastry made with 8oz (200gm) flour (see Basic recipes, page 100)
8oz (200gm) cream cheese
2 tablespoons milk
salt and pepper
halved walnuts or black grapes

1. Preheat oven to moderately hot, 400 deg F or gas 6 (200 deg C).
2. Roll the pastry out to a ¼-inch thickness.
3. Cut out as many rounds as possible using a 1-inch (2·5-cm) cutter.
4. Gather up the scraps, re-roll the pastry and cut out more rounds.
5. Place on baking sheets and bake for about 10 minutes until golden brown. Cool on a wire tray.
6. Beat the cheese with milk and seasoning.
7. Put the cheese into a large piping bag with a large star pipe.
8. Pipe a star on to each biscuit and garnish with either halved walnuts or halved and stoned grapes.

CELERY BOATS
Makes 30

1 head celery
1oz (25gm) butter
3oz (75gm) Stilton cheese
little milk
salt and pepper
paprika pepper

1. Wash the celery sticks well and dry them.
2. Beat the butter until it is soft then beat in the cheese with milk, if necessary, to make a creamy consistency.
3. Season the mixture well then spread it into the inside of the celery sticks.
4. Sprinkle each stick with paprika pepper and cut into 2-inch lengths.
5. Arrange on large trays with the cheese delights.

TASTY BITEFULS
Makes 25

1lb (½ kilo) sausagemeat
1 medium onion, peeled and finely chopped
cooking oil for frying
1 can (14oz or 350gm) tomatoes
1 packet dried vegetable soup
½ pint (250ml) chicken stock
few drops Worcestershire sauce
salt and pepper

1. Mix the sausagemeat with the onion then divide the mixture into small pieces and roll each into the size of a whole walnut.
2. Heat some oil in a frying pan and add the balls. Fry them slowly until evenly brown and cooked to the centre. Drain on absorbent paper.
3. Meanwhile put the tomatoes, soup powder, stock and Worcestershire sauce into a pan.
4. Stirring all the time, bring the sauce to the boil and simmer, uncovered, for 10 minutes.
5. Check the seasoning. Pour into a dish, insert a cocktail stick into each sausage ball and place in the sauce.
6. Serve hot.

PORTUGUESE FISH ROLLS
Makes 24

8 slices fresh white bread
1½oz (37gm) butter
1 can (4oz or 100gm) sardines in oil
3oz (75gm) Cheddar cheese, grated
salt and pepper

1. Cut the crusts from the bread and roll each slice thinner with a rolling pin. Spread thinly with some of the butter.
2. Put the sardines, two-thirds of the cheese and seasoning into a bowl and mash it to a paste with a fork.
3. Spread the paste on the buttered bread and roll each slice lengthways.
4. Cut each roll into three and place them close together on the grill pan.
5. Melt the remainder of the butter, brush it over the tops of the rolls and sprinkle them with the rest of the cheese.
6. Just before they are to be served, place the rolls under a preheated grill to brown.

PARTY PARCELS
Makes 20

3 hard-boiled eggs
6oz (150gm) liver sausage
½ level teaspoon curry powder
1 medium onion, peeled and grated
salt and pepper
shortcrust pastry made with 1lb (½ kilo) flour (see Basic recipes, page 100)
little milk to glaze

1. Preheat oven to moderate to moderately hot, 375 deg F or gas 5 (190 deg C).
2. Chop the eggs roughly then rub through a sieve into a small bowl.
3. Beat in the liver sausage with the curry powder, onion and seasoning.
4. Roll out the pastry to about an ⅛-inch thickness and cut out an equal number of rounds using a 2-inch (5-cm) cutter.
5. Gather up the scraps and re-roll the pastry to cut out more rounds.
6. Place ½ teaspoon of the filling on half the rounds.
7. Dampen the edges with water, place the remaining pastry rounds on top and seal the two edges together with the blunt end of a 1½-inch (3·8-cm) cutter.
8. Place the parcels on baking sheets and brush with milk.
9. Bake on the top two shelves of the oven for 20–25 minutes. Serve hot or cold.

DEVILS ON HORSEBACK
(Illustrated on page 53)
Makes 15

1 can (15½oz or 387gm) prunes
little sweet chutney
12oz (300gm) streaky bacon rashers
watercress to garnish

1. Preheat oven to hot, 425 deg F or gas 7 (220 deg C).
2. Drain the prunes and carefully remove the stones.
3. Place a little chutney in the cavity left by the stone.
4. Cut the rind from the bacon and, with the back of a knife, stretch it to about double its original length.
5. Cut the bacon in half and wrap a piece around each prune.
6. Put the rolls into an ovenproof dish and cook in the centre of the oven for about 10 minutes, until the bacon is crisp.
7. Arrange in a dish and serve garnished with watercress. Have a small glass of cocktail sticks at hand to make eating them easier.

ONION DIP
Serves 25

4 cartons natural yogurt
2 packets dried onion soup
few onion rings to garnish

1. At least 1 hour before the party, mix the yogurt with the dried soup.
2. Serve the dip in a bowl with a few onion rings on top.
3. Hand a good selection of biscuits with the dip, as well as raw vegetables such as sticks of carrots, cucumber and celery and sprigs of cauliflower. Bread sticks are also excellent with a dip.

BOTTLE PARTY

A party where your guests provide the drink and you provide the food. However, I do suggest you serve an inexpensive punch just to start the party off with a swing. I have catered for 16 people but the recipes can be doubled or trebled to suit your number of guests.

MENU
Serves 16

Tuna and tomato pancakes
Savoury stack
Waldorf salad
Green salad (see page 16)

Lemon meringue pie
Blackcurrant whip

Cider cup

TUNA AND TOMATO PANCAKES

(Illustrated on page 53)
Serves 10

oil for frying
½ pint (250ml) pancake batter (see Basic recipes, page 100)
2 cans tuna fish
1oz (25gm) dripping
8oz (200gm) mushrooms
pinch of rosemary
salt and pepper
1oz (25gm) margarine
1 onion, peeled and chopped
2 level tablespoons plain flour
1 can (2lb 3oz or approximately 1 kilo) tomatoes
1 bayleaf
few parsley stalks
1 level teaspoon caster sugar
few drops Worcestershire sauce
1 level dessertspoon tomato purée
1 garlic clove, crushed
chopped parsley to garnish

1. Preheat oven to moderate, 350 deg F or gas 4 (180 deg C).
2. Heat a little oil in a small frying pan.
3. When it is quite hot, pour off all that will run, leaving only the few drops that cling to the base.
4. Heat the pan again then lift it off the heat and pour about 2 tablespoons of batter into the base. Tip the pan at the same time so it swirls round the pan and coats the bottom thinly.
5. Immediately return the pan to the heat and cook the pancake on both sides until brown.
6. Turn it on to a teatowel and fry the others in the same way, piling them on top of each other.
7. The pan will need regreasing every 5 or 6 pancakes.
8. Drain the oil from the fish and flake it.
9. Melt the dripping and fry the mushrooms for 3–4 minutes; add them to the fish with the rosemary and seasoning.
10. Melt the margarine in the same pan as the mushrooms were fried in and add the onion. Fry gently for 2–3 minutes without colouring. Stir in the flour and tomatoes.
11. Stir over a gentle heat until the mixture comes to the boil.
12. Add the bayleaf, parsley stalks, caster sugar, Worcestershire sauce, tomato purée, crushed garlic, salt and pepper. Cover and simmer for 25 minutes.
13. Sieve the sauce, then return it to the pan and boil for a few minutes, without the lid so it reduces slightly.
14. Stir a little sauce into the tuna mixture to bind the ingredients together.
15. Divide the filling between all but two of the pancakes, roll up and arrange in a large ovenproof dish.
16. Pour the remaining sauce over the top. Cut the remaining pancakes into strips; make each strip about ⅓ inch wide.
17. Lattice the top of the dish with the strips then place in the centre of the oven for 40–50 minutes.
18. Just before serving, sprinkle chopped parsley in every alternate diamond formed by the lattice.

SAVOURY STACK

Serves 8

1½lb (¾ kilo) minced beef
1 onion, peeled and chopped
4oz (100gm) mushrooms
1 can (15oz or 375gm) oxtail soup
salt and pepper
few drops Worcestershire sauce
pinch of mixed herbs
½ pint (250ml) pancake batter (see Basic recipes, page 100)
2oz (50gm) butter
2oz (50gm) cheese, grated

1. Preheat oven to moderate, 350 deg F or gas 4 (180 deg C).
2. Fry the beef and onion together until the meat is lightly brown.
3. Add the chopped mushrooms to the pan with the soup, seasoning, Worcestershire sauce and herbs.
4. Bring the mixture to the boil, stirring, then reduce the heat and simmer, uncovered for 1 hour, or until it has slightly reduced and the ingredients are cooked.
5. Follow the directions for making the pancakes in the previous recipe and stack them in layers with the filling on an ovenproof plate.
6. Brush the top and sides with butter.
7. Sprinkle the cheese over the top and heat through in the centre of the oven for 30 minutes, or until the top starts to brown.
8. Cut into wedges like a cake and serve immediately.

To freeze: arrange unfilled pancakes, one on top of the other, in a polythene bag. Seal and label. Thaw at room temperature for 3 hours, then fill and use as required.

WALDORF SALAD

Serves 16

1 head celery
$1\frac{1}{2}$lb ($\frac{3}{4}$ kilo) potatoes, cooked and diced
2oz (50gm) walnuts, chopped
6 tablespoons mayonnaise
salt and pepper
2 red-skinned apples
2 green-skinned apples
little lemon juice

1. Wash and trim the celery sticks, then cut them into small pieces.
2. Put the celery into a bowl with the potatoes and walnuts and mix the ingredients well together.
3. Stir in the mayonnaise and season with salt and pepper if required.
4. Quarter, core and slice the apples, keeping the different coloured skins separate.
5. Toss the apple slices in lemon juice.
6. Turn the salad on to a large plate and arrange the apple slices around the edge, alternating red and green skinned pieces.
7. Keep in a cool place until required. It will stay fresh, if covered with a piece of polythene, for about 1 hour.

LEMON MERINGUE PIE

Serves 8–10

shortcrust pastry made with 8oz (200gm) flour (see Basic recipes, page 100)
2 large lemons
2oz (50gm) cornflour
$\frac{3}{4}$ pint (375ml) water
8oz (200gm) caster sugar
2 egg yolks
2 egg whites
4oz (100gm) caster sugar

1. Preheat oven to moderate to moderately hot, 375 deg F or gas 5 (190 deg C).
2. Roll out the pastry and use to line an $8\frac{1}{2}$-inch (21-cm) fluted flan ring, placed on a baking sheet.
3. Cover the base with crumbled tissue paper and fill with baking beans or dry crusts.
4. Bake the flan case blind in the centre of the oven for 30 minutes.
5. Remove the paper, beans and flan ring and bake the pastry case for a further 10 minutes. Remove the flan from the oven and reduce the oven heat to cool, 300 deg F or gas 2 (150 deg C).
6. Put the finely grated rind and the juice from the lemons into a saucepan.
7. Add the cornflour then blend in the water and sugar.
8. Over a gentle heat, and stirring all the time, bring the mixture to the boil and simmer for a few minutes to thicken.
9. Remove from the heat and stir 2 tablespoons of the filling into the egg yolks.
10. Stir this into the main bulk of the filling and pour it into the flan case.
11. Whisk the egg whites until stiff.
12. Add 2 level tablespoons of the sugar, then rewhisk the mixture until as stiff as before.
13. Fold in the remaining sugar and put the meringue into a piping bag fitted with a star pipe.
14. Pipe trellis on the lemon mixture with the meringue.
15. Cook in the centre of the oven for about 30 minutes, or until the meringue is tinged golden brown.
16. Serve hot or cold, with single cream.

BLACKCURRANT WHIP

Serves 8–10

1 can (15oz or 375gm) blackcurrants
1 blackcurrant jelly
1 large can unsweetened evaporated milk, chilled
juice of half a lemon
$\frac{1}{2}$ red-skinned apple
1 glacé cherry

1. Strain the blackcurrants and put the juice into a pan.
2. Add the jelly and, over a very low heat, dissolve the jelly – do not allow it to boil.
3. Stir the blackcurrants into the melted jelly and leave the mixture on one side to cool.
4. Put the evaporated milk and the lemon juice into a bowl and whisk the ingredients until they are really stiff. (It is ready only when a definite trail is left when the whisk is lifted out of the mixture.)
5. When the jelly is cold and almost at setting point, stir it carefully into the evaporated milk.
6. Turn the whip into a serving bowl and leave it to set in a cool place.
7. To decorate, core and slice the apple then arrange the slices, overlapping, in the centre of the whip, with the cherry in the middle to form a flower.
8. Serve with single cream.

CIDER CUP

Serves 16–20

2 oranges
2 apples
2 pints (approximately 1 litre) cider
2 pints (approximately 1 litre) lemonade or soda water
1 pint (approximately $\frac{1}{2}$ litre) apple juice
ice cubes

1. Slice the fruit, without removing the peel, and put it into a large bowl.
2. Pour over the cider, lemonade or soda water and apple juice.
3. Stir to mix the flavours together.
4. Add the ice cubes and serve immediately.

FOOD FOR THE WHIST DRIVE

It is normal, when catering for a whist drive, to have the food prepared in various people's homes and then transported to the hall where the function is to be held. All the recipes in the following menu come under this heading, with the exception of the bridge rolls, which can be buttered and the filling prepared at home; I advise that you do not assemble the bridge rolls until at the hall.

MENU
Serves 24

Bridge rolls
Stuffed eggs
Savoury toasts
Pork fingers
Battenburg
Gingerbread
Crispy biscuits
Tropical cakes

Tea

BRIDGE ROLLS
Makes 48

24 bridge rolls
8oz (200gm) butter

Pâté filling:
4oz (100gm) streaky bacon rashers
4oz (100gm) liver sausage
1 teaspoon Worcestershire sauce
cucumber slices and mustard and cress to garnish

Tuna filling:
1 can (7½oz or 187gm) tuna fish
2 level tablespoons mayonnaise
squeeze lemon juice
salt and pepper
tomato slices, mustard and cress and lettuce to garnish

1. Split the rolls in half and spread each half with butter.
2. For the pâté filling, cut the rind and any small bones from the bacon.
3. Chop the bacon finely and fry quickly in a pan without any extra fat. Place in a bowl.
4. Add the liver sausage and Worcestershire sauce and beat the ingredients together until they are soft.
5. Spread the mixture over half of the buttered rolls and garnish with cucumber slices and mustard and cress.
6. For the tuna filling, mix the tuna fish with the mayonnaise.
7. Beat in the lemon juice and seasoning.
8. Spread the filling over the remaining buttered bridge rolls.
9. Garnish the rolls with tomato slices and mustard and cress.
10. Serve the bridge rolls on large plates lined with lettuce.

STUFFED EGGS
Serves 24

12 hard-boiled eggs
3oz (75gm) margarine
1 onion, peeled and finely chopped
2 level teaspoons curry powder
parsley to garnish

1. Shell the eggs and cut them in half.
2. Scoop out the yolks, with a teaspoon, and place in a bowl.
3. Cut a little off the base of any of the egg white cases that do not stand firmly.
4. Melt the margarine in a small pan, add the onion and fry it until soft but not coloured.
5. Stir in the curry powder and continue to cook the ingredients together for a few minutes.
6. Mash the egg yolks with a fork then stir in the curry mixture and check the filling for seasoning.
7. Spoon the filling back into the egg white cases (it can be piped in if liked).
8. Garnish the top of each with a very small piece of parsley and put the stuffed eggs on to a tray, packed together quite tightly, to transport to the whist drive.

SAVOURY TOASTS
Serves 24

2 cans sardines in oil
2oz (50gm) fresh white breadcrumbs
1 dessertspoon Worcestershire sauce
1 level dessertspoon made English mustard
6 thick bread slices
2oz (50gm) butter or margarine
4oz (100gm) cheese, grated
2 tomatoes

1. Preheat the grill.
2. Mash the sardines together with their oil.
3. Stir in the breadcrumbs, Worcestershire sauce and mustard and mix the ingredients together.
4. Toast the bread on one side and remove the crusts.
5. Butter the untoasted side and spread the filling over the slices.
6. Sprinkle the cheese over the top.
7. Cut each bread slice into quarters.
8. Cut each tomato into six slices; cut each slice in half.
9. Arrange a piece of tomato on each savoury toast and place under the grill for about 5 minutes, or until golden brown.
10. Arrange on large plates or trays with the pork fingers.
11. These savouries can be served hot or cold.

PORK FINGERS
Serves 32

8 bread slices
tomato ketchup
8oz (200gm) pork sausagemeat

1. Preheat the grill.
2. Toast the bread on both sides lightly.
3. Spread one side thinly with tomato ketchup then cover it with the sausagemeat.
4. Grill slowly until the sausagemeat is cooked.
5. Cut the crusts off the slices, then cut each slice into four fingers and place a blob of tomato ketchup on each.
6. Serve with the savoury toasts.

BATTENBURG
Serves 12

Two of these cakes will be required for the whist drive.

6oz (150gm) margarine
9oz (225gm) caster sugar
3 large eggs
6oz (150gm) self-raising flour
few drops red food colouring
6oz (150gm) ground almonds
3oz (75gm) icing sugar, sifted
1 egg yolk
little lemon juice
sieved apricot jam
little cornflour

1. Preheat oven to moderate, 350 deg F or gas 4 (180 deg C).
2. Cut a piece of cardboard the length of a tin, 10 inches (25cm) by 6 inches (15cm), and a little higher. Cover the cardboard in kitchen foil.
3. Brush the tin with melted fat and line the base with a piece of greaseproof paper cut to fit.
4. Brush the paper lining, position the piece of card down the centre of the tin and brush that also with melted fat.
5. Beat the margarine to a soft cream.
6. Add 6oz (150gm) of the caster sugar and beat the ingredients together until light and fluffy in both colour and texture.
7. Beat the eggs together then gradually add them to the creamed mixture, beating well between each addition.
8. Sift the flour and, using a metal spoon, fold it into the creamed mixture.
9. Turn half the mixture into one side of the tin.
10. Colour the other half pink and put it in the other side.
11. Smooth the surface of each then bake in the centre of the oven for 25 minutes, until springy to the touch.
12. Leave to cool on a wire tray and remove the division and greaseproof paper.
13. Mix the ground almonds with the remaining caster sugar and the sifted icing sugar.
14. Stir in the egg yolk with sufficient lemon juice to make a consistency similar to shortcrust pastry.
15. Trim the top of each cake so it is level then sandwich the two together with jam. Cut in half lengthways.
16. Brush one cut side with jam then sandwich the two pieces back together having reversed one half, so the colours alternate.
17. Sprinkle a working surface with cornflour and roll the almond icing into a rectangle large enough to wrap around the cake.
18. Brush the almond icing with jam and place the cake along one edge.
19. Roll the cake up in the almond icing and make sure the join is secure.
20. Trim the ends of the cake neatly.
21. With the back of a knife, mark the top of the cake in diamonds.
22. Finish the cake by pinching the almond icing into a scalloped effect down each side of the rectangle.
23. Cut into slices for serving.

To freeze: this cake is ideal for freezer storage, before it is almond-iced; place in a polythene bag, seal and label. Store for up to 3 months. Thaw at room temperature.

GINGERBREAD
Serves 24

It is advisable to make the gingerbread at least 1 day before it is required.

8oz (200gm) margarine
8oz (200gm) soft brown sugar
8oz (200gm) black treacle
12oz (300gm) plain flour
2 level dessertspoons ground ginger
3 level teaspoons ground cinnamon
2 large eggs
½ pint (250ml) milk
2 level teaspoons bicarbonate of soda

1. Preheat oven to cool, 300 deg F or gas 2 (150 deg C).
2. Brush a deep tin, 8 inches (20cm) by 11 inches (28cm) with melted fat and line the base with a piece of greaseproof paper cut to fit. Brush the paper lining.
3. Put the margarine, soft brown sugar and treacle in a pan.
4. Melt these ingredients together until dissolved. (Do not allow to get too hot.)
5. Sift the flour, ground ginger and cinnamon together.
6. Stir them into the melted ingredients with the 2 eggs, lightly beaten.
7. Warm the milk to blood heat, pour it on to the bicarbonate of soda and stir the liquid into the mixture.
8. Pour the mixture into the prepared tin and bake in the centre of the oven for about 1½ hours, or until firm to the touch.
9. Cover the top lightly after the first hour, with a piece of greaseproof paper.
10. Leave to cool in the tin for 30 minutes then turn on to a wire tray to cool completely.
11. Serve buttered, cut into small slices.

To freeze: place in a polythene bag, seal and label. Gingerbread will store for at least 3 months. Thaw at room temperature for about 3 hours.

CRISPY BISCUITS
Makes about 24

6oz (150gm) margarine, softened
5oz (125gm) caster sugar
1 large egg
few drops vanilla essence
10oz (250gm) self-raising flour
2oz (50gm) porridge oats
walnut pieces

1. Preheat oven to moderate, 350 deg F or gas 4 (180 deg C).
2. Beat the margarine until it is soft and creamy.
3. Add the sugar and cream together until well combined.
4. Beat in the egg and vanilla essence, then fold in the flour.
5. Divide the mixture into 24 even pieces and roll each piece into a ball.
6. Roll the balls in the porridge oats so they are well coated.
7. Put on to baking sheets and flatten each slightly with a fork.
8. Place a piece of walnut on top then bake on the two top shelves of the oven for 15–20 minutes, or until golden brown.
9. Leave to cool on a wire tray and store in a tin until required.

To freeze: biscuits store well in the freezer; place in a polythene bag, seal and label. Store for up to 6 months and thaw at room temperature.

TROPICAL CAKES
Makes 32

4oz (100gm) margarine
4oz (100gm) caster sugar
2 large eggs
grated rind and juice of 1 orange
4oz (100gm) self-raising flour
pinch of ground cinnamon
1 can (15oz or 375gm) crushed pineapple
1 level tablespoon arrowroot
8 glacé cherries, chopped

1. Preheat oven to moderate to moderately hot, 375 deg F or gas 5 (190 deg C).
2. Cream the margarine until it is soft then add the sugar and beat together until light and fluffy in colour and texture.
3. Beat the eggs together, then beat in the orange rind and add to the creamed mixture gradually, beating well between each addition.
4. Sift the flour and cinnamon and, using a metal spoon, fold into the creamed mixture.
5. Arrange 32 paper cases on baking sheets and place about 1 teaspoonful in each.
6. Bake on the two top shelves of the oven for 15–20 minutes. Cool on a wire tray.
7. Drain the pineapple, put the arrowroot into a pan and gradually blend in the pineapple juice.
8. Over a low heat and stirring all the time, bring the sauce to the boil and boil for 2-3 minutes.
9. Stir in the orange juice with the crushed pineapple and chopped cherries.
10. Divide the topping between the cakes, spreading it to the sides of the cakes.
11. Carry them in shallow cake tins to the hall then arrange on plates for serving.

TEA

Allow 36 cups of tea for the whist drive – this amount is sufficient for second cups.

2–3oz (50–75gm) tea, depending on the strength desired
1 gallon (approximately 4½ litres) boiling water
2 pints (approximately 1 litre) milk

1. Make the tea with only half the boiling water so it is really strong.
2. Keep a kettle full of boiling water.
3. Fill each cup, when required, only half full of milk and tea and top up with boiling water.
4. This gives a really hot and delicious cup of tea and will mean the tea to be served stays hot all through the refreshment time.

CHEESE AND WINE PARTY

A party popular all the year round and suitable for so many gatherings. You can cater with ease for any number of people. Choose a selection of cheeses, different in colour, flavour and texture and have bowls of chutney, pickled onions and gherkins to compliment the cheese. Bowls of fruit are ideal to follow but if you feel you would like to serve a sweet course, apple pie or fruit cake, with coffee to follow is a good choice.

QUANTITIES

Cheese
Allow 3oz (75gm) cheese per person and buy it, if possible, on the day of the party from a shop which has a good turnover of products so you can be assured of its freshness. Make sure the selection you choose gives your guests as wide a choice as possible, combining flavour, texture and colour. It is fun to choose from the selection of English cheeses available – Cheddar, Stilton, Red Cheshire, Wensleydale and Leicester. Make a good display which can, of course, include some of the Continental cheeses such as Brie, Edam and Gorgonzola. Obviously the larger the gathering the wider the selection of cheese can be served.

Bread
Allow 2 rolls or slices of French bread per person but also serve a selection of biscuits, not forgetting crispbreads for the slimmers. Serve a selection of butter, English, French and Danish and allow 1lb (½ kilo) for 20 people.

Wine
There is such a good selection of reasonably-priced wine on the market nowadays that the choice is far easier than it used to be. It is best to buy large bottles as it works out cheaper and a litre bottle is sufficient for four people. For small gatherings too many wines to choose from makes serving difficult, so I suggest you just serve chilled rosé which is usually to everyone's taste. For larger gatherings, however, more choice in wines can be offered. White wines, always served chilled, are ideal with the milder cheeses such as Wensleydale; rosé also served chilled is delicious with Cheshire and Leicester and red wine served at room temperature with Stilton and Cheddar. Always open red wine at least an hour before it is to be served to give it time to breathe. Do not forget to cater for the non-alcoholic drinkers either. A punch with a base of cider is quite a good idea for them. Buy the wine from a wine merchant, if possible on a sale or return basis and enquire if you can borrow glasses as well. It is normal for wine merchants to hire out glasses free of charge, providing you buy the wine from them. You would have to pay for any breakages.

Arranging the tables
Serve the cheese on boards with plenty of cheese knives around. If possible, label the cheeses to help your guests with their choice. Garnish the boards with fruit, nuts, celery and watercress to add colour to the table. Have plates, napkins and knives at either end of the table so as not to create large queues of people. Place the drinks on a separate table away from the main one so as not to add to the confusion of serving.

If the cheese and wine party is for an organization and a large number of people are expected, work out a rota for serving the wine or one man could be left with the job the whole evening and not have any fun himself.

APPLE PIE
Serves 6–8

shortcrust pastry made with 8oz (200gm) flour (see Basic recipes, page 100)
1lb (½ kilo) cooking apples
4oz (100gm) granulated sugar
6 cloves
little milk and caster sugar to glaze

1. Preheat oven to moderate to moderately hot, 375 deg F or gas 5 (190 deg C).
2. Roll out half the pastry to a circle and use to line an 8-inch (20-cm) ovenproof plate.
3. Peel, core and thinly slice the apples and layer them on to the pastry-lined plate with the sugar and cloves.
4. Roll the other piece of pastry into a circle 1 inch larger than the plate, moisten the edges of the pastry on the plate and lift the other piece of pastry on a rolling pin over the apples.
5. Seal the two edges together and trim them with the back of a knife. Pinch the edges into scallops.
6. Brush the top with milk, dust it thickly with caster sugar and make two holes in the centre.
7. Bake in the centre of the oven for approximately 40 minutes, until the pastry is golden brown.
8. Serve warm if possible, with single cream.

FRUIT CAKE
Gives about 36 pieces

8oz (200gm) currants
8oz (200gm) sultanas
8oz (200gm) large raisins, chopped
4oz (100gm) mixed chopped candied peel
4oz (100gm) glacé cherries, chopped
2oz (50gm) walnuts, chopped
grated rind of 1 orange
10oz (250gm) margarine
10oz (250gm) soft brown sugar
5 standard eggs
3 level dessertspoons black treacle
10oz (250gm) plain flour
1 level teaspoon baking powder
2 level teaspoons mixed spice
3 tablespoons milk

1. Preheat oven to very moderate, 325 deg F or gas 3 (170 deg C).
2. Line an 8-inch (20-cm) square tin with two strips of greaseproof paper, crossing them over the base and coming 1 inch above the top of the tin.
3. Brush the paper lining with melted fat.
4. Mix the currants, sultanas, raisins, peel, cherries, walnuts and orange rind together in a bowl.
5. Beat the margarine until it is soft, add the sugar and beat the ingredients together until soft and fluffy.
6. Beat the eggs together and gradually beat them into the creamed mixture.
7. Beat in the black treacle.
8. Finally stir in the flour, sifted with the baking powder and mixed spice and the prepared fruit with the milk.
9. Turn the mixture into the prepared tin and hollow out the centre slightly.
10. Bake in the centre of the oven for 30 minutes, then turn the heat down to cool, 300 deg F or gas 2 (150 deg C) and bake for a further 3 hours, until a skewer, inserted into the cake, comes out clean.
11. Leave to cool in the tin for 30 minutes, then finish cooling on a wire tray.
12. Wrap in foil or a polythene bag until the party.

A COFFEE PARTY

Whether it is in the morning or the evening, a coffee party is a very pleasant and informal way of entertaining friends.

The coffee
Make it strong using either instant or ground coffee. Allow 1 pint (approximately ½ litre) coffee for every three people and 1 pint (approximately ½ litre) milk for every nine people, not forgetting second cups.

Instant: mix 1 level tablespoon of instant coffee with 1 pint (approximately ½ litre) boiling water.

Ground: use freshly ground coffee if possible as the flavour and aroma is always superior. Use 2 rounded tablespoons to every 1 pint (approximately ½ litre) of water. If you have no percolator spoon the coffee into a large, warm jug, pour in the boiling water and stir for 1–2 seconds with a metal spoon. Leave the jug in a warm place for about 10 minutes to allow the grounds to settle, then strain through a fine sieve or muslin and reheat the coffee in a pan when required – do not allow it to boil.

MENU
Serves 8–10

Quiche Lorraine
Walnut fudge cake
Chocolate éclairs
Crusty lemon bake
Shortbread biscuits
Florentines

QUICHE LORRAINE
Serves 6–8

shortcrust pastry made with 6oz (150gm) flour (see Basic recipes, page 100)
9 spring onions or 1 medium onion
4oz (100gm) streaky bacon rashers
2 large eggs
¼ pint (125ml) milk
2oz (50gm) cheese, grated
salt and pepper

1. Preheat oven to moderate to moderately hot, 375 deg F or gas 5 (190 deg C).
2. Roll the pastry into a circle and use to line an 8-inch (20-cm) flan ring placed on a baking sheet.
3. Leave the lined flan ring in a cool place while preparing the filling.
4. Trim the spring onions or peel and slice the medium onion.
5. Cut the rind from the bacon and cut it into pieces.
6. Fry the bacon without any extra fat until it is cooked and scatter the pieces in the flan ring.
7. Fry the onions in the pan after the bacon, for a few minutes then place with the bacon.
8. Beat the eggs together, mix in the milk and half the cheese.
9. Season the mixture and pour it into the flan ring.
10. Sprinkle over the rest of the cheese then bake in the centre of the oven for about 40 minutes, until it is set and well risen.
11. Serve hot or cold.

WALNUT FUDGE CAKE
(Illustrated on page 54)
Serves 8–10

6oz (150gm) soft margarine
6oz (150gm) light soft brown sugar
3 large eggs
6oz (150gm) self-raising flour
pinch of salt
2oz (50gm) walnuts, chopped
2 tablespoons milk

Filling and decoration:
6oz (150gm) margarine
2 tablespoons milk
1 level tablespoon malted milk powder
12oz (300gm) icing sugar, sifted
2oz (50gm) walnuts, chopped

1. Preheat oven to moderate to moderately hot, 375 deg F or gas 5 (190 deg C).
2. Grease two 7½-inch (19-cm) sandwich tins with melted fat and line the base of each with a circle of greaseproof paper.
3. Put the margarine, sugar, eggs, flour, salt, walnuts and milk into a bowl.
4. Using a wooden spoon mix all the ingredients together then beat them for a minute.
5. Divide the mixture between the two tins and level the surface.
6. Bake in the centre of the oven for 25–30 minutes, until the cakes feel springy to the touch and they are coming away from the sides of the tin.
7. Leave on a wire tray to cool and remove the greaseproof paper.
8. Melt the margarine for the filling, then remove the pan from the heat and add the milk and malted milk powder.
9. Gradually beat in the sifted icing sugar and when it has all been added and the icing is smooth, leave it on one side to cool and thicken.
10. Sandwich the two cakes together with half the icing.
11. Spread the remainder on top letting it flow down the sides of the cake slightly.
12. Sprinkle the chopped walnuts on the top for decoration.

CHOCOLATE ECLAIRS
Makes 14

2½oz (62gm) plain flour
2oz (50gm) margarine
¼ pint (125ml) water
2 standard eggs
1 egg white
2 level teaspoons caster sugar
¼ pint (125ml) double cream
4oz (100gm) icing sugar, sifted
1 level tablespoon cocoa powder
3 level tablespoons drinking chocolate

1. Preheat oven to hot, 425 deg F or gas 7 (220 deg C).
2. Sift the flour on to a piece of greaseproof paper.
3. Melt the margarine over a low heat, add the water and bring the mixture to the boil.
4. Remove the pan from the heat and add the flour.
5. Immediately beat the mixture with a wooden spoon until it leaves the sides of the pan clean.
6. Beat the eggs together and when the mixture has cooled beat them in gradually.
7. Fill a piping bag, with a ½-inch pipe attached, with the mixture and pipe on to greased sheets, 3-inch lengths, leaving a space between each éclair.
8. Bake on the two top shelves of the oven for 15–20 minutes, until golden and well risen.
9. Immediately they come out of the oven slit one side open to release any steam. Cool on a wire tray.
10. Whip the egg white stiffly then whisk in the caster sugar.
11. Whip the cream until it holds its shape then fold in the egg white.
12. Fill the éclairs with the cream – the easiest way is to pipe it in.
13. Sift the icing sugar, cocoa and drinking chocolate into a bowl and mix in sufficient water to make a thick coating consistency.
14. Spoon a teaspoonful of icing along each éclair. Leave to set, then serve.

CRUSTY LEMON BAKE
Serves 24

6oz (150gm) butter
6oz (150gm) brown sugar
2 large eggs
6oz (150gm) self-raising flour
about 4oz (100gm) caster sugar
juice of 1 large lemon

1. Preheat oven to moderate, 350 deg F or gas 4 (180 deg C).
2. Brush a 9-inch (23-cm) by 13-inch (32·5-cm) Swiss roll tin with melted fat.
3. Cut the butter into small pieces, place it in a pan and, over a very low heat, melt it.
4. Remove from the heat and stir in the sugar.
5. Beat the eggs and stir them into the mixture with the sifted flour.
6. Turn the mixture into the tin and level the surface.
7. Bake in the centre of the oven for about 40 minutes, or until the surface is golden brown.
8. Remove from the oven, immediately mix enough caster sugar with the lemon juice to make a thin paste and spread it over the surface.
9. The lemon sinks into the surface leaving the top crispy.
10. Cut into pieces to serve.

SHORTBREAD BISCUITS
Makes 36

12oz (300gm) plain flour
8oz (200gm) butter
2oz (50gm) caster sugar
caster sugar to sprinkle

1. Preheat oven to very moderate, 325 deg F or gas 3 (170 deg C).
2. Sift the flour into a basin and rub the butter in until the mixture resembles breadcrumbs.
3. Stir in the caster sugar, then knead the mixture into a ball.
4. Roll it out to a ¼-inch thickness and cut out rounds with a 2-inch (5-cm) cutter.
5. Gather up the scraps, re-roll the dough and cut out more rounds.
6. Place the rounds on baking sheets and sprinkle with extra caster sugar.
7. Bake on the centre and lower shelves of the oven for about 20 minutes. Cool on a wire tray.
8. These biscuits store well in an airtight tin.

FLORENTINES
Makes 12–16

3½oz (87gm) butter
4oz (100gm) caster sugar
3½oz (87gm) chopped mixed peel
2oz (50gm) glacé cherries, chopped
2oz (50gm) flaked almonds
2oz (50gm) blanched almonds, chopped
2 level tablespoons whipped cream
4–6oz (100–150gm) plain chocolate

1. Preheat oven to moderate, 350 deg F or gas 4 (180 deg C).
2. Melt the butter, add the sugar and bring the mixture very slowly to the boil.
3. Remove the pan from the heat and stir in the peel, cherries and flaked and chopped almonds.
4. Finally stir in the cream.
5. Put teaspoonfuls of the mixture, well spaced on to greased baking sheets.
6. Bake on the second shelf of the oven for 3 minutes.
7. Remove the sheet from the oven and, with a fork, neaten the edges of each florentine so the mixture forms a neat round about 3 inches in diameter.
8. Return the tray to the oven and continue baking for 4–5 minutes.
9. Leave to cool and set slightly before running a sharp knife underneath each to loosen it from the sheet.
10. Cool on a wire tray while baking the other batches.
11. When all the florentines are cooked and cold, melt the chocolate on a plate over a pan of hot water.
12. Spread the base of each biscuit with some chocolate, mark it with a fork then leave the chocolate to set.
13. Store in an airtight tin.

EASTER TEA FOR TEN

MENU

Tasty ham sandwiches
Bombay sandwiches
Cheese scones
Fruit malt loaf
Simnel cake
Ginger oaties
Cream horns
Easter bonnets
Hot cross buns

TASTY HAM SANDWICHES

Makes 20

The butter is mixed into the filling so there is no need to butter the bread before making the sandwiches.

4oz (100gm) ham
1 level tablespoon mustard pickle
2oz (50gm) butter, melted
10 thin slices bread

1. Mince the ham into a bowl.
2. Mix in the mustard pickle and melted butter.
3. Divide the filling between 5 slices of the bread.
4. Cover with the other slices, cut off the crusts then cut the sandwiches into four.
5. Arrange the sandwiches on a plate and cover them with polythene until required.

BOMBAY SANDWICHES

Makes 20

As with the tasty ham sandwich recipe, the butter is in the filling.

2oz (50gm) butter
little black pepper
½ level teaspoon curry powder
4oz (100gm) cooked chicken, minced
10 thin slices bread

1. Beat the butter until it is soft, then beat in the black pepper and curry powder.
2. Finally mix in the minced chicken.
3. Spread the filling over 5 slices of bread.
4. Cover with the other slices.
5. Cut off the crusts and cut each round into four.
6. Arrange on a plate for serving.

CHEESE SCONES

Makes 16

6oz (150gm) self-raising flour
pinch of salt
pinch of cayenne pepper
1oz (25gm) margarine
7½oz (187gm) cheese, grated
about 6 tablespoons milk
2oz (50gm) butter
few parsley sprigs to garnish

1. Preheat oven to hot, 425 deg F or gas 7 (220 deg C).
2. Sift the flour, salt and cayenne pepper into a bowl.
3. Add the margarine and rub it in until evenly distributed.
4. Mix in 1½oz (37gm) of the cheese, then bind the ingredients together to form a soft dough with the milk.
5. Turn the dough on to a floured working surface and roll it out to just over a ½ inch thick.
6. Cut out as many scones as possible.
7. Gather up the scraps, re-roll them and cut out more scones.
8. Place them on a baking sheet and bake in the centre of the oven for just under 10 minutes, or until lightly brown. Cool on a wire tray.
9. Split in half and butter each piece.
10. Pile the remaining grated cheese on top and garnish each scone half with a sprig of parsley.

To freeze: scones freeze well. Store them in polythene bags, seal and label. Use as required.

FRUIT MALT LOAF

Makes about 20 slices

12oz (300gm) self-raising flour
1½ level teaspoons bicarbonate of soda
4oz (100gm) sultanas
¼ pint (125ml) milk
3 level tablespoons malt extract
3 level tablespoons golden syrup
2 large eggs

1. Preheat oven to moderate, 350 deg F or gas 4 (180 deg C).
2. Brush a 2-lb (½-kilo) loaf tin with melted fat.
3. Sift the flour and bicarbonate of soda into a bowl and mix in the fruit.
4. Heat the milk, malt and syrup together in a pan over a low heat.
5. Beat the eggs together.
6. Stir the eggs and melted mixture into the flour and fruit so they are all combined. Do not beat the mixture.
7. Turn the mixture into the tin.
8. Bake in the centre of the oven for 20 minutes, then reduce the heat to very moderate, 325 deg F or gas 3 (170 deg C) and bake for a further 40 minutes.
9. Cool on a wire tray.
10. Serve sliced and buttered.

SIMNEL CAKE

Marzipan:
8oz (200gm) ground almonds
4oz (100gm) icing sugar, sifted
4oz (100gm) caster sugar
1 standard egg, beaten
little lemon juice

Cake:
4oz (100gm) currants
4oz (100gm) sultanas
3oz (75gm) glacé cherries, chopped
3oz (75gm) walnuts, chopped
1oz (25gm) chopped mixed peel
finely grated rind of 1 lemon
5oz (125gm) plain flour
pinch of salt
1 level teaspoon baking powder
1 level teaspoon mixed spice
4oz (100gm) margarine
4oz (100gm) soft dark brown sugar
1 level dessertspoon black treacle
2 large eggs
2 tablespoons milk

Decoration:
2 level tablespoons apricot jam
½ beaten egg
broken shell from 1 egg
2 small toy chicks

1. Preheat oven to very moderate, 325 deg F or gas 3 (170 deg C).
2. Brush a 6-inch (15-cm) tin with melted fat and line the base and sides with greaseproof paper. Brush the paper lining.
3. Mix the ground almonds, icing sugar and caster sugar together in a bowl.
4. Add the beaten egg with enough lemon juice to make a fairly stiff dough.
5. Keep the marzipan covered until required.
6. Mix the currants, sultanas, cherries, walnuts, mixed peel and lemon rind together.
7. Sift the flour, salt, baking powder and mixed spice on to a piece of paper and mix 2 tablespoons with the dried fruit.
8. Beat the margarine until it is soft then add the sugar and cream the ingredients together.
9. Stir in the black treacle.
10. Beat the eggs then add them gradually to the creamed mixture, beating well between each addition.
11. Stir in the flour, dried fruit and milk and turn half the mixture into the prepared tin.
12. Cut one-third from the marzipan, roll it into a 6-inch circle and rest it on the cake mixture in the tin.
13. Turn the remainder of the cake mixture on top, smooth over the surface, then hollow out the centre slightly so the cake cooks level.
14. Bake in the centre of the oven for 2 hours, or until a skewer, inserted, comes out clean.
15. Cool on a wire tray and remove the greaseproof paper.
16. Roll half the remaining marzipan into a 6-inch circle.
17. Make the cake level if necessary, then turn it over and use the base as the top.
18. Warm the jam, brush it over the top then put the marzipan in place, neatening the edges with a palette knife.
19. Divide the rest of the marzipan into 12 pieces, roll them into balls and place them around the top edge.
20. Brush the marzipan with the beaten egg.
21. Wrap a band of greaseproof paper around the side of the cake deep enough to hold the marzipan in place.
22. Put the cake in a very moderate oven, 325 deg F or gas 3 (170 deg C) for about 10 minutes until the marzipan is golden brown.
23. Remove the greaseproof band, encircle the cake with a piece of ribbon and place the chicks and the broken egg shell on top.

GINGER OATIES
Makes 18

8oz (200gm) rolled oats
2 level teaspoons ground ginger
4oz (100gm) soft brown sugar
4oz (100gm) margarine
2 level tablespoons golden syrup

1. Preheat oven to moderate, 350 deg F or gas 4 (180 deg C).
2. Brush a 7½-inch (19-cm) square shallow tin with melted fat.
3. Put the rolled oats, ginger and sugar into a bowl and mix them well together.
4. Melt the margarine and syrup together over a gentle heat.
5. Stir them into the dry ingredients and mix well.
6. Turn into the tin and level the surface.
7. Bake in the centre of the oven for 20–25 minutes, until golden brown.
8. Leave in the tin to cool, then turn out and cut into 18 fingers.

CREAM HORNS
Makes 10

puff pastry made with
8oz (200gm) flour (see Basic recipes, page 100)
1 egg white
little caster sugar
¼ pint (125ml) double cream
1 small carton single cream
3 tablespoons raspberry jam
little sifted icing sugar to sprinkle

1. Preheat oven to moderate to moderately hot, 400 deg F or gas 6 (200 deg C).
2. On a lightly floured working surface, roll the pastry into a rectangle 18 inches by 12 inches.
3. Trim the edges then cut 10 strips each 18 inches long and just over 1 inch wide.
4. Brush 10 cream horn tins with a little melted fat, and the strips of pastry with water.
5. Starting at the tip of each mould, wind a strip of pastry around each tin, overlapping the strip slightly as you work.
6. Place the horns on a baking sheet with the ends underneath.
7. Beat the egg white lightly then brush it over the horns and sprinkle them with caster sugar.
8. Leave in a cool place for about 10 minutes to rest the pastry.
9. Bake in the centre of the oven for 20 minutes, or until golden brown and cooked.
10. Carefully twist the moulds from the horns and leave on a wire tray to cool.
11. Whip the creams together until they are stiff.
12. Put the whipped cream into a large piping bag with a large star pipe (No. 6) attached.
13. Place a little jam in the base of each horn and pipe a swirl of cream to fill the end.
14. Dust with icing sugar before serving.

EASTER BONNETS
(Illustrated on page 54)
Makes 14

3oz (75gm) margarine
3oz (75gm) caster sugar
6oz (150gm) plain flour
finely grated rind of 1 lemon
little beaten egg
2oz (50gm) butter
2oz (50gm) icing sugar, sifted
little coffee essence
crystallized violets and mimosa

1. Preheat oven to moderate to moderately hot, 400 deg F or gas 6 (200 deg C).
2. Beat the margarine and sugar together until soft and fluffy.
3. Mix in the flour and grated lemon rind with enough beaten egg to make a dough of shortcrust pastry consistency.
4. On a lightly floured working surface roll the dough out to just under an ⅛-inch thickness.
5. Cut out an even number of large and small rounds using 2½-inch (6·3-cm) and 1¼-inch (3·2-cm) fluted cutters.
6. Gather up the scraps and cut out more rounds.
7. Place the biscuits on a baking sheet and cook in the centre of the oven for about 8 minutes. (The smaller ones will be ready first.) Cool on a wire tray.
8. Beat the butter to a soft cream, then gradually beat in the icing sugar with enough coffee essence to flavour and colour.
9. Place the filling in a piping bag with a star pipe attached.
10. Pipe a swirl just slightly off centre of the larger biscuits.
11. Top with a small biscuit to make the crown of the bonnet.
12. Decorate with crystallized violets and mimosa for trimmings.

HOT CROSS BUNS
Makes 18

½oz (12gm) dried yeast
3oz (75gm) soft brown sugar
½ pint (250ml) water
1lb (½ kilo) strong plain flour
pinch of salt
4 level teaspoons mixed spice
2oz (50gm) margarine
3oz (75gm) currants
1oz (25gm) sultanas
1oz (25gm) chopped mixed peel

Topping:
1oz (25gm) plain flour
1 level dessertspoon caster sugar
2 dessertspoons milk

1. Preheat oven to hot, 425 deg F or gas 7 (220 deg C).
2. Put the dried yeast into a bowl with 1 teaspoon of the sugar.
3. Warm the water to blood heat.
4. Whisk half of it into the yeast and leave the bowl in a warm place for about 10 minutes, or until the liquid has a thick froth on top.
5. Sift the flour, salt and mixed spice into a bowl and rub in the margarine.
6. Make a well in the centre and pour into it the rest of the sugar, dissolved in the remaining water and the dissolved yeast.
7. Using your hand, mix the ingredients together until they form a dough.
8. Beat the dough in the bowl until it is soft, then turn it on to a floured working surface and knead for at least 5 minutes, until it is smooth.
9. Knead in the fruit and peel and, when it is evenly distributed, place the dough in a greased bowl, cover it with a piece of greased polythene and leave it in a warm place to rise to double its size.
10. Again turn the dough on to a lightly floured working surface and knock it back gently.
11. Cut the dough into 18 even pieces and form each into a round.
12. Place the buns on a greased baking sheet.
13. For the topping, mix the flour with a little water to make it a stiff batter.
14. Spoon it into a greaseproof paper piping bag, snip off the end and pipe a cross on top of each bun.
15. Leave the buns to prove for 15 minutes in a warm place.
16. Bake in the centre of the oven for 15–20 minutes, or until golden brown.
17. Meanwhile, dissolve the sugar in the milk, over a low heat, then increase the heat and bring the glaze to the boil.
18. Brush it over the buns as soon as they come out of the oven to give them a good gloss.

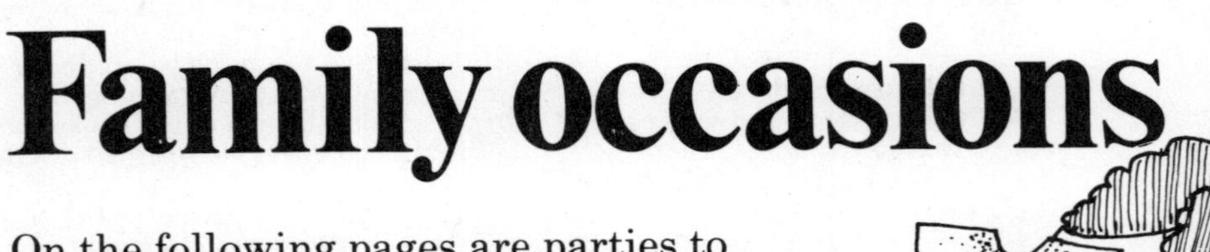

Family occasions

On the following pages are parties to celebrate all the happy family occasions, such as christening, engagement, coming of age and wedding.

A CHRISTENING PARTY

The christening party takes the form of a tea for 12 people. All the recipes can be arranged attractively on the table before leaving for the church. As long as they are covered with teatowels or sheets of polythene, the food will come to no harm while you are out.

MENU
Serves 12

The christening cake
Tongue whirls
Cucumber sandwiches
Sea savouries
Brandy snaps
Chocolate truffles
Viennese buns
Fruit trifle

THE CHRISTENING CAKE

In case you cannot use the top tier of your wedding cake, here is a delicious recipe for a cake which is iced with American frosting and suitably decorated for the occasion.

8oz (200gm) margarine
8oz (200gm) caster sugar
3 large eggs plus 2 egg yolks
8oz (200gm) self-raising flour
2oz (50gm) glacé cherries, chopped
2oz (50gm) crystallized pineapple, chopped
2oz (50gm) crystallized ginger, chopped
little milk
2 egg whites
12oz (300gm) granulated sugar
¼ level teaspoon cream of tartar
4 tablespoons water

1. Preheat the oven to moderate to moderately hot, 375 deg F or gas 5 (190 deg C).
2. Brush two 8-inch (20-cm) sandwich tins with melted fat and line the base of each with a circle of greaseproof paper; brush the paper lining.
3. Beat the margarine until it is soft and creamy.
4. Add the caster sugar and beat the ingredients together until light and fluffy in colour and texture.
5. Beat the eggs and egg yolks and add them gradually to the creamed mixture beating well between each addition.
6. Finally stir in the sifted flour with the cherries, pineapple, ginger and milk.
7. Turn the cake mixture into the prepared tins and hollow out the centre slightly so they rise evenly.
8. Bake in the centre of the oven for 25–30 minutes, until they are shrinking away from the sides of the tin and are golden brown in colour. Cool on a wire tray.
9. Put the egg whites for the frosting into a bowl with the sugar, cream of tartar and water.
10. Place the bowl over a pan of simmering water and stir gently until every grain of sugar has dissolved – it will take about 10 minutes.
11. Whisk the mixture, still over the water, until it is thick and leaves a clear trail when the whisk is lifted out of the bowl.
12. Remove the bowl from the heat and whisk the frosting for a further minute.
13. Sandwich the two cakes together with a little of the icing.
14. Spoon the rest on top of the cake and quickly spread it over the top and down the sides leaving the surface rough.
15. Position a cradle or stork ornament on top of the cake and surround it with artificial flowers.
16. Place the cake on a board or plate for serving.

Vols-au-vent (see page 74)

Sea savouries (see page 73)

Kipper cream (see page 80)

Taj Mahal chicken (see page 80)

Special mince pies (see page 87)

Chocolate log cake (see page 87)

Fudge (see page 88)

Roast turkey (see page 94)

TONGUE WHIRLS
Makes 50

Make these the day before they are required.

1 large uncut white sandwich loaf
about 8oz (200gm) butter
8oz (200gm) tongue, thinly sliced
little French mustard
watercress to garnish

1. Using a very sharp knife cut the top crust from the loaf.
2. Soften the butter and spread some along the loaf.
3. Cut a thin slice of bread the length of the loaf then cut off the crusts.
4. Cover the slice with the tongue and spread the meat with a little mustard.
5. Roll the slice tightly down the length and put it into a polythene bag.
6. Cut more slices and make more roles in the same way using up the tongue.
7. Leave the rolls tightly wrapped in polythene in a cool place overnight.
8. Next day cut the rolls into ½-inch slices, arrange on a plate and garnish with watercress.

CUCUMBER SANDWICHES
Makes 44

8oz (200gm) butter
1 thinly sliced brown loaf
1 small cucumber
1 dessertspoon vinegar
salt and pepper

1. Soften the butter and use it to butter the slices of bread.
2. Peel and thinly slice the cucumber. Place in a bowl.
3. Add the vinegar and seasoning and mix them together.
4. Lay the slices of bread out on a board and divide the filling between 11 slices. Top with remaining slices.
5. Cut off the crusts then cut each round into four triangles.
6. Arrange on a large plate and cover with polythene until required.

SEA SAVOURIES
(Illustrated on page 71)
Makes about 15

1 packet (3oz or 75gm) cream cheese
1 can (8oz or 200gm) pilchards in tomato sauce
pepper
small savoury biscuits
pickled cocktail onions or stuffed olives

1. Beat the cream cheese to a soft consistency.
2. Add the pilchards in tomato sauce and, using a fork, beat the mixture to a soft and pliable consistency. Season with pepper.
3. Place the filling in a large piping bag and pipe stars on to savoury biscuits.
4. Garnish with onions or slices of stuffed olive.

BRANDY SNAPS
Makes 20

2oz (50gm) margarine
2 level tablespoons golden syrup
1½oz (37gm) caster sugar
grated rind of half a lemon
1½oz (37gm) plain flour
1 level teaspoon ground ginger
¼ pint (125ml) double cream

1. Preheat oven to cool, 300 deg F or gas 2 (150 deg C).
2. Melt the margarine with the syrup, sugar and lemon rind over a low heat.
3. Sift the flour and ginger together and mix them into the melted ingredients.
4. Grease several baking sheets with melted fat.
5. Put 4 or 5 teaspoonfuls of the mixture, well spaced out, on to each sheet.
6. Bake in several batches in the centre of the oven for 10 minutes, until a light brown colour.
7. As a sheet is ready, run a palette knife under each brandy snap to loosen it.
8. Turn it over and immediately, while it is still hot, roll it around an oiled wooden spoon handle.
9. Slip it off, when curled, to cool completely and roll the rest in the same way. (If the brandy snaps start to cool and harden put them back into the oven to soften again so they can be rolled.)
10. Whip the cream until it is stiff and put it into a piping bag with a star pipe attached.
11. Just before they are to be served, pipe a swirl of cream in each end of the rolls.

CHOCOLATE TRUFFLES
(Illustrated on page 54)
Makes 18 large cakes or 36–40 small sweets

This mixture may be made in a mixer, when all the ingredients are placed in the bowl and the machine is switched on low until they are combined.

1lb (½ kilo) cake crumbs
8oz (200gm) icing sugar, sifted
4oz (100gm) cocoa powder
¼ pint (125ml) milk
1 dessertspoon rum
chocolate strands

1. Put the cake crumbs into a bowl and mix in the sifted icing sugar.
2. Sift in the cocoa powder.
3. Bind the ingredients together with the milk and rum to make a fairly stiff mixture.
4. Divide it into 18 even-sized, large pieces or 36–40 small pieces and roll them in your hands to make balls.
5. Place the chocolate strands in a polythene bag.
6. Add the balls two at a time and shake the bag so the balls are well coated with the strands.
7. Place each chocolate truffle in a paper case or sweet case for serving.

VIENNESE BUNS
Makes 16

8oz (200gm) butter
2oz (50gm) caster sugar
8oz (200gm) plain flour
pinch of salt
few drops vanilla essence
icing sugar
1 tablespoon raspberry jam

1. Preheat oven to moderate, 350 deg F or gas 4 (180 deg C).
2. Beat the butter until it is soft.
3. Add the caster sugar and beat again until the mixture is very light and creamy.
4. Sieve the flour and salt.
5. Mix the flour gradually into the butter and sugar with the vanilla essence, beating well between each addition, until the mixture is light and soft.
6. Put it into a piping bag fitted with a large star pipe and pipe a whirl of mixture in 16 paper cases. Place on a baking sheet.
7. Bake on the second shelf from the top of the oven for about 15 minutes, or until very light brown. Cool.
8. To serve, sprinkle the tops with icing sugar and place a small dab of jam in the centre of each cake.

FRUIT TRIFLE
Serves 12

6 trifle sponges
12oz (300gm) raspberry jam
5 tablespoons milk or sherry
1 can (1lb 13oz or 725gm) sliced peaches
4 level tablespoons custard powder
3 level tablespoons caster sugar
1½ pints (approximately ¾ litre) milk
¼ pint (125ml) double cream
1 glacé cherry

1. Split the sponge cakes and spread them with the jam.
2. Cut into small pieces and place them in a 4-pint (approximately 2-litre) glass dish.
3. Pour over the sherry or milk and syrup from the can of fruit and leave the base to soak.
4. Put the custard powder and sugar into a pan and blend to a smooth paste with a little milk.
5. Blend in the rest of the milk and put the pan over the heat.
6. Stirring all the time, bring the custard to the boil and cook for a few minutes to thicken.
7. Leaving 7 peach slices for decoration, place the rest into the bowl on top of the sponge.
8. Pour over the slightly cooled custard and leave to cool completely, overnight if liked.
9. To decorate the trifle, whip the cream until it just holds its shape and spread it over the custard.
10. Arrange the peach slices in the centre of the trifle with a glacé cherry in the centre so the design resembles a flower.
11. Keep in a cool place until required.

A COMING-OF-AGE PARTY

I have suggested a finger buffet for this party. However, if you would prefer to serve a fork buffet, the menu for the wedding reception would be ideal.

MENU
Serves 24

Ham and haddock and tomato vols-au-vent
Sausage rolls
Chicken drumsticks
Asparagus rolls
Scotch eggs
Chocolate fancy cakes
Peach turnovers
Meringues

Cider punch or Rosé wine cup

VOLS-AU-VENT
(Illustrated on page 71)
Makes 48

You will require 48 vol-au-vent cases – they can be bought from your baker ready made or frozen, but uncooked, or you can make them yourself. Fill them several hours before the buffet is to be served and place them on baking sheets. Heat them through in a moderate oven, 325 deg F or gas 3 (170 deg C) for about 15 minutes.

For the cases:
puff pastry made with 2lb (1 kilo) flour (see Basic recipes, page 100)
little beaten egg to glaze

1. Preheat oven to hot, 450 deg F or gas 8 (230 deg C).
2. Divide the pastry in four and roll out each piece into a rectangle 9 inches by 13 inches.
3. Using a 2-inch (5-cm) fluted cutter cut out 24 circles from each piece.
4. Press a 1-inch cutter lightly into the centre of 12 of them, but leave the centre in position.
5. Brush the tops of the uncut circles with a little water, lift a marked pastry piece on top and

press the two circles together.
6. Put the cases on to baking sheets and leave in a cool place for 30 minutes.
7. Brush the tops with egg glaze then bake near the top of the oven for 8–10 minutes, until golden brown and cooked. Cool on a wire tray and remove the tiny centres.

The fillings

HAM
Fills 24 cases

8oz (200gm) cooked ham shoulder
1 level dessertspoon piccalilli
1 pint (approximately ½ litre) white sauce (see Basic recipes, page 100)

1. Chop the ham finely and cut up any large pieces in the piccalilli.
2. Stir these ingredients into the sauce and check for seasoning.
3. Divide the filling between the cases using a teaspoon.

HADDOCK AND TOMATO
Fills 24 cases

12oz (300gm) smoked haddock fillet
3 large tomatoes
1 pint (approximately ½ litre) white sauce (see Basic recipes, page 100)
pinch of mace
salt and pepper

1. Wipe the fish, place it in enough cold water to cover the fillets and, over a very low heat, bring the water to the boil.
2. Simmer the fish for about 5 minutes, then remove it from the pan and place it on a plate.
3. Remove any skin and bones and flake the fish.
4. Plunge the tomatoes into boiling water for 20 seconds, then transfer them to cold water and peel off the skins.
5. Chop the tomatoes roughly and mix them into the sauce with the fish and the mace.
6. Check the filling for seasoning, then divide it between the cases, using a teaspoon for filling each case.

SAUSAGE ROLLS
Makes about 24

flaky pastry made with 8oz (200gm) flour (see Basic recipes, page 100)
1lb (½ kilo) pork sausagemeat
1 medium onion, peeled and finely chopped
little beaten egg to glaze

1. Preheat oven to hot, 425 deg F or gas 7 (220 deg C).
2. On a lightly floured working surface, roll the pastry into a 14-inch square.
3. Cut it into four strips with a sharp knife.
4. Divide the sausagemeat into four and, using some flour, roll each quarter out to the same length as the pastry.
5. Place a strip of meat on each strip of pastry and sprinkle them all with the onion.
6. Moisten a long edge, roll the other side over the sausagemeat and press the edges firmly together.
7. Brush the rolls with the egg glaze.
8. Assemble the rolls, side by side, and with a sharp knife, cut them in half, then each half into three to make 24 rolls in all.
9. Make a snip in the top of each with a pair of scissors and place them on baking sheets.
10. Leave the sausage rolls in a cool place for 15 minutes, then bake in the centre of the oven for 10 minutes.
11. Reduce the heat to moderate to moderately hot, 375 deg F or gas 5 (190 deg C) and cook the sausage rolls for 15 minutes, until they are golden brown.
12. Cool on a wire tray and serve them hot or cold when required.

To freeze: sausage rolls can be stored in a freezer. Pack in polythene bags, seal and label. Use as required. There is no need to thaw them out, just reheat in a moderate oven, 350 deg F or gas 4 (180 deg C) for 15–20 minutes.

CHICKEN DRUMSTICKS
Makes 24

24 chicken drumsticks
2oz (50gm) butter
2 level tablespoons chopped parsley
1 garlic clove, crushed
salt and pepper

1. Preheat oven to moderate to moderately hot, 375 deg F or gas 5 (190 deg C).
2. Wipe the chicken drumsticks and put them into an ovenproof dish.
3. Beat the butter to a soft cream, together with the parsley, garlic and seasoning. Spread it over the chicken.
4. Bake the chicken in the centre of the oven for about 45 minutes, until the meat is tender and the skin golden brown.
5. Place a cutlet frill on each drumstick so they are easier to eat. Serve hot.

ASPARAGUS ROLLS
Makes about 50

2 small brown loaves (1 day old if possible)
8oz (200gm) butter, softened
2 cans cut asparagus spears
tomato quarters to garnish

1. Cut the crusts from the loaves.
2. Slice the bread very thinly then roll it flat with a rolling pin.
3. Butter each slice with the softened butter.
4. Drain the asparagus spears and wrap a slice of bread around each.
5. Arrange on a plate and cover with polythene until ready to serve.
6. Garnish the dish with tomato quarters.

SCOTCH EGGS
Serves 28

7 hard-boiled eggs
1½lb (¾ kilo) sausagemeat
1 large egg, beaten
browned breadcrumbs
deep fat for frying
watercress to garnish

1. Shell the eggs.
2. Divide the sausagemeat into seven equal pieces.
3. Flatten each piece out on a floured working surface.
4. Place an egg in the centre of each round and work the meat over the egg so it is completely smooth without any cracks in the meat.
5. Brush each Scotch egg with beaten egg then toss in the breadcrumbs so the surface is evenly coated.
6. Heat the fat, which should be deep enough to cover the eggs, in a pan.
7. Put the Scotch eggs into the deep fat basket and lower them into the fat.
8. Fry for about 5 minutes and place them on absorbent paper to drain. Leave to cool.
9. Cut the eggs into quarters, arrange on a dish and garnish with watercress.

CHOCOLATE FANCY CAKES
Makes 30

The cake can be made the day before it is required and kept wrapped in polythene.

6oz (150gm) margarine
6oz (150gm) caster sugar
3 large eggs
5oz (125gm) self-raising flour
1oz (25gm) cocoa powder
10oz (250gm) icing sugar
1oz (25gm) cocoa powder
crystallized violets
angelica diamonds

1. Preheat oven to moderate to moderately hot, 375 deg F or gas 5 (190 deg C).
2. Brush a Swiss roll tin with melted fat and line the base with a piece of greaseproof paper. Brush the paper lining.
3. Melt the margarine very gradually then pour it into a mixing bowl with the caster sugar.
4. Beat the two together then add the eggs one at a time, beating well between each addition.
5. Sift the flour and cocoa powder together and fold them into the mixture.
6. Turn into the prepared tin and hollow out the centre slightly, so the cake will be level when baked.
7. Bake in the centre of the oven for about 20 minutes, or until well risen and springy to the touch. Turn on to a wire tray to cool. Remove the greaseproof paper.
8. When the cake is cold cut it into 2-inch squares but keep the pieces together in their original shape.
9. Sift the icing sugar and cocoa powder into a bowl and stir in sufficient cold water to make a thick coating consistency.
10. Pour the icing on to the centre of the cake and spread it over the surface with a palette knife.
11. Pull the cakes apart and leave the icing to set for at least 10 minutes.
12. Trim the edges with a sharp knife.
13. Decorate each square with a piece of crystallized violet and angelica.

PEACH TURNOVERS
Makes 20

5oz (125gm) plain flour
3oz (75gm) butter
2oz (50gm) caster sugar
2 egg yolks (keep the whites for the meringues)
1 can (15oz or 375gm) sliced peaches
caster sugar to sprinkle

1. Preheat oven to moderate to moderately hot, 400 deg F or gas 6 (200 deg C).
2. Sieve the flour into a bowl.
3. Rub the butter in and when the mixture resembles breadcrumbs stir in the caster sugar.
4. Bind the mixture together with the egg yolks to make a pliable dough.
5. Wrap the dough in greaseproof paper and leave it in a cool place for about 30 minutes.
6. Divide the pastry into two and roll each half into a 20-inch square.
7. Cut both pieces into 2-inch squares, making 20 in all.
8. Put a peach slice, diagonally across each square, then damp the two opposite corners and fold one up over the other so the peach still shows at both ends.
9. Sprinkle the turnovers with sugar and place them on baking sheets.
10. Bake on the two top shelves of the oven for about 10 minutes. Cool on a wire tray.

MERINGUES
Makes about 30 whole meringues

4 egg whites
8oz (200gm) caster sugar
½ pint (250ml) double cream
¼ pint (125ml) single cream

1. Preheat oven to very cool, 225 deg F or gas ¼ (110 deg C).
2. Brush 2 baking sheets with a little oil then dust them with flour and shake off the surplus.
3. Put the egg whites into a bowl and whisk them until very stiff.
4. Add 4 level tablespoons of the caster sugar and rewhisk the mixture until it is as stiff as it was before any sugar was added.
5. Fold in the rest of the sugar lightly and quickly.
6. Fill a piping bag fitted with a large star pipe with some meringue mixture.
7. Pipe swirls of the mixture on to the sheets, spacing them quite closely together as they spread very little. (The mixture should make about 60 halves.)
8. Bake on third and fourth shelves of the oven for about 4 hours, or until they can be lifted straight off the sheets. Cool. (The meringues can now be stored for up to a month in an airtight tin.)
9. To fill them whisk the creams together until stiff.
10. Sandwich the meringues together in pairs with the cream and place each in a paper case.
11. Serve soon after filling as the meringues will start to soften.

CIDER PUNCH
Gives 20 glasses

4 pints (approximately 2 litres) cider
1½ pints (approximately ¾ litre) ginger ale
4 level tablespoons clear honey
grated rind and juice of 6 oranges
ice cubes
orange slices to garnish

1. At the last minute pour the cider and ginger ale into a punch bowl.
2. Mix the honey with the orange rind and juice and stir it into the other ingredients.
3. Add plenty of ice and serve with a few slices of orange floating on top.

ROSÉ WINE CUP
Gives 35 glasses

4 pints (approximately 2 litres) rosé wine
4 tablespoons brandy
4 pints (approximately 2 litres) lemonade
ice cubes
few cucumber slices
1 apple, thinly sliced

1. Mix the wine with the brandy and lemonade in a large punch bowl.
2. Add the ice cubes, cucumber and apple.
3. Stir the ingredients together and serve chilled.

AN ENGAGEMENT PARTY

A small gathering of 15–20 people to celebrate an engagement. The party is a finger buffet to make serving easy.

MENU
Serves 15–20

The engagement cake
Ham and gherkin puffs
Open sandwiches
Savoury porcupine
Cheese straws
Strawberry shortcakes
Chocolate mint squares

THE ENGAGEMENT CAKE

Cake:
8oz (200gm) margarine
8oz (200gm) caster sugar
4 large eggs
8oz (200gm) self-raising flour
pinch of salt
little milk

Filling:
8oz (200gm) margarine, softened
1lb (½ kilo) icing sugar, sifted
little coffee essence
chocolate vermicelli

Icing and decoration:
12oz (300gm) icing sugar, sifted
little coffee essence
little chocolate spread

1. Preheat oven to moderate to moderately hot, 375 deg F or gas 5 (190 deg C).
2. Brush a 7-inch (18-cm) round and a 7-inch (18-cm) square sandwich tin with melted fat; line the base of each with a piece of greaseproof then brush the paper lining.
3. For the cake, beat the margarine until it is soft.
4. Add the sugar and cream the ingredients together until light and fluffy in colour and texture.
5. Beat the eggs together then add them gradually to the creamed mixture, beating well between each addition.
6. Sift the flour and salt, then using a metal spoon fold them into the mixture with enough milk to make a soft dropping consistency.
7. Divide the mixture between the tins and spread it to the sides. Hollow out the centre, then bake in the centre of the oven for 30–35 minutes, or until they feel springy to the touch and are starting to shrink away from the sides of the tins.
8. Cool on a wire tray and remove the greaseproof paper.
9. Beat the margarine for the filling, then gradually beat in the icing sugar with enough coffee essence to flavour.
10. When the cakes are cold slice them in half and spread with a little of the filling. Sandwich together again.
11. Place the square cake on a board angled like a diamond. Cut the round cake in half across the width and position the pieces against the top two sides of the diamond to form a heart.
12. Spread the sides with most of the remaining filling and press chocolate vermicelli into the sides.
13. Mix the sifted icing sugar with enough water and coffee essence to give a smooth icing.
14. Spoon it on to the top of the cake and spread it over the surface.
15. Put the chocolate spread into a greaseproof paper icing bag, snip off the end and pipe, diagonally, across the cake a large arrow with the names of the engaged couple on either side.
16. Finally, pipe the remaining filling in a shell border around the top of the cake.

To freeze: the sponges can be stored in a freezer for up to 2 months. Place in a polythene bag, seal and label. Thaw at room temperature.

HAM AND GHERKIN PUFFS

Serves 14–16

puff pastry made with 8oz (200gm) flour (see Basic recipes, page 100)
4oz (100gm) ham
6 small pickled gherkins
1 level tablespoon tomato ketchup
salt and pepper
little beaten egg to glaze

1. Preheat oven to hot, 425 deg F or gas 7 (220 deg C).
2. Roll the pastry, on a lightly floured working surface, into a large square about ⅛-inch thickness.
3. Using a 2½-inch (6·3-cm) fluted cutter, cut out an equal number of rounds.
4. Carefully gather up the scraps, lay them on top of each other and re-roll the pastry to make more rounds.
5. Lay half the rounds on baking sheets, leaving the remainder for lids.
6. Finely chop the ham and gherkins and mix them together with the tomato ketchup and salt and pepper.
7. Divide the filling between the pastry bases, placing about ½ teaspoonful in the centre of each.
8. Brush one side of the lids with water, cover the filling and seal the edges well. Make a hole in the centre of each.
9. Brush with egg glaze then bake in the centre of the oven for 15–20 minutes, until golden brown and risen.

To freeze: place the puffs in polythene bags; seal and label. Store for up to 2 months. To reheat, place, still frozen, on baking sheets and heat in a moderate oven, 350 deg F or gas 4 (180 deg C) for 15–20 minutes.

OPEN SANDWICHES

Open sandwiches originate from the Scandinavian countries. They are a base of bread – white, rye, granary or crispbread – which has been buttered, and then garnished with a selection of food. They are normally eaten with a knife and fork but for the purpose of this party I suggest you use only half a slice of bread per sandwich so they can be eaten with the fingers. The list of ingredients that can be used for this recipe is endless so below you will find a few suggestions for some sandwiches and I leave you to create any more that you may require. Allow 2 sandwiches per person.

TOMATO, EGG AND CRESS

3 peeled tomato slices
3 shelled hard-boiled egg slices
½ slice brown bread, buttered
salt and pepper
1 dessertspoon mayonnaise (see Basic recipes, page 100)
little mustard and cress

1. Lay overlapping slices of tomato and egg, side by side across the bread.
2. Season with salt and pepper and spoon the mayonnaise down the centre.
3. Sprinkle the centre with a little mustard and cress.

OPEN HAM SANDWICH

1 slice ham
½ slice rye bread, buttered
little shredded lettuce
1 pickled onion
4 beetroot slices

1. Roll up the ham.
2. Cover the bread with shredded lettuce and place the ham diagonally on top.
3. Secure it to the bread with a cocktail stick and place the onion on top.
4. Garnish either side of the roll with 2 overlapping slices of beetroot.

OPEN FISH SANDWICH

1 small lettuce leaf
½ slice white bread, buttered
1 sardine
2 cucumber slices
3 radishes, chopped
1 dessertspoon mayonnaise (see Basic recipes, page 100)
little paprika pepper

1. Place the lettuce leaf on the slice of bread.
2. Place the sardine down one side.
3. Cut the slices of cucumber to the centre, twist the slices and place them over the fish.
4. Arrange the chopped radishes on the other side.
5. Cover with mayonnaise and sprinkle a little paprika pepper on the top for colour.

SAVOURY PORCUPINE

(Illustrated on page 54)

Makes 1 large porcupine for the centre of the table. There are about 4 savouries per person.

1lb (½ kilo) chipolata sausages
4oz (100gm) clear honey
few drops Worcestershire sauce
little dry mustard
4oz (100gm) Cheddar cheese
4oz (100gm) green grapes
1 jar (3½oz or 87gm) button mushrooms in brine
1 small can pineapple chunks
1 large firm cabbage

1. Prepare all the food before putting together the porcupine.
2. Keeping the sausages still in a string, twist each into two.
3. Heat the honey, Worcestershire sauce and mustard in a pan and, when it has melted, add the string of sausages.
4. Cook them gently, turning occasionally, for 20–30 minutes, until they are golden brown, cooked and glazed.
5. Drain on a wire tray.
6. Cut the cheese into ½-inch cubes and wash the grapes.
7. Drain the mushrooms.
8. Cut the pineapple into smaller pieces if too large.
9. Remove any discoloured leaves from the cabbage and cut the base so the cabbage stands firm.
10. Arrange 32 cocktail sticks evenly around the cabbage, separate the sausages and spear one on to each stick.
11. Fill up the space between the sausages with cocktail sticks speared with a selection of the other ingredients – cheese and a grape, pineapple and mushroom.

CHEESE STRAWS

Makes 36

cheese pastry made with 8oz (200gm) flour (see Basic recipes, page 100)
1 level teaspoon vegetable extract

1. Preheat oven to moderate to moderately hot, 400 deg F or gas 6 (200 deg C).
2. Roll the pastry thinly and cut it into 6-inch strips.
3. Blend the vegetable extract with a little water and brush it over the pastry.
4. Using a sharp knife, cut off fingers of pastry about a ½ inch wide. (Cut straight down with the knife. If it is dragged through the dough it will spoil the shape of the fingers.)
5. Arrange fairly closely together on baking sheets, then bake, in batches, in the centre of the oven for 7–10 minutes, until golden brown. Cool on the sheets.
6. Serve in bowls or glasses.

To freeze: place in an airtight container or polythene bag; seal and label and store for up to 3 months. Reheat, from the frozen state, in a cool oven, 300 deg F or gas 2 (150 deg C).

STRAWBERRY SHORTCAKES

Makes 15–20

If strawberries are not available, 1 can (11oz or 275gm) mandarin oranges can be used instead.

6oz (150gm) plain flour
3oz (75gm) rice flour
6oz (150gm) butter
3oz (75gm) caster sugar
½ pint (250ml) double cream
1 punnet strawberries

1. Preheat oven to very moderate, 325 deg F or gas 3 (170 deg C).
2. Sift the flour and rice flour into a mixing bowl.
3. Add the butter and rub it in until evenly distributed.
4. Stir in the sugar and knead the ingredients into a dough.
5. On a lightly floured working surface, roll the dough a ¼-inch thickness and cut out an equal number rounds, using a 2-inch (5-cm) and a 2½-in (6·3-cm) fluted cutter.
6. Gather up the scraps and re-roll them to the same thickness to make more large and small rounds.
7. Place on baking sheets and bake on the top two shelves of the oven for about 25 minutes, or until just starting to brown.
8. Sprinkle with caster sugar then cool on a wire tray.
9. Whip the cream until it holds its shape and spoon one-third into a large piping bag fitted with a star pipe (No 8).
10. Wipe the strawberries and put 7–10 on one side for decoration.
11. Hull the rest and chop them roughly.
12. Stir the strawberry pieces into the cream.
13. Place about 1 teaspoonful on each large biscuit.
14. Top with a smaller biscuit and pipe a star of cream on each.
15. Cut each strawberry in half and use to decorate the shortcakes.

CHOCOLATE MINT SQUARES

Makes 24

2oz (50gm) margarine
2oz (50gm) caster sugar
1 large egg
few drops peppermint essence
5oz (125gm) self-raising flour
6oz (150gm) plain chocolate

1. Preheat oven to moderate to moderately hot, 375 deg F or gas 5 (190 deg C).
2. Brush an 8-inch (20-cm) by 12-inch (30-cm) Swiss roll tin with melted fat.
3. Melt the margarine in a pan over a low heat.
4. Remove from the heat and stir in the sugar.
5. Beat the egg and add it to the mixture with the peppermint essence and sifted flour.
6. When the ingredients are well blended, turn them into the tin and spread the mixture level.
7. Bake in the centre of the oven for 20–25 minutes.
8. Break the chocolate into pieces and as soon as the cake is cooked, scatter the pieces over the top – the heat will melt the chocolate.
9. Smooth it all over the top and while still warm cut the cake into 24 2-inch squares.
10. Leave to cool completely in the tin, then carefully lift the pieces out on to a serving plate.

A WEDDING RECEPTION

To cater for your own wedding reception is a great challenge but one that can be surmounted with much reward if the occasion is well planned and there are several friends prepared to help on the day. After all you do not want to be cooking right up to the last minute!

The reception will, no doubt, be held in a large hall. Arrange the food down one side on trellis tables covered with white sheets and, if possible, drape green ivy around the sides. Have plenty of small tables with chairs around the room for people to sit down at if they wish; I suggest you serve the drinks away from the food so as not to cause too much congestion in one area.

When your guests arrive it is usual to offer them a sherry and one bottle is sufficient for 16 glasses. Serve a white or red wine with the meal (8 glasses of wine can be poured from a bottle), then toast the bride and groom with champagne, a sparkling wine such as Spumante or a champagne cup. This buffet is sufficient for 50 people.

MENU
Serves 50

Kipper cream
Melon à l'orange

Taj Mahal chicken
Whole baked ham
Cumberland sauce
Celery salad
Potato salad
Chicory and grape salad
Green salad (see page 16)

Shortbread gâteau
Lemon mousse

Champagne cup

KIPPER CREAM
(Illustrated on page 71)
Make 3 for the reception

1lb (½ kilo) kipper fillets
½ pint (250ml) thick white sauce (see Basic recipes, page 100)
¼ pint (125ml) mayonnaise (see Basic recipes, page 100)
pinch of ground nutmeg
2 large eggs, separated
1 dessertspoon lemon juice
salt and pepper
½oz (12gm) powdered gelatine
3 tablespoons cold water
½ cucumber, thinly sliced

1. Make the cream the day before it is required. Cook the kipper fillets and leave them to cool.
2. Remove the skin and any bones and place the flesh in a bowl.
3. Mix in the white sauce, mayonnaise, nutmeg, egg yolks and lemon juice.
4. Check the mixture for seasoning.
5. Dissolve the gelatine in the water over a gentle heat then stir it into the kipper mixture.
6. Finally whisk the egg whites until stiff and, with a metal spoon, fold into the mixture.
7. Lightly oil a 2-pint (approximately 1-litre) dish and pour the cream into it.
8. Smooth over the surface then leave to set.
9. To serve, either leave it in the dish and arrange the cucumber slices around the edge or loosen the cream from the dish, turn it on to a plate and arrange whole cucumber slices around the base and halved cucumber slices around the top of the cream.

MELON A L'ORANGE
Serves 32

4 large melons
4 oranges
32 maraschino cherries

1. Cut the melons in half.
2. Remove all the seeds from inside.
3. Divide each half into 4 slices.
4. Run a knife between the flesh and the skin on each slice to separate it, then cut the flesh into 1-inch pieces.
5. Push each piece out on alternate sides.
6. Cut the oranges into 32 slices.
7. Secure a slice to a cocktail stick to resemble the sail of a boat and place a cherry on top; insert into a melon slice.
8. Decorate each slice in the same way and serve the melon with sugar and ground ginger.

TAJ MAHAL CHICKEN
(Illustrated on page 71)
Serves 36

2 tablespoons cooking oil
1 large onion, peeled and finely chopped
3 level dessertspoons curry powder
1 level tablespoon curry paste
¼ pint (125ml) red wine
juice of 1 lemon
6 level tablespoons apricot jam
2 pints (approximately 1 litre) mayonnaise (see Basic recipes, page 100)
salt and paprika pepper
3 cooked chickens (each about 3lb or 1½ kilo)
2½lb (1¼ kilo) long-grain rice
French dressing using 16 tablespoons olive oil (see Basic recipes, page 100)
4oz (100gm) flaked almonds, browned

1. The sauce can be made the week before it is required so long as it is stored in a cool place.
2. Heat the oil in a frying pan, add the onion and fry it gently until tender but not coloured.
3. Add the curry powder and paste and cook the mixture for a few more minutes.
4. Stir in the red wine, lemon juice and jam and cook all the ingredients over a brisk heat for

about 3 minutes until they have reduced.
5. Leave this mixture to cool completely before stirring it into the mayonnaise.
6. Check the sauce for seasoning.
7. On the day before the wedding remove all the meat from the chicken and cut it into small pieces.
8. Cook the rice on the actual day in boiling, salted water, for about 12 minutes.
9. Drain the rice thoroughly, then run cold water through the grains to separate them and remove excess starch.
10. Leave the rice to drain for a little while then turn it into a bowl and mix in the French dressing.
11. Divide the rice between two large dishes and arrange it around the edge.
12. Mix the chicken with the curried mayonnaise and divide it between the two dishes, placing it in the centre of the rice.
13. Scatter the flaked almonds over the top of each dish.

WHOLE BAKED HAM

1 whole gammon
1oz (25gm) demerara sugar
4oz (100gm) brown breadcrumbs

1. Preheat oven to moderate to moderately hot, 375 deg F or gas 5 (190 deg C).
2. Check the weight of the gammon and calculate the cooking time, allowing 20 minutes to every lb (½ kilo).
3. Soak the gammon in cold water for at least 24 hours, changing the water once or twice during the time.
4. Remove it from the water and pat it dry, then scrape the surface with a knife to remove any bloom.
5. Rub the cut surfaces with the sugar and leave it on one side for 5 minutes.
6. Place the gammon in a large roasting tin and cover it completely with kitchen foil, securing all the edges well.
7. Bake the gammon on the third shelf of the oven for the calculated cooking time.
8. When it is cooked peel off the skin and while it is still warm press the breadcrumbs into the surface where the skin was.
9. It is advisable to slice some of the gammon and leave a carving knife and fork beside the joint for people to help themselves to more.

CUMBERLAND SAUCE
Makes about 1 pint (approximately ½ litre)

8oz (200gm) redcurrant jelly
½ pint (250ml) inexpensive red wine
finely grated rind and juice of 2 oranges
finely grated rind and juice of 1 large lemon
3 level teaspoons cornflour

1. Put the redcurrant jelly and wine into a pan.
2. Over a low heat melt the ingredients together.
3. Stir in the grated rind and juice of the oranges and lemon.
4. Blend the cornflour with a little water to make a smooth paste.
5. Stir a little of the sauce into the cornflour then return it to the main bulk in the pan.
6. Bring the sauce to the boil, stirring it all the time so it thickens.
7. Leave the sauce to cool before serving in two separate sauce boats.
8. Place the sauce near the whole gammon.

CELERY SALAD
Serves 30

2 large heads celery
2 green-skinned dessert apples
2 red-skinned dessert apples
4oz (100gm) sultanas
4oz (100gm) walnut halves
French dressing using 8 tablespoons olive oil (see Basic recipes, page 100)

1. Trim the roots from the celery then cut away any damaged parts and remove all the leaves.
2. Wash the celery sticks then cut them into 1-inch lengths and place in a bowl.
3. Quarter and core the apples, then cut them into thin slices and place them in the bowl together with the sultanas.
4. Chop all but 10 walnut halves and mix the pieces into the bowl with the other ingredients.
5. Toss the salad in the dressing and divide it between two serving dishes.
6. Arrange the walnut halves on top before serving.

POTATO SALAD
Serves 30

6lb (3 kilo) potatoes, peeled
French dressing using 8 tablespoons olive oil (see Basic recipes, page 100)
mayonnaise using ¾ pint (375ml) oil (see Basic recipes, page 100)
1 punnet mustard and cress

1. Cook the potatoes in salted water until tender.
2. Drain them well then cut into neat pieces or cubes.
3. Place in a bowl, pour over the French dressing and turn the potatoes occasionally as they cool so all the dressing is absorbed.
4. Toss the potatoes, when completely cold, in the mayonnaise.
5. Divide the potato salad between two bowls and garnish with the mustard and cress.

CHICORY AND GRAPE SALAD
Serves 25

6 heads chicory
4oz (100gm) black grapes
4oz (100gm) green grapes
½ pint (250ml) soured cream
salt and pepper

1. Wash the chicory and remove any damaged leaves.
2. Cut it into rings and place the pieces in a bowl.
3. Wash and halve the grapes and remove the pips.
4. Stir the grapes into the bowl with the soured cream and some seasoning and turn the salad into a serving dish.

SHORTBREAD GATEAU
Make 3 for the reception – each will serve 12

6oz (150gm) plain flour
3oz (75gm) cornflour
6oz (150gm) butter
3oz (75gm) caster sugar
½ pint (250ml) double cream
¼ pint (125ml) single cream

Suggested fruit fillings:
2 cans mandarin oranges or
2 cans stoned cherries or
1lb (½ kilo) mincemeat mixed with 1 grated apple or
1 large can fruit cocktail or
a mixture of 1 diced apple, 2 sliced bananas and 1 orange cut into segments

1. Preheat oven to cool, 300 deg F or gas 2 (150 deg C).
2. Sift the flour and cornflour into a mixing bowl and rub in the butter.
3. Stir in the caster sugar then knead the mixture together to form a dough.
4. Weigh the dough out into 2 pieces, 10oz (250gm) and 8oz (200gm), and roll the larger piece into a 12-inch circle.
5. Roll the other piece into a 10-inch circle and cut it into 12 pieces.
6. Place the rounds on to baking sheets and cook, in batches, in the centre of the oven for 40–45 minutes. Cool on a wire tray.
7. Whip the creams together and place about one-quarter into a piping bag fitted with a large star pipe.
8. Spread the rest of the cream on to the larger circle placed on the serving dish.
9. Drain the canned fruits if being used and reserve 12 pieces for decoration. If you are using the mincemeat and apple as a filling, decorate the gâteau with glacé cherries and angelica.
10. Place the filling on the cream, then arrange the 12 triangular pieces in a circle on top leaving a space between each piece to show the filling.
11. Pipe a star on each piece of shortbread and a large swirl in the centre.
12. Finally decorate the stars with the reserved fruit.
13. This gâteau can be made at least 3 hours before it is required, but must be kept in a cool place.

LEMON MOUSSE
Make 3 for the reception – each will serve 8–10

1 lemon jelly
¼ pint (125ml) water
grated rind and juice of 2 lemons
4 large eggs, separated
6oz (150gm) caster sugar
glacé cherries and angelica diamonds to decorate

1. Break the jelly into pieces and put it into a pan with the water.
2. Dissolve the jelly over a gentle heat then remove the pan from the heat and stir in the lemon rind and juice.
3. Leave the jelly to cool slightly.
4. Beat the egg yolks and caster sugar together until creamy in colour and texture then stir in the jelly.
5. Leave this mixture until it is almost set then whisk the egg whites until really stiff.
6. Using a metal spoon fold them into the mousse as lightly and quickly as possible.
7. Turn the mousse into a 3-pint (approximately 1½-litre) glass dish and leave in a cool place to set overnight.
8. Decorate the mousse just before it is to be served with the cherries and angelica.

CHAMPAGNE CUP
Gives 50 glasses

ice cubes
1 miniature Curaçao
6 tablespoons brandy
1 miniature cherry brandy
3 bottles champagne or sparkling white wine
3 large bottles soda water
sliced oranges and fresh or canned cherries

1. Mix this at the very last minute.
2. Put plenty of ice cubes into a punch bowl (this can usually be hired from the wine merchant, as can the glasses).
3. Pour in the Curaçao, brandy and cherry brandy, then add the champagne or sparkling white wine and the soda water.
4. Stir all the drinks together and float the orange slices and cherries into the bowl before serving the drink, with the cake.

SILVER WEDDING BUFFET

MENU

Serves 15–20

Cheese bites
Smoked salmon rolls

Sausage and sweetcorn flan
Chicken and mushroom flan
Cold meat platter
Rice salad
Cabbage coleslaw
Tomato and orange salad

Silver wedding fruit salad
Anniversary pudding
(Serve the first course to your guests while they are having their drinks)

CHEESE BITES

Makes 24

The cheese mixture will keep in an airtight container in a cool place for at least a week.

2oz (50gm) margarine
4oz (100gm) Cheddar cheese
1 level teaspoon dry mustard
2 tablespoons milk
6 slices white bread
3 level tablespoons chutney

1. Preheat the grill.
2. Melt the margarine over a low heat then remove the pan from the heat.
3. Stir in the cheese, dry mustard and milk and beat them together until the mixture is well blended.
4. Toast the bread on one side and spread the untoasted side with the chutney.
5. Cover this with the cheese mixture. You will find that the chutney and cheese tend to mix together as you spread.
6. Cook under the preheated grill until golden brown and bubbling.
7. Cut off the crusts, then cut each slice into four, arrange on a plate and serve immediately.

SMOKED SALMON ROLLS

Makes 24

6 medium slices brown bread, buttered
6oz (150gm) smoked salmon
black pepper
1 lemon, cut into wedges
parsley sprigs

1. Cut the crusts from the bread.
2. Cut each slice into four squares.
3. Place a small roll of smoked salmon on each and sprinkle with black pepper.
4. Place the squares on a dish and garnish the platter with the lemon wedges and a few sprigs of parsley.

SAUSAGE AND SWEETCORN FLAN

Serves 16

shortcrust pastry made with 6oz (150gm) flour (see Basic recipes, page 100)
1 can (11oz or 275gm) sweetcorn kernels
8oz (200gm) chipolata sausages
2 large eggs
½ pint (250ml) milk
pinch of mixed herbs
salt and pepper

1. Preheat oven to moderate to moderately hot, 375 deg F or gas 5 (190 deg C).
2. Roll out the pastry to a rectangle larger than an 8-inch (20-cm) by 12-inch (30-cm) Swiss roll tin. Lift the pastry into the tin and press it into the base and sides.
3. Trim off the extra pastry around the edge and very lightly prick the base.
4. Drain the sweetcorn and scatter the kernels over the pastry base.
5. Fry or grill the sausages until they are brown.
6. Cut them in half lengthways and arrange them in two rows over the sweetcorn.
7. Beat the eggs together, add the milk with the herbs and seasoning and stir the mixture together.
8. Pour into the flan case.
9. Bake in the centre of the oven for about 45 minutes.
10. Cut into 16 fingers and arrange on a serving dish.

CHICKEN AND MUSHROOM FLAN
Serves 18

shortcrust pastry made with 6oz (150gm) flour (see Basic recipes, page 100)
1oz (25gm) margarine
6oz (150gm) mushrooms
1 level tablespoon plain flour
1 can condensed mushroom soup
8oz (200gm) cooked chicken
1 large egg
4 tablespoons milk
salt and pepper

1. Preheat oven to moderate to moderately hot, 375 deg F or gas 5 (190 deg C).
2. Line an 8-inch (20-cm) by 12-inch (30-cm) Swiss roll tin with the pastry (see the previous recipe).
3. Melt the margarine in a pan, add the sliced mushrooms and fry over a low heat for about 5 minutes; stir in the flour.
4. Remove the pan from the heat and stir in the soup with the chicken which has been shredded.
5. Beat the egg, add the milk and stir it into the soup with the seasoning.
6. Pour the filling into the flan case, making sure the pieces of chicken and mushroom are evenly distributed.
7. Bake in the centre of the oven for about 45 minutes.
8. Cut the flan into 18 pieces and place on a large serving dish with the pieces of sausage and sweetcorn flan, so they can be kept warm until ready to serve.

COLD MEAT PLATTER

Buy a selection of ready sliced cooked meats such as beef, pork, salami, tongue and ham and arrange them on a large platter. Garnish the dish with curls of butter, carrot or radishes and sprigs of watercress.

RICE SALAD
Serves 15–20

1½lb (¾ kilo) long-grain rice
2 large packets frozen mixed vegetables
3oz (75gm) walnuts, chopped
4oz (100gm) sultanas
French dressing using 8 tablespoons olive oil (see Basic recipes, page 100)

1. Cook the rice in plenty of boiling, salted water for 10 minutes.
2. Add the frozen vegetables and cook for a few more minutes.
3. Drain and run cold water through to separate the grains and refresh the vegetables.
4. Leave to cool and drain completely.
5. Stir in the walnuts and sultanas with the French dressing and turn the salad into a large bowl for serving.

CABBAGE COLESLAW
Serves 15–20

2 level tablespoons granulated sugar
2 level dessertspoons plain flour
salt and pepper
2 level dessertspoons made mustard
½ pint (250ml) vinegar
1oz (25gm) butter
2 eggs
milk
1½lb (¾ kilo) white cabbage
1½lb (¾ kilo) carrots, peeled
1 head celery
2 apples

1. The basic dressing will keep, undiluted, for several days in a cool place.
2. Put the sugar, flour, salt, pepper and mustard into a pan.
3. Mix in a little vinegar to make a smooth paste then stir in the rest.
4. Put the pan over a low heat and, stirring all the time, bring it to the boil.
5. Reduce the heat and simmer the dressing for 5 minutes.
6. Take the pan off the heat and stir in the butter.
7. Beat the eggs in a bowl and gradually pour on the vinegar, stirring all the time.
8. Leave to cool then beat in sufficient milk to dilute the dressing to the required consistency and taste.
9. Shred the cabbage finely and put it in a bowl.
10. Grate the carrots coarsely and stir them into the cabbage.
11. Trim the head of celery, removing any damaged leaves, then wipe the sticks, cut them into 1-inch pieces and stir them into the cabbage and carrots.
12. At the last minute, quarter, core and slice the apple and stir it through the salad with the diluted dressing.
13. Spoon into a bowl for serving.

TOMATO AND ORANGE SALAD
Serves 10–12

4 large oranges
1lb (½ kilo) firm tomatoes
French dressing (see Basic recipes, page 100)

1. Peel the rind from 1 orange, using a potato peeler.
2. Cut the peel into shreds; put in a pan, cover with cold water and bring to the boil. Drain.
3. Slice the tomatoes thinly and arrange them overlapping down one side of a dish.
4. Using a sharp knife cut the peel and pith from the oranges working spirally around them with the knife just below the pith but above the flesh.
5. Cut the oranges into thin slices and arrange them down the other side of the dish.
6. Sprinkle over the French dressing just before the salad is to be served and scatter over the pieces of drained orange peel.

SILVER WEDDING FRUIT SALAD
Serves 16–20

A fruit salad with a difference – select canned fruit that can be piped with cream, and arranged on large trays covered with foil. Your guests can choose exactly what fruit they would like at a glance instead of searching through a large bowl.

1 can (1lb 13oz or 725gm) peach halves
1 can (1lb 13oz or 725gm) pear halves
1 can (15oz or 375gm) pineapple rings
½ pint (250ml) double cream
2oz (50gm) chocolate, grated

1. Drain the fruits well and arrange them on the covered trays.
2. Whip the cream until it just holds its shape.
3. Fill a piping bag, fitted with a large star pipe, and pipe whirls of cream in the centre of each fruit.
4. Decorate with the grated chocolate.
5. The fruits will keep in a cool place for several hours.
6. Serve with Nice biscuits.

ANNIVERSARY PUDDING
Serves 10–12

An ideal pudding for a party as it can be made 2 days before it is required and kept in a cool place.

28 sponge finger biscuits
apricot jam
6 trifle sponges
2 tablespoons sherry
2 small cans unsweetened evaporated milk, chilled
finely grated rind and juice of 1 lemon
½oz (12gm) powdered gelatine
¼ pint (125ml) double cream
¼ pint (125ml) single cream
4oz (100gm) caster sugar
¼ pint (125ml) soured cream
1 can (15oz or 375gm) blackcurrant pie filling

1. Line the sides of an 8-inch (20-cm) spring form tin or loose-bottomed cake tin with the sponge fingers sticking them together with a little jam spread down each side.
2. Put the trifle sponges in the base of the tin, cutting them to fit if necessary; pour over the sherry.
3. Put the evaporated milk into a bowl, add the lemon rind and whisk the ingredients together until thick and creamy.
4. Melt the powdered gelatine in the lemon juice, over a low heat. Do not allow it to boil.
5. Stir it into the evaporated milk and leave the mixture in a cool place to start to set.
6. Whip the double and single creams together until they just hold their shape.
7. Fold the sugar and soured cream into the evaporated milk mixture, then fold in the whipped cream.
8. Turn the filling, which should be starting to set, into the lined tin.
9. Level the surface and keep the pudding in a cool place until ready to serve.
10. Remove the pudding from the tin by pushing up from the base or undoing the spring clip.
11. Place the pudding, still on the cake base, on a pretty plate.
12. Encircle the pudding with a piece of ribbon tied in a bow.
13. Lastly, turn the pie filling on top of the pudding and spread it to the edges.
14. Serve with single cream if liked.

The festive season

You will find here all the traditional Christmas recipes, plus plenty of party ideas for the festive season.

CHRISTMAS CAKE

8oz (200gm) currants
12oz (300gm) sultanas
6oz (150gm) seedless raisins
4oz (100gm) glacé cherries, chopped
4oz (100gm) mixed chopped peel
2oz (50gm) almonds, blanched and finely chopped
2oz (50gm) ground almonds
grated rind of 1 orange
10oz (250gm) plain flour
1 level teaspoon baking powder
pinch of salt
2 level teaspoons mixed spice
10oz (250gm) margarine
10oz (250gm) soft dark brown sugar
4 large eggs
3 level dessertspoons black treacle
2 level dessertspoons milk
3 level dessertspoons rum

Almond icing:
12oz (300gm) ground almonds
6oz (150gm) caster sugar
6oz (150gm) icing sugar, sifted
2 egg yolks (keep the whites in a screw-topped jar in a cool place for the royal icing)
lemon juice
about 8oz (200gm) apricot jam, sieved

Royal icing:
4 egg whites
2 teaspoons lemon juice
1 teaspoon glycerine
about 2lb (1 kilo) icing sugar, sifted

1. Preheat oven to very moderate, 325 deg F or gas 3 (170 deg C).
2. Brush a 9-inch (23-cm) round cake tin with melted fat then line the base and sides with double thickness of greaseproof paper. Brush the lining with melted fat.
3. Mix the currants, sultanas, raisins, glacé cherries and peel together.
4. Stir in the chopped and ground almonds with the grated orange rind.
5. Sift the flour with the baking powder, salt and mixed spice.
6. Cream the margarine, then add the sugar and beat together until soft and fluffy.
7. Beat the eggs then gradually add them to the creamed mixture, beating well between each addition.
8. Beat in the treacle.
9. Finally, using a metal spoon, fold in the prepared fruit with the dry ingredients, milk and rum.
10. Turn the mixture into the tin and hollow out the centre slightly.
11. Bake the cake in the centre of the oven for 30 minutes, then reduce the heat to cool, 300 deg F or gas 2 (150 deg C) and cook for a further $3\frac{1}{4}$–$3\frac{1}{2}$ hours. Test to see if cooked with a skewer.
12. Leave the cake to cool completely, then wrap it in foil until 10 days before Christmas.
13. To almond ice the cake, remove the greaseproof paper and turn the cake over so the base is used for the top. Trim the top to make it stand level if necessary.
14. Mix the ground almonds with the sugars then stir in the egg yolks with enough lemon juice to make a shortcrust pastry consistency.
15. Use half of the almond icing for the top of the cake, sticking it to the surface with warmed apricot jam.
16. Roll the other half out the depth and circumference of the side of the cake, trimming it to the correct size if necessary.
17. Secure this piece on to the cake with warmed apricot jam.
18. Place the cake on a wire tray and cover it with a teatowel. Leave it in a cool place for at least 4 days for the almond icing to dry.
19. Beat the egg whites with the lemon juice then beat in the glycerine with enough sifted icing sugar to make the icing fairly stiff.
20. Stick the cake on to an 11-inch (28-cm) board and turn the icing on top.
21. Spread the icing over the top and down the sides of the cake, leaving it rough as you work.
22. Decorate the cake with Christmas decorations, then leave to set in a cool place.

CHOCOLATE LOG CAKE

(Illustrated on page 72)

If preferred, this recipe can be made using a bought chocolate Swiss roll.

3 large eggs
3oz (75gm) caster sugar
2oz (50gm) plain flour
1oz (25gm) cocoa powder
1½ level teaspoons baking powder
caster sugar to sprinkle
6oz (150gm) butter
12oz (300gm) icing sugar
1½oz (37gm) cocoa powder
1 egg
holly and a little sifted icing sugar to decorate

1. Preheat oven to moderate to moderately hot, 375 deg F or gas 5 (190 deg C).
2. Cut a rectangle of greaseproof paper 1 inch larger all round than the base of an 8-inch (20-cm) by 12-inch (30-cm) Swiss roll tin.
3. Cut a 1-inch slit from each corner diagonally towards the centre.
4. Brush the tin with fat, place the lining into it and press it into the sides and base overlapping the slits so they fit neatly into the corners.
5. Brush the paper lining.
6. Put the eggs and sugar into a bowl placed over a pan of hot water and whisk the mixture for about 10 minutes.
7. The whisk, lifted out of the mixture should leave a clear trail which should be light and creamy in consistency.
8. Sift the flour, cocoa powder and baking powder together.
9. Fold them into the whisked mixture lightly and carefully, using a metal spoon.
10. Immediately pour the mixture into the tin and tip the tin so the mixture runs and levels into the corners.
11. Bake in the centre of the oven for about 18 minutes.
12. In the meantime place a teatowel on a working surface and cover it with a large piece of greaseproof paper – larger than the Swiss roll tin.
13. Sprinkle the paper thickly with caster sugar.
14. When the sponge is cooked – it should feel springy to the touch – turn it on to the paper and remove the paper lining.
15. Trim the edges and score deeply across the sponge a ½ inch in from one short side.
16. Turn up this end then, using the paper as a guide, roll up the sponge.
17. Wrap it in the teatowel and leave it to cool.
18. Beat the butter until it is light and fluffy.
19. Sift the icing sugar and cocoa together and beat it into the butter with the egg.
20. Unwrap the roll carefully and spread it with some of the butter cream and roll it up again.
21. Spread the rest of the buttercream over the roll marking it with a knife to give the appearance of bark. Sprinkle with a little sifted icing sugar.
22. Arrange the holly at one end then place the cake on a board or plate for serving.

MINCEMEAT

Makes about 6lb (3 kilo)

Make the mincemeat at least 2 weeks before it is required to give the fruit time to mellow and the flavour improve. Always store mincemeat in a cool, dry cupboard.

12oz (300gm) soft light brown sugar
12oz (300gm) sultanas
12oz (300gm) currants
12oz (300gm) mixed chopped candied peel
1lb (½ kilo) seeded raisins
12oz (300gm) shredded suet
¼ level teaspoon ground nutmeg
¼ level teaspoon ground ginger
¼ level teaspoon mixed spice
1 large cooking apple
6oz (150gm) blanched almonds
juice of 2 oranges
juice of 2 lemons
¼ pint (125ml) sherry

1. Put the sugar, sultanas, currants, peel, raisins, suet and spices together in a bowl.
2. Mix these ingredients together well.
3. Then, using the coarsest disc on the mincer, mince all these ingredients together. (If no mincer is available the ingredients can be chopped.)
4. Peel and core the apple and chop it finely with the blanched almonds.
5. Stir into the main bulk in the bowl and bind the mixture with the orange and lemon juice and the sherry.
6. When the ingredients are well mixed pack the mincemeat firmly into clean, dry jam jars.
7. Cover with waxed discs and jam pot covers and seal as for jam.
8. Wipe the jars free of stickiness, label and store until required.

SPECIAL MINCE PIES

(Illustrated on page 72)

Makes 18–20

The pastry for these pies is a special shortcrust; wrapped in greaseproof paper it will keep in the refrigerator for a week or more.

4 tablespoons water
7oz (175gm) lard
9oz (225gm) plain flour
1½oz (37gm) cornflour
½ level teaspoon baking powder
pinch of salt
generous 8oz (200gm) mincemeat
icing sugar to sprinkle

1. Preheat the oven to moderate to moderately hot, 400 deg F or gas 6 (200 deg C).
2. Put the water and lard into a fairly large pan and, over a low heat, melt the lard.
3. Sift the flour, cornflour, baking powder and salt together on to a piece of paper.
4. Shoot the dry ingredients into the liquid and stir well to form a soft dough.
5. Wrap the dough in foil or greaseproof paper and leave it in a cool place overnight.
6. Next day roll out the pastry and cut out an equal number of large and small rounds, using 2½-inch (6·3-cm) and 2-inch (5-cm) cutters.
7. Line deep tartlet tins with the larger rounds and fill each with 1 teaspoon of mincemeat.
8. Moisten the pastry edges and put on the tops.
9. Using the rim of an upturned wine glass, press the two joined edges firmly together.
10. Make a hole in the centre of each pie with a skewer.
11. Bake in the centre of the oven for 35–40 minutes, until the pastry is light golden brown.
12. Dust the mince pies with icing sugar before serving hot or cold.

HOME-MADE SWEETS

A selection of home-made sweets are ideal to serve in small dishes at any of the Christmas festivities, or to wrap up and put in pretty boxes to give as Christmas presents.

SULTANA TOFFEE
Makes 49 pieces

1lb (½ kilo) demerara sugar
¼ pint (125ml) plus 4 tablespoons water
2 level tablespoons golden syrup
1 teaspoon vinegar
1½oz (37gm) butter
4oz (100gm) sultanas

1. Brush a 7-inch (18-cm) shallow square tin lightly with cooking oil.
2. Put the sugar, water, syrup, vinegar and butter into a pan.
3. Over a low heat, dissolve the sugar stirring it occasionally.
4. When all the sugar has melted bring the toffee to the boil.
5. Boil steadily, without stirring, for about 10–12 minutes, or until it is a good golden colour.
6. Remove the pan from the heat and put a few drops into a cup of cold water. If it forms a ball the toffee is ready, if not, boil it for a little longer before trying the test once more.
7. Stir in the sultanas and pour the toffee straight into the tin.
8. Mark it into small squares when it has nearly set then leave it to cool completely.
9. Turn it out when cold and cut or break it following the marks.

FUDGE
(Illustrated on page 72)
Makes 49 pieces

3oz (75gm) butter
1½lb (¾ kilo) granulated sugar
1 large can unsweetened evaporated milk
few drops vanilla essence

1. Brush a 7-inch (18-cm) shallow square tin with a little oil.
2. Melt the butter in a large metal, not enamel, pan.
3. Add the sugar and evaporated milk and stir occasionally over a gentle heat until the sugar has dissolved. (Do not allow the mixture to boil before every grain of sugar has melted.)
4. When the sugar has melted turn up the heat to bring the fudge to the boil.
5. Boil the mixture steadily for about 30–45 minutes watching it very carefully all the time and stirring it when necessary. As the mixture cooks it will thicken and darken.
6. To test the mixture, take the pan off the heat. Drop a teaspoonful of the mixture into a cup of cold water. Leave it for a few seconds then roll it between the fingers into a ball. The ball should be firm though soft.
7. Beat in the vanilla essence and continue beating (off the heat) with a wooden spoon until it cools and thickens.
8. While it is still soft pour into the tin.
9. Leave the fudge until it is almost cold and set then cut it into squares with an oiled knife.
10. Leave to cool completely then place each square in a sweet paper case for serving.

CHERRY BITES
Makes about 50

6oz (150gm) margarine
2oz (50gm) icing sugar, sifted
few drops vanilla essence
4½oz (112gm) plain flour
1½oz (37gm) cornflour
13 glacé cherries, quartered

1. Preheat oven to moderate to moderately hot, 375 deg F or gas 5 (190 deg C).
2. Put the margarine in a bowl and beat it until soft.
3. Add the sifted icing sugar gradually, beating well between each addition. (The mixture should be very soft and creamy when it has all been added.)
4. Beat in the vanilla essence.
5. Sift the flour with the cornflour and, using a metal spoon, fold them into the creamed ingredients.
6. Put the mixture into a large forcing bag with a fairly large star pipe attached.
7. Put 50 sweet paper cases on to a baking sheet and pipe a star of mixture into each.
8. Top with a piece of cherry and bake in the centre of the oven for about 10 minutes. Cool and store in an airtight tin until required.

COCONUT ICE
Makes 36 pieces

1lb (½ kilo) granulated sugar
¼ pint (125ml) milk
4oz (100gm) desiccated coconut
little pink food colouring

1. Brush a 6-inch (15-cm) square cake tin with oil.
2. Put the sugar and milk into a pan and, over a very low heat, dissolve the sugar.
3. When every grain has melted increase the heat and boil the mixture steadily for approximately 15 minutes, or until it becomes light cream in colour and syrupy in texture.
4. Remove the pan from the heat and stir the mixture for about 3 minutes, or until it starts to thicken.
5. Stir in the coconut then pour half the mixture into the tin and spread it level with a palette knife.
6. Quickly mix pink colouring into the rest of the mixture still in the pan, and turn it on top of the white coconut ice.
7. Again spread it level then leave the tin in a cool place to set.
8. When set turn out of the tin and cut the block into small squares.

CARAMELIZED GRAPES
Makes about 20

8oz (200gm) granulated sugar
$\frac{1}{4}$ pint (125ml) water
8oz (200gm) black or green grapes

1. Put the sugar and water into a fairly large saucepan and dissolve the sugar over a low heat. (The mixture must not boil until every grain has melted or it will crystallize when it is brought to the boil.)
2. When all the sugar has dissolved, bring the syrup to the boil and boil it briskly, without a lid.
3. When it starts to change colour and becomes golden brown, after about 10–15 minutes, remove the pan from the heat. (Take it off the heat a shade lighter than you require as it will continue to darken for a few seconds.)
4. Divide the grapes into pairs, keeping them attached by the stalks.
5. Let the bubbles in the caramel subside, then support one side of the pan on a kitchenweight to make a deep pool of caramel.
6. Rub your hands with a little oil to prevent the caramel sticking to them should any drips fall on your fingers.
7. Using a pair of tweezers or a fork, dip one pair of grapes at a time into the caramel.
8. Lift the grapes out of the caramel and let them drip for a few seconds then place carefully on an oiled baking sheet.
9. Leave the pairs of grapes to set completely before putting into sweet paper cases for serving.

TURKISH DELIGHT
Makes 36 pieces

1oz (25gm) powdered gelatine
$\frac{1}{4}$ pint (125ml) cold water
1lb ($\frac{1}{2}$ kilo) granulated sugar
$\frac{1}{4}$ pint (125ml) warm water
few drops peppermint essence and a little green food colouring or few drops vanilla essence and a little pink food colouring
sifted icing sugar to sprinkle

1. Brush a 6-inch (15-cm) square cake tin with a little corn oil.
2. Put the gelatine into a bowl and pour on the cold water.
3. Put the sugar into a pan, pour on the warm water and, over a low heat, dissolve the sugar slowly until every grain has melted.
4. Add the softened gelatine and water and simmer the mixture, without stirring and uncovered, for 30 minutes.
5. To test if it is ready, dip a wooden spoon into the mixture then take a little off the spoon with the first finger.
6. Press it against the thumb then draw the fingers apart and a thread should form for about a $\frac{1}{2}$ inch before it breaks. If the thread does not form simmer the mixture for a little longer before testing again.
7. Stir in the colouring and desired flavouring then pour the mixture into the tin and leave it to set.
8. When the mixture is ready, turn it on to a working surface dusted with icing sugar.
9. Using a sharp knife, cut the Turkish delight into small pieces dusting each with more icing sugar.
10. Store in a cool dry place.

CAROL SINGERS' SUPPER

A supper for 12 carol singers after a very enjoyable but rather chilly evening raising money for a local charity. What could be more welcome as they come through the doorway than the aroma of French onion soup on the simmer? Then with plenty of other delicious dishes as well as a hot punch – wassail – the party is complete.

MENU
Serves 12

French onion soup
Savoury scone rounds
Sausages with tomato dip
Hot baked potatoes
Star mince tart
Lantern squares

Wassail

FRENCH ONION SOUP
Serves about 12–16

2lb (1 kilo) onions
6oz (150gm) margarine
2 tablespoons corn oil
salt and pepper
1 level dessertspoon caster sugar
1oz (25gm) plain flour
4 pints (approximately 2 litres) beef stock
2 bayleaves
1 small French loaf
4oz (100gm) Cheddar cheese, grated

1. Peel and thinly slice the onions.
2. Heat 2oz (50gm) of the margarine and the oil in a large pan.
3. Add the onions with plenty of salt and the sugar and fry over a fairly high heat, turning frequently until golden brown and cooked.
4. Sprinkle over the flour and remove the pan from the heat.
5. Gradually blend in the stock, add the bayleaves and return the pan to the heat.
6. Bring the soup to the boil, stirring occasionally, then put the lid on the pan and simmer the soup gently for 30 minutes.
7. Test it for seasoning.
8. Meanwhile, cut the bread into slices and toast one side only.
9. Spread the untoasted side with the remaining margarine and arrange the slices on a grill pan.
10. Sprinkle the slices liberally with the cheese and cook under a preheated grill until the cheese is golden brown, melted and bubbling.
11. Put a piece of toasted cheesebread into each soup bowl and ladle the soup on top.
12. The bread will rise immediately to the surface; serve the soup straight away.

SAVOURY SCONE ROUNDS
Makes 2 rounds
– each round serves 8

1lb ($\frac{1}{2}$ kilo) self-raising flour
good pinch of salt
3oz (75gm) margarine
3oz (75gm) cheese, grated
1 large egg
scant $\frac{1}{2}$ pint (250ml) milk

Topping:
6oz (150gm) cheese, grated
1lb ($\frac{1}{2}$ kilo) tomatoes
1 can skippers

1. Preheat oven to moderate to moderately hot, 400 deg F or gas 6 (200 deg C).
2. Sift the flour and salt into a mixing bowl.
3. Add the margarine and, using your fingertips only, rub the fat in until it is evenly distributed.
4. Stir in the cheese.
5. Beat the egg and stir it into the dry ingredients with enough milk to make a soft though not sticky dough.
6. Cut the dough in half and knead each piece into a round about 8 inches in diameter.
7. Put them on to baking sheets.
8. Sprinkle the cheese on top of each round.
9. Slice the tomatoes and arrange all but 2 slices overlapping around the edge of each round on the cheese.
10. Divide the skippers between the 2 rounds, arranging them as the spokes of a wheel and place a slice of tomato in the centre.
11. Bake the savouries on the two top shelves of the oven for 20 minutes, until the scone base is light brown and cooked.
12. Leave to cool then cut into slices.

SAUSAGES
Serves 12

If liked the sausages can be cooked on the shelf below the baked potatoes – they will take about 45 minutes and should be basted and turned once.

2lb (1 kilo) chipolata sausages
2oz (50gm) dripping

1. Melt the dripping in a large frying pan.
2. Add the sausages, separated, and, over a gentle heat, fry them slowly so they do not split.
3. Turn the sausages occasionally to brown them evenly.
4. They should be cooked right through in 10–15 minutes.
5. Drain them and serve in a dish with the tomato dip in the centre.

TOMATO DIP
Makes $\frac{1}{2}$–$\frac{3}{4}$ pint (250–375ml)

2oz (50gm) margarine
1 onion, peeled and finely chopped
1 level teaspoon dry mustard
1 level teaspoon demerara sugar
pinch of paprika pepper
pinch of mixed herbs
3 tablespoons vinegar
2 level tablespoons horseradish sauce
1 tablespoon Worcestershire sauce
$\frac{1}{2}$ pint (250ml) tomato juice
1 can (14oz or 350gm) tomatoes
salt and pepper

1. Melt the margarine in a pan.
2. Add the prepared onion and fry until cooked and just starting to colour.
3. Then add all the other ingredients except the salt and pepper and bring the dip to the boil very slowly.
4. Reduce the heat and simmer the mixture, uncovered, for about 60 minutes, or until it has reduced by half.
5. Check the dip for flavour and add any salt and pepper if required.
6. Serve the dip warm, but it can be made in advance, if stored in a covered jar in a cool place. It will keep for at least a week – in fact, the flavour improves as all the ingredients have time to mellow.

HOT BAKED POTATOES
Serves 12

12 medium potatoes
salt
6oz (150gm) butter

1. Preheat oven to moderate to moderately hot, 375 deg F or gas 5 (190 deg C).
2. Scrub the potatoes. Rub salt into the skins and prick them all over with a fork.
3. Place the potatoes on the oven shelves and cook for about $1\frac{1}{2}$ hours, or until they feel soft.
4. Remove them from the oven and cut a fairly deep cross the length and width of each potato, using a sharp knife.
5. Then, holding the potato in a cloth, push the sides towards the middle so the centre of the potato comes up and the cross opens.
6. Serve a pat of butter in the centre of each potato and hand them round wrapped in gay serviettes.

STAR MINCE TART
Serves 12

shortcrust pastry made with 12oz (300gm) flour (see Basic recipes, page 100)
12oz (300gm) mincemeat
little caster sugar

1. Preheat oven to moderate to moderately hot, 400 deg F or gas 6 (200 deg C).
2. On a lightly floured working surface, roll half the pastry and use to line a 10-inch (25-cm) ovenproof plate.
3. Spread the mincemeat over the pastry to within a $\frac{1}{2}$ inch of the edges.
4. Roll out the other piece of pastry slightly larger than the plate.
5. Moisten the edges of the pastry on the plate then lift the other piece into position on a rolling pin.
6. Seal the edges firmly together and trim off any surplus pastry with a sharp knife.
7. Using a fork decorate the edge.
8. Cut an eight-pointed star in the centre of the tart through the pastry lid, making each point about 2 inches in length.
9. Fold back the pieces to reveal the centre and make the star pattern on the pastry lid. Mincemeat will have stuck to the

points of the star when they are folded back – do not worry as it just makes the design more prominent.
10. Brush the pastry surface with water and sprinkle it thickly with sugar.
11. Bake in the centre of the oven for 20 minutes, then reduce the heat to moderate, 350 deg F or gas 4 (180 deg C) and bake for a further 30 minutes.

LANTERN SQUARES
Makes 24 pieces

3oz (75gm) margarine
3oz (75gm) caster sugar
1 large egg
3oz (75gm) self-raising flour
8oz (200gm) tangerine jam
6oz (150gm) plain chocolate

1. Preheat oven to moderate, 350 deg F or gas 4 (180 deg C).
2. Brush an 8-inch (20-cm) by 12-inch (30-cm) Swiss roll tin with melted fat.
3. Cut the margarine into small pieces, put it into a mixing bowl.
4. Leave the bowl in a warm place for a few minutes.
5. When the fat starts to oil remove the bowl from the heat and stir in the sugar.
6. Beat the egg and add it to the mixture with the sifted flour.
7. Turn the mixture into the greased tin and smooth over the surface.
8. Bake the base in the centre of the oven for about 30 minutes. (It is ready when lightly brown but the surface is still soft.) Cool in the tin.
9. Heat the jam if slightly stiff then, when the base is cold, spread it over the surface.
10. Break the chocolate into pieces, put them on a plate then place the plate over a pan of hot water.
11. Allow the chocolate to melt slowly then pour it over the jam and, very carefully, spread it all over the surface – the jam and chocolate may merge together slightly.
12. Leave the topping to set completely, then cut into 24 pieces.

WASSAIL
Gives 16 glasses

A heart-warming drink served traditionally at Christmas time.

scant ½oz (12gm) root ginger
6 cloves
1 level teaspoon ground nutmeg
1 blade of mace
½ level teaspoon coriander seeds
½ level teaspoon cardamom seeds
8oz (200gm) granulated sugar
2 lemons
½ pint (250ml) water
4 pints (approximately 2 litres) dry cider
2 egg yolks
6 small cooking apples
demerara sugar

1. Preheat oven to moderate to moderately hot, 375 deg F or gas 5 (190 deg C).
2. Bruise the root ginger with a hammer.
3. Put the pieces into a large pan with the cloves, ground nutmeg, mace, coriander, cardamom and granulated sugar.
4. Finely grate the lemon rinds and put them into the pan with the water.
5. Slowly dissolve the sugar then bring the liquid to the boil and simmer the mixture for 5 minutes.
6. Squeeze the lemons and add the juice to the pan with the cider.
7. Heat the punch slowly.
8. Put the egg yolks into a large punch bowl and gradually blend in ½ pint (250ml) of the hot – not boiling – liquid. This should make a good froth.
9. When the main bulk of the liquid is almost at boiling point, whisk it all into the bowl.
10. Meanwhile, core the apples and put them into a roasting pan.
11. Fill the centre of each with demerara sugar and bake them in the centre of the oven for 20 minutes.
12. Put them into the punch when it is to be served. (Do not forget to warm the glasses.)

CHRISTMAS EVE

Christmas Eve is so often the time when the last few presents are wrapped or the turkey is stuffed. But if you do not have to cook the Christmas lunch this year why not drop a note to your friends inviting them to start the festive season with a drink at your home? Do not state any particular time, as that could prove difficult for some people, just keep the punch and the soup on the simmer to welcome your guests as they arrive.

MENU
Serves 20

Hot spicy punch
Minestrone soup
Cheese cones
Savoury peanut loaf
Sausage roll circle
Crab dip
Pleasure peaches
Apple squares

HOT SPICY PUNCH
Gives 20 glasses

5 pints (approximately 2½ litres) cider
1 lemon
2 oranges
8 cloves
2-inch piece cinnamon stick
2 level teaspoons ground nutmeg
2 level tablespoons caster sugar
5 tablespoons brandy

1. Pour the cider into a large pan.
2. Stud the lemon and oranges with the cloves and put them into the pan with the cinnamon, nutmeg and sugar.
3. Over a very low heat bring the punch to just below boiling point.
4. Stir in the brandy and ladle the punch into heatproof tumblers.
5. Keep the punch warm if possible, but do not allow it to boil at any time.

MINESTRONE SOUP
Serves 20

1lb (½ kilo) leeks
1lb (½ kilo) tomatoes
2oz (50gm) margarine
1lb (½ kilo) potatoes, peeled and diced
8oz (200gm) carrots, peeled and diced
1lb (½ kilo) onions, peeled and diced
1lb (½ kilo) cabbage, finely shredded
2 garlic cloves
6 pints (approximately 3 litres) stock or water
salt and pepper
3oz (75gm) small pasta shapes
grated Parmesan cheese

1. Wash and slice the leeks making sure all the grit and sand is removed.
2. Plunge the tomatoes into boiling water for 20 seconds, transfer them to cold water and peel off the skins.
3. Cut the tomatoes into small pieces.
4. Melt the margarine in a large pan.
5. Add the potatoes, carrots, leeks, onions, cabbage and tomatoes and cook them covered over a low heat for about 10 minutes, shaking the pan occasionally.
6. Add the crushed garlic to the vegetables with the stock and seasoning.
7. Bring the soup to the boil, cover the pan and simmer the soup over a low heat for about 1 hour, or until the vegetables are tender.
8. About 10 minutes before the end of the cooking time, add the pasta shapes and check the soup for seasoning.
9. Serve the soup either as your guests arrive or prior to their departure, with grated Parmesan cheese to sprinkle on top.

CHEESE CONES
Makes 22

1 large white sliced loaf
2oz (50gm) butter
12oz (300gm) Wensleydale cheese
6 tomatoes
1 level dessertspoon made mustard
salt and paprika pepper

1. Preheat oven to moderate to moderately hot, 375 deg F or gas 5 (190 deg C).
2. Cut a circle from each slice of bread using a 3-inch (7·5-cm) plain cutter.
3. Cut a small triangle from each circle.
4. Butter patty tins and wrap a circle of bread around the inside of each to form a cone.
5. Bake the cases in the centre of the oven for about 20 minutes, until crisp and golden. Cool on a wire tray.
6. Grate the cheese into a bowl.
7. Chop the tomatoes finely and stir them into the cheese.
8. Mix in the mustard and salt and paprika pepper and check the mixture for seasoning.
9. When the cones are cool, divide the filling between them.
10. Serve the cheese cones on a bed of lettuce.

SAVOURY PEANUT LOAF
Serves 24

It is best to make this loaf the day before the party.

1lb (½ kilo) plain flour
pinch of salt
pinch of cayenne pepper
1 level teaspoon bicarbonate of soda
1 level teaspoon cream of tartar
2oz (50gm) margarine
1 medium onion, peeled and finely chopped
2oz (50gm) peanuts, chopped
3oz (75gm) Cheddar cheese, grated
1 large egg
½ pint (250ml) plus 2 tablespoons milk

1. Preheat oven to moderate, 350 deg F or gas 4 (180 deg C).
2. Brush a 2-lb (1-kilo) loaf tin with melted fat.
3. Sift the flour, salt, cayenne pepper, bicarbonate of soda and cream of tartar into a bowl.
4. Rub in the margarine until it is evenly distributed.
5. Mix in the onion, peanuts and grated cheese.
6. Beat the egg, mix in the milk then add the liquid to the dry ingredients and stir them in to form a fairly wet consistency.
7. Turn the mixture into the tin, smooth the surface and bake in the centre of the oven for about 2½ hours. Test with a warmed skewer.
8. Cool on a wire tray; wrap in foil until required.
9. To serve, cut the loaf into fairly thick slices and serve spread with butter.

SAUSAGE ROLL CIRCLE
Serves 12

flaky pastry made with 8oz (200gm) flour (see Basic recipes, page 100)
1 tablespoon chutney
4oz (100gm) sausagemeat
little beaten egg to glaze
watercress to garnish

1. Preheat oven to hot, 425 deg F or gas 7 (220 deg C).
2. Roll the pastry into a rectangle 18 inches by 4 inches and trim the edges.
3. Spread the chutney over the pastry then spread the sausagemeat over the chutney, leaving a ¾-inch edge along one long side.
4. Damp this edge with water then roll up the pastry towards the edge.
5. Form the roll into a ring and place it on a baking sheet with the join underneath and the two ends joined firmly together.
6. Make slits from the edge of the circle almost to the centre at about 1½-inch intervals and open the slits slightly.
7. Brush the pastry with a little beaten egg.
8. Bake in the centre of the oven for 20–25 minutes, or until the pastry is golden brown.
9. Place the ring on a plate and garnish with watercress.

CRAB DIP
Serves about 16

3 level tablespoons natural yogurt
1 level tablespoon tomato ketchup
1 tablespoon lemon juice
salt and cayenne pepper
6oz (150gm) cream cheese
1 can (7½oz or 187gm) crab meat

1. Put the yogurt, tomato ketchup and lemon juice with the salt and cayenne pepper into a liquidizer goblet.
2. Cut the cheese into pieces.
3. Switch on the machine and gradually add the cheese until it is all added and the mixture smooth.
4. Drain the crab meat and discard any tendons.
5. Add the fish to the liquidizer and switch it on just long enough to roughly chop it.
6. Turn it into a small bowl or glass dish and serve with crisps, biscuits or bread sticks.

PLEASURE PEACHES
Serves 30

1lb (½ kilo) gingernut biscuits
2oz (50gm) ground almonds
¼ pint (125ml) milk or peach juice from the can
30 peach halves, fresh or canned
8 glacé cherries, quartered

1. Preheat the grill.
2. Put the biscuits into a polythene bag and, with a rolling pin, crush them to crumbs.
3. Tip the crumbs into a bowl and mix in the ground almonds.
4. Bind these together with the milk or juice.
5. Place the peach halves, cut side uppermost, on the grill pan and divide the filling between them, leaving it fairly rough.
6. Put a piece of cherry on each then put the pan under the grill.
7. Grill for 3–5 minutes, or until the filling starts to brown.
8. Transfer the pleasure peaches to a large flat serving dish and hand them round hot or cold.

APPLE SQUARES
Makes 20

4oz (100gm) margarine
4oz (100gm) caster sugar
1 large egg
8oz (200gm) self-raising flour
½ level teaspoon ground cinnamon
pinch of salt
8oz (200gm) cooking apples
4 tablespoons milk
caster sugar to sprinkle

1. Preheat oven to moderate, 350 deg F or gas 4 (180 deg C).
2. Brush an 8-inch (20-cm) by 10-inch (25-cm) Swiss roll tin with melted fat.
3. Cream the margarine until it is soft, then add the caster sugar.
4. Beat the ingredients together until they are light and fluffy in colour and texture.
5. Beat the egg and add it to the mixture.
6. Sift the flour, cinnamon and salt together.
7. Peel, core and roughly chop the apples.
8. Stir the flour and apple into the creamed mixture with the milk.
9. Turn it into the prepared tin and spread it evenly over the base.
10. Cook in the centre of the oven for 25–30 minutes, until the cake is golden brown and springy to the touch.
11. Sprinkle with sugar as soon as it comes out of the oven. Then leave it in the tin to cool.
12. Cut the cake into 20 squares to serve and decorate the dish with a few holly leaves and berries.

CHRISTMAS LUNCH FOR SIX

Christmas Day is when the cook herself should also relax and enjoy the company of her family, so everything must be well organized. Some of the food can be prepared on Christmas Eve, providing you have a cool place in which to store it.

1. Prepare and stuff the turkey. If you have bought a frozen turkey, make sure you give it plenty of time to thaw out at room temperature – it will take anything from 36–48 hours and do not forget to remove the giblets.
2. Prepare the potatoes, carrots and parsnips and leave them covered with cold water in bowls.
3. Trim the Brussels sprouts and store them in a polythene bag in the bottom of the refrigerator or a cool place.

MENU

Grilled grapefruit

Roast turkey
Boiled bacon
Roast potatoes
Roast parsnips
Brussels sprouts
Buttered carrots
Bread sauce
Cranberry sauce

Christmas pudding
Brandy butter
Sharp lemon sauce
Holly pudding

Suggested wines: Niersteiner Domthal, a German medium dry to medium sweet white wine. Médoc, a French dry and light-bodied, red wine. Serve 1 bottle of each or 2 bottles of one variety.

see overleaf for recipes

GRILLED GRAPEFRUIT
Serves 6

3 grapefruit
4oz (100gm) icing sugar, sifted
6 maraschino cherries

1. Preheat the grill.
2. Cut the grapefruit in half.
3. Using a grapefruit knife, cut out the flesh then remove all the membranes and place the segments back into each grapefruit half.
4. Just before serving sprinkle the halves thickly with icing sugar.
5. Place them on a grill pan under the grill.
6. Cook them until the icing sugar has caramelized.
7. Serve immediately with a cherry in the centre of each.

ROAST TURKEY
(Illustrated on page 72)
Serves 6

1 turkey (about 10lb or 5 kilo)
1lb (½ kilo) fresh chestnuts or 1 can (10oz or 250gm) whole chestnuts in water
8oz (200gm) pie pork or veal, minced
6oz (150gm) streaky bacon, minced
salt and pepper
pinch of ground nutmeg
1lb (½ kilo) streaky bacon, fairly thickly sliced
1lb (½ kilo) chipolata sausages
1 level tablespoon plain flour
¾ pint (375ml) stock made from the giblets
watercress to garnish

1. Preheat oven to moderate to moderately hot, 400 deg F or gas 6 (200 deg C).
2. Weigh the bird and calculate the cooking time by allowing 20 minutes to the lb (½ kilo) plus an extra 20 minutes.
3. If using fresh chestnuts, snip the top of each chestnut with a pair of scissors then place them in a pan of water.
4. Bring the water to the boil and boil the chestnuts for 2 minutes, then remove them from the heat.
5. Remove the outer and inner shells, keeping the chestnuts as whole as possible and place them in a mixing bowl. (Drain the canned chestnuts.)
6. Add the minced pork or veal and bacon with plenty of seasoning and the ground nutmeg.
7. Bind the ingredients together to form a stuffing.
8. Starting at the neck end work the stuffing very carefully in between the skin and the breast to about halfway along the breast.
9. Do not split the skin if possible or the stuffing will burst out during cooking. Push the stuffing under the breast skin, making sure the shape of the bird is retained. The stuffing helps to keep the breast moist as well as giving it a good flavour.
10. Tuck the loose skin which covered the neck under the wings to help keep the stuffing in place.
11. Put the turkey in a roasting tin and cover it completely with the rashers of streaky bacon starting at the legs, then cover the tin with foil.
12. Roast the bird in the centre of the oven for 1 hour then reduce the heat to moderate, 350 deg F or gas 4 (180 deg C) for the rest of the cooking time. (If the bird is really large, that is above 18lb or 9 kilos, reduce the heat after the first hour to cool, 300 deg F or gas 2 (150 deg C).
13. Baste the bird after the first hour.
14. Half an hour before the end of the cooking time remove the foil and bacon so the skin can brown. Place pricked sausages around the turkey.
15. Transfer the cooked turkey to a plate and surround with the sausages. Leave in a warm place while making the gravy.
16. Drain almost all the fat from the tin leaving about 1 tablespoon.
17. Stir in the flour then gradually blend in the stock.
18. Place the tin over the heat, and stirring all the time, bring the gravy to the boil.
19. Check it for seasoning before pouring it into a gravy boat.
20. Serve the turkey garnished with watercress.

BOILED BACON
Serves 6

1 piece bacon collar (4lb or 2 kilo)
6 peppercorns
1 bayleaf
2oz (50gm) dried breadcrumbs

1. Soak the bacon in cold water for 24 hours, changing the water occasionally.
2. Weigh the joint and calculate the cooking time allowing 20 minutes to the lb (½ kilo) plus 20 minutes.
3. Put the bacon into a large pan, add the peppercorns and bayleaf and enough water to completely cover the joint.
4. Bring the water slowly to the boil uncovered. Then cover the pan and simmer the joint for the calculated cooking time. (Keep the water only at simmering point. If it boils the meat will only toughen.)
5. When the bacon is cooked, remove it from the water.
6. Peel off the skin carefully, then press the crumbs into the fat under the skin.
7. Serve hot or cold.

ROAST POTATOES AND ROAST PARSNIPS
Serves 6

2lb (1 kilo) potatoes
1½lb (¾ kilo) parsnips
2oz (50gm) lard or dripping

1. Preheat oven to moderate, 350 deg F or gas 4 (180 deg C).
2. Wash and peel the potatoes and parsnips.
3. Place in a pan of cold, salted water, bring to the boil and simmer for 5 minutes.
4. Place the fat in a roasting pan and put it in the oven to melt.
5. Drain the potatoes and parsnips then, holding each in turn in a clean teatowel, scrape the surface with the prongs of a fork – this helps to make them crisp.
6. Place the parsnips and potatoes into the pan of melted fat and baste them all thoroughly.
7. Place the pan above the turkey and cook the vegetables for 1½ hours, until crisp and golden.
8. Place in a tureen for serving.

BRUSSELS SPROUTS
Serves 6

1. Trim off the stalks from 2lb (1 kilo) Brussels sprouts and remove any damaged leaves.
2. Wash thoroughly.
3. Cook the Brussels sprouts in a pan of boiling, salted water, uncovered for about 10 minutes, or until they are just tender.
4. Drain well and toss in melted butter before serving in a tureen.

BUTTERED CARROTS
Serves 6

1. Peel $1\frac{1}{2}$lb ($\frac{3}{4}$ kilo) carrots and cut them into rings. Rinse in cold water.
2. Cook in boiling, salted water for 7–10 minutes.
3. Drain well then toss in melted butter and chopped parsley.

BREAD SAUCE
Serves 6

1 onion, stuck with 8 cloves
$\frac{3}{4}$ pint (375ml) milk
4oz (100gm) stale bread, crusts removed
pinch of ground mace
$\frac{1}{2}$oz (12gm) butter
salt and pepper

1. Put the onion into a pan with the milk and gently heat it.
2. Break the bread into small pieces and place it in the pan.
3. Cover the pan and leave it to soak for at least 1 hour.
4. Stir in the mace and butter and season the sauce to taste.
5. Bring the sauce to the boil, stirring it occasionally.
6. Remove the onion and cloves and, with a fork, beat the sauce until it is smooth.
7. Check again for seasoning before turning it into a small dish for serving.

CRANBERRY SAUCE
Serves 6

4oz (100gm) cranberries
$\frac{1}{4}$ pint (125ml) water
3–4oz (75–100gm) caster sugar

1. Place the cranberries in a pan with the water and simmer until tender and the liquid is slightly reduced.
2. Stir in sugar to taste.
3. Turn the sauce into a small dish for serving.

CHRISTMAS PUDDING
Serves 6–8

These ingredients make either 1 large pudding, cooked in a 3-pint (approximately $1\frac{1}{2}$-litre) basin or 2 smaller ones. Make the pudding on one day then steam it on the next.

8oz (200gm) currants
8oz (200gm) sultanas
8oz (200gm) stoned raisins, chopped
4oz (100gm) chopped mixed peel
8oz (200gm) fresh white breadcrumbs
8oz (200gm) demerara sugar
8oz (200gm) shredded suet
finely grated rind and juice of 1 lemon
4oz (100gm) blanched almonds, chopped
8oz (200gm) plain flour
pinch of salt
1 level teaspoon ground nutmeg
1 level teaspoon ground cinnamon
1 level teaspoon mixed spice
3 large eggs
$\frac{1}{2}$ pint (250ml) stout

1. Mix the currants, sultanas, raisins and peel together in a large basin.
2. Stir in the breadcrumbs, sugar, suet, lemon rind and almonds.
3. Sift the flour, salt and spices together.
4. Beat the eggs and add the lemon juice and stout to them.
5. Mix the flour and the egg mixtures into the other ingredients.
6. Cover the bowl and leave it overnight.
7. Next day brush the basin with melted fat and fill it with the pudding mixture.
8. Take a large sheet of double greaseproof paper, brush it with fat, make a pleat down the centre then tie it over the bowl with string.
9. Steam the large pudding for 8 hours or the smaller ones for at least 6 hours.
10. When the pudding is cold replace the greaseproof paper and store it in a cool dry place until required.

On Christmas morning if you have not already done so, cover the pudding with a double layer of greaseproof paper. Then:
1. Tie the paper in position with string, making a handle over the top so the pudding can easily be removed from the steamer.
2. Put it into the steamer so it steams for at least 2 hours, replenishing the water with boiling water when necessary.
3. To serve, remove the paper, loosen the pudding from the bowl and turn it on to a plate.
4. Sprinkle a little rum or brandy over the top and quickly set the alcohol alight.
5. Serve the pudding with brandy butter or sharp lemon sauce.

BRANDY BUTTER
Serves 6

4oz (100gm) slightly salted butter
pinch of ground nutmeg
grated rind of 1 lemon
8oz (200gm) icing sugar, sifted
2 tablespoons brandy

1. Beat the butter until soft and fluffy then beat in the nutmeg and lemon rind.
2. Add the sifted icing sugar with the brandy, gradually, beating well between each addition.
3. When it has all been incorporated, turn the butter into a small dish and leave it in a cool place until required. (The brandy butter will keep for at least 1 week, so it can be made in advance of the festivities.)

SHARP LEMON SAUCE
Makes about ½ pint (250ml)

Serve this as an alternative to the brandy butter, which some people find too rich.

3oz (75gm) caster sugar
2 level tablespoons cornflour
pinch of salt
¼ pint (125ml) plus 4 tablespoons water
1 large egg
grated rind and juice of 1 lemon
1oz (25gm) butter

1. Blend the sugar, cornflour and salt in a pan with a little of the water.
2. Put the pan over a low heat and, stirring all the time, bring it to the boil.
3. Boil the sauce for 3 minutes, until it is smooth and clear.
4. Remove the pan from the heat.
5. Beat the egg in a small bowl with the lemon juice and rind.
6. Blend in a little of the cornflour sauce then return it all to the pan.
7. Stir the egg into the cornflour sauce thoroughly and slowly bring just to the boil, stirring continuously.
8. Turn off the heat, stir in the butter and when it has melted serve the sauce immediately.

HOLLY PUDDING
Serves 6

Serve this as an alternative to Christmas pudding.

2 oranges
2 bananas
1 small can pineapple tidbits
1 level tablespoon soft brown sugar
2 tablespoons rum
6 level tablespoons custard powder
1 pint (approximately ½ litre) milk
¼ pint (125ml) single cream
½oz (12gm) powdered gelatine
2 tablespoons cold water
2oz (50gm) desiccated coconut
sugar to taste

1. Peel and slice the oranges and the bananas and place them in a bowl with the drained pineapple.
2. Add the soft brown sugar and the rum and leave the mixture in a cool place to soak.
3. Blend the custard powder with a little of the milk in a pan, then stir in the rest.
4. Place the pan over the heat and, stirring all the time, bring it to the boil. Cook until thickened.
5. Remove the pan from the heat and pour the cream on top to prevent a skin forming.
6. Leave the custard to cool.
7. Put the gelatine into a small pan with the water and, over a low heat, melt the gelatine.
8. Stir into the custard and mix in the coconut and enough sugar to taste.
9. Stir in the fruits and any juice they have formed then turn the pudding into a dish.
10. Leave it in a cool place to set and decorate with a sprig of holly before serving.

BOXING DAY

For some people the thought of eating turkey again is unwelcome on Boxing Day, but with so much meat in the larder it must be used somehow. This is why I have devised the following recipe – it uses not only the turkey meat but some cold sausages as well and is really very tasty served with the suggested vegetables and a fresh fruit salad to follow – what could be nicer?

MENU
Serves 6

Turkey pie
Sauté potatoes
Garden peas (see page 10)

Fresh fruit salad
Mince pies

TURKEY PIE
Serves 8–10

shortcrust pastry made with 12oz (300gm) flour (see Basic recipes, page 100)
6 cold cooked sausages
1½lb (¾ kilo) cooked turkey meat
4oz (100gm) cooked long-grain rice (raw weight)
grated rind of 1 lemon
1 small onion, peeled and chopped
salt and pepper
¼ pint (125ml) stock
8oz (200gm) tomatoes, skinned and sliced
2 hard-boiled eggs
little beaten egg to glaze

1. Preheat oven to moderate to moderately hot, 400 deg F or gas 6 (200 deg C).
2. Cut off a quarter of the pastry for the lid.
3. Roll the rest of the pastry into a large circle and use to line the base and sides of an 8-inch (20-cm) loose-bottomed cake tin.
4. Lay the sausages in the base of the tin.
5. Chop the turkey meat and mix it into the rice with the lemon rind, chopped onion and salt and pepper.
6. Stir in the stock.
7. Place half this filling in the pie over the sausages.
8. Lay the tomatoes on top with the hard-boiled eggs, shelled and sliced.
9. Spread the rest of the filling on top of the eggs.
10. Roll the reserved pastry out for the lid.
11. Damp the edges, lift the lid into place and seal the edges firmly together.
12. Trim the pie then decorate with any pastry scraps.
13. Brush the top with egg glaze and make a hole in the centre.
14. Bake in the centre of the oven for 40 minutes, then reduce the heat to moderate 350 deg F or gas 4 (180 deg C) for a further hour, or until the pastry is golden brown.

SAUTE POTATOES

Serves 6

If you have several roast potatoes left from the Christmas lunch, a good way of using them is to add them, sliced, to the sauté potatoes as they start to cook.

2lb (1 kilo) potatoes
3 tablespoons cooking oil
1½oz (37gm) butter
salt and pepper
1 level dessertspoon chopped parsley

1. Scrub the potatoes then cook for 25 minutes, in their skins, until tender.
2. Drain thoroughly then peel and slice them.
3. Heat a frying pan, add the oil then the butter.
4. When the butter has melted, add the potatoes.
5. Sprinkle over the seasoning, then keep turning the potatoes until they are golden brown and crisp.
6. Remove from the heat, sprinkle over the parsley and turn the potatoes into a serving dish.

FRESH FRUIT SALAD

Serves 6

3 oranges
1 lemon
12oz (300gm) granulated sugar
1 pint (approximately ½ litre) water
4oz (100gm) black grapes
4oz (100gm) green grapes
1 pear
1 red-skinned apple
1 green-skinned apple
2 bananas

1. The syrup can be made before Christmas and stored in a cool place. Using a potato peeler, remove the rind from 1 orange and the lemon, taking as little of the white pith as possible.
2. Put the rind into a saucepan with the sugar and water.
3. Place the pan over a low heat and dissolve the sugar.
4. When the sugar has melted bring the syrup to the boil and boil rapidly for 3 minutes.
5. Strain it into a basin and leave to cool. When the syrup is to be used, stir in the juice from the rindless orange and lemon and turn the syrup into a large mixing bowl.
6. Using a sharp knife, cut the skin from the remaining 2 oranges in a spiral fashion, keeping the knife between the fruit and the white pith and using a sawing action as you work.
7. Cut the oranges into thin slices and add them to the bowl of syrup.
8. Wash the grapes, cut them in half and remove the pips before adding them to the bowl.
9. Peel, quarter and core the pear, then cut it into slices. Add them to the bowl.
10. Wipe the apples, cut them in quarters, remove the cores then slice them and stir into the bowl.
11. Leave the fruit salad in a cool place for a few hours so the flavours can combine.
12. Peel and slice the bananas and add them at the last moment.
13. Serve the fruit salad with single cream.

MINCE PIES

Makes 16

shortcrust pastry made with 8oz (200gm) flour (see Basic recipes, page 100)
1lb (½ kilo) mincemeat
icing sugar to sprinkle

1. Preheat oven to moderate to moderately hot, 400 deg F or gas 6 (200 deg C).
2. Roll half the pastry out to an ⅛-inch thickness and cut out 16 rounds using a 3-inch (7·5-cm) fluted cutter.
3. Press these into tartlet tins.
4. Fill each with 1 teaspoonful of mincemeat.
5. Roll out the remaining pastry and cut out the smaller rounds for the tops.
6. Moisten the rims of the pies then press the tops securely into position.
7. Make a hole in the centre of each with a skewer.
8. Bake in the centre of the oven for 20 minutes.
9. Dust with icing sugar, then serve them warm with any brandy butter left from the Christmas lunch.

NEW YEAR'S EVE PARTY

Greet your friends as they arrive with a glass of mulled wine – it will be very welcome on a cold winter's night. Start the party with a choice of dips, then serve one substantial dish for the main course and finish with fruit gâteaux or a cheese board. Also included is a cold, wine-based punch to drink throughout the meal. The party is for 20 people.

MENU
Serves 20

Mulled wine

Indian dip
Spicy ham dip

Midnight spaghetti
Mimosa salad
Cucumber salad

Fruit gâteaux
Cheese board

Twelve o'clock punch

MULLED WINE

Gives 20 glasses

1 pint (approximately ½ litre) cold water
3-inch cinnamon stick
1 level teaspoon ground nutmeg
3oz (75gm) demerara sugar
2 oranges
3 bottles Spanish Burgundy wine or 1 jar (½ gallon or approximately 2¼ litres)

1. Put the water, cinnamon stick, nutmeg and sugar into a pan.
2. Peel the rind from the oranges with a potato peeler and add it to the pan with the orange juice.
3. Put the pan over a low heat and dissolve the sugar.
4. When all the grains have dissolved, bring the syrup to the boil then remove the pan from the heat.
5. Leave it on one side for all the flavours to infuse – this takes about 15 minutes.
6. Add the wine, return the pan to the heat and, very slowly, warm the drink. Do not allow it to boil.
7. Keep on a low heat until required and serve in warm glasses.

INDIAN DIP

Serves 15

½ pint (250ml) mayonnaise (see Basic recipes, page 100)
1 level tablespoon curry paste
1 large cooking apple
2oz (50gm) sultanas
2 hard-boiled eggs
little lemon juice
salt and pepper

1. Put the mayonnaise into a bowl and stir in the curry paste.
2. Peel, core, then coarsely grate the apple and add it to the curry mayonnaise with the sultanas.
3. Shell the eggs, cut them in half and, using a potato masher, chop them finely.
4. Stir the chopped eggs into the dip, with the lemon juice, and check it for seasoning.
5. Turn into a bowl and serve with small biscuits or cubes of bread. Have cocktail sticks at hand for dipping the bread.

SPICY HAM DIP

Serves 15

8oz (200gm) cream cheese
2 level tablespoons tomato purée
6oz (150gm) ham, minced
dash of Worcestershire sauce
dash of Tabasco sauce
salt and pepper

1. Beat the cream cheese until it is soft.
2. Stir in the tomato purée with the ham.
3. Finally mix in the Worcestershire sauce, Tabasco sauce and salt and pepper.
4. Check the flavour before turning the dip into a small bowl for serving.
5. Serve with a selection of vegetables, cut into convenient sizes, such as carrots, celery, cauliflower sprigs, etc.

MIDNIGHT SPAGHETTI

Serves 20

3oz (75gm) margarine
3oz (75gm) lard
2lb (1 kilo) onions
12oz (300gm) streaky bacon rashers, chopped
8oz (200gm) mushrooms, sliced
2 large cans tomatoes (each 2lb 3oz or approximately 1 kilo)
1 large can tomato soup
1 level dessertspoon mixed herbs
2lb (1 kilo) short-cut spaghetti
4 tablespoons oil
salt and pepper
pinch of ground nutmeg
5lb (2½ kilo) cooked turkey or chicken meat
1½lb (¾ kilo) cooked chipolata sausages
grated Parmesan cheese

1. Melt the margarine and lard in a large pan.
2. Peel and slice the onions and add to the melted fat.
3. Fry the onions slowly so they cook but do not colour.
4. Add the bacon and mushrooms to the onions, when tender, and cook together for a few more minutes.
5. Stir in the tomatoes, with their juice, the soup and mixed herbs.
6. Bring the mixture to the boil and boil it rapidly without a lid for 15–20 minutes, or until it becomes thicker, stirring occasionally.
7. Meanwhile cook the spaghetti in a large pan of boiling salted water, for about 15 minutes.
8. Drain it thoroughly and run hot water through the strands to keep them separate.
9. Heat the oil in the pan with pepper and nutmeg then return the spaghetti to it, put the lid on and toss the pasta in the oil.
10. Stir the meat and sausages into the sauce and heat them through for about 5–10 minutes.
11. Heap the spaghetti on to a large or two smaller serving dishes and pile the meat sauce down the centre.
12. Serve with Parmesan cheese.

To freeze: the sauce and meats can be frozen separately – they will keep for 2–3 months. To thaw, remove from the freezer at least 24 hours before the party and thaw slowly. Heat the sauce first, thoroughly, before adding the meats.

MIMOSA SALAD
Serves 15

2 lettuces
1 red pepper
French dressing (see Basic recipes, page 100)
1 hard-boiled egg

1. Wash the lettuce, dry the leaves and shred them finely.
2. Cut the pepper in half, remove the core and seeds and cut the flesh into thin strips.
3. Blanch them in boiling water for 1 minute then transfer immediately to cold water and drain.
4. Mix the lettuce and pepper together then toss in the French dressing.
5. Place the salad on a serving dish.
6. Shell the egg, rub it through a sieve and sprinkle it down the centre of the salad before serving.

CUCUMBER SALAD
Serves 15

1 cucumber
salt
little French dressing (see Basic recipes, page 100)
chopped mint if available

1. Peel and thinly slice the cucumber. (A potato peeler is the ideal utensil for this job.)
2. Lay the slices in a shallow dish and sprinkle them with salt.
3. Leave the dish in a cool place for at least 1 hour for the salt to extract as much liquid as possible.
4. Drain off the water and pat the slices dry.
5. Sprinkle over the French dressing, just enough to moisten the surface and sprinkle over a little chopped mint if available.

FRUIT GATEAUX

For 20 people make either three 10-inch (25-cm) sponges or four 8-inch (20-cm) sponges. For a 10-inch sponge use the quantities below; for an 8-inch one use a 2 egg mixture and cook the cake for 20 minutes.

3 standard eggs
3oz (75gm) caster sugar
3oz (75gm) plain flour
1 level teaspoon baking powder
¼ pint (125ml) double cream
2oz (50gm) grated chocolate or desiccated coconut, browned
1 large can pineapple rings and 1 can red cherries, stoned or 8oz (200gm) black and white grapes, 1 can apricot halves and 1 small orange, peeled and segmented or
1 can peach slices and 8oz (200gm) strawberries
¼ pint (125ml) canned fruit juice
2 level teaspoons arrowroot

1. Preheat oven to moderate to moderately hot, 375 deg F or gas 5 (190 deg C).
2. Brush a 10-inch (25-cm) sponge tin with melted fat and line the base with a circle of greaseproof paper cut to fit. Brush the paper lining.
3. Break the eggs into a mixing bowl and add the sugar.
4. Place the bowl over a pan of hot water and, using a wire or rotary whisk, whip the ingredients together until very thick and creamy.
5. The whisk, when lifted out of the mixture, should leave a definite trail.
6. Take the bowl off the saucepan and whisk the mixture for a further 1 minute.
7. Sift the flour and baking powder together and, using a metal spoon, fold them lightly and quickly into the mixture.
8. Turn it into the tin, level the surface then bake in the centre of the oven for 25 minutes, or until it starts to shrink away from the sides of the tin. Cool on a wire tray.
9. Whip the double cream and spread a little around the side of the sponge.
10. Put the chocolate or coconut on to a piece of paper and roll the sponge in them so they adhere to the sides.
11. Stand the cake on a serving plate and decorate the top of the sponge with one of the suggested groups of fruit.
12. Put the rest of the cream into a piping bag and pipe it around the top edge.
13. Blend the arrowroot with a little water to form a smooth paste.
14. Stir in the fruit juice then, over a gentle heat and stirring all the time, bring the glaze to the boil when it will clear.
15. Allow to cool, then spoon it over the fruit so it is completely coated.

To freeze: place the undecorated sponges, separately, in polythene bags; seal and label. Store for 3 months. Thaw overnight.

CHEESE BOARD

Serve a cheese board that has a selection of cheese with different flavours, textures and colours. Arrange them attractively with grapes, apples, plums and nuts if they are available. Hand round a selection of biscuits and crispbread and do not forget the butter. Store the cheeses, wrapped in polythene or greaseproof paper and foil in a cool place, such as a larder or refrigerator, but remove them at least an hour before they are to be served.

TWELVE O'CLOCK PUNCH
Gives 30 glasses

½ gallon (approximately 2¼ litres) rosé wine
1 pint (approximately ½ litre) apple juice
2 pints (approximately 1 litre) soda water
1 red-skinned apple
1 green-skinned apple
ice cubes

1. Mix the wine and apple juice together.
2. Just before serving, stir in the soda water and float the apple slices on top.
3. Add ice cubes to cool the drink.

Basic recipes

FRENCH DRESSING

4 tablespoons olive oil
½ level teaspoon salt
¼ level teaspoon caster sugar
½ level teaspoon freshly ground pepper
2 tablespoons white wine vinegar

1. Put oil into a basin and add salt, sugar and pepper.
2. Whisk in the vinegar drop by drop and continue beating until mixture thickens slightly.

Variations
Add a few chopped fresh herbs, a little crushed garlic or a dash of mustard etc.

ASPIC JELLY
Makes ½ pint or 250ml

½oz (12gm) gelatine
½ pint (250ml) boiling water
¼oz (6gm) caster sugar
½ level teaspoon salt
2 tablespoons tarragon vinegar
2 tablespoons lemon juice

1. Dissolve gelatine in boiling water. Add all other ingredients.
2. Leave to cool and thicken.
3. Use as required either before or after it has set as the recipe demands.

Note
Alternatively, thicken a can of consommé with approximately 2 teaspoons gelatine. Or dilute clear meat extract or a bouillon cube with ½ pint (250ml) water and add approximately 2 teaspoons gelatine.

MAYONNAISE
Makes ¾ pint (375ml)

3 egg yolks
3 level teaspoons French mustard
good pinch of caster sugar
salt and pepper
¾ pint (375ml) oil
about 2 tablespoons distilled white vinegar

1. Put the egg yolks into a bowl with the mustard, sugar, salt and pepper.
2. Measure the oil into a jug, then add a drop at a time to the yolks, beating all the time with a wooden spoon.
3. When the mayonnaise starts to thicken the oil can be added a little more quickly.
4. When it is really thick, add a little vinegar to thin it to the right consistency.
5. Check the mayonnaise for seasoning then store it in a screw-topped jar in a cool place until it is required.
6. To make the mayonnaise in a liquidizer, put the *whole* eggs into the goblet with the mustard, sugar, salt and pepper.
7. Blend the ingredients together for a few seconds then add the oil in a steady thin stream.
8. As it starts to thicken add the oil more quickly then adjust the consistency with the vinegar.

WHITE SAUCE
Makes ½ pint or 250ml

½oz (12gm) butter or margarine
½oz (12gm) flour
½ pint (250ml) cold milk (or milk and stock or water mixed)
salt and pepper

1. Melt the butter or margarine in a pan over a gentle heat.
2. Stir in flour and cook without browning for 2 minutes, stirring all the time.
3. Remove pan from heat and gradually beat in the liquid. Alternatively, add all the liquid and whisk thoroughly.
4. Return to heat and bring to boil, stirring well. Simmer gently for 2–3 minutes and add seasoning. If sauce is to be kept, cover it with greaseproof paper or foil to prevent a skin forming.

THICK WHITE SAUCE
Makes ½ pint or 250ml

Make exactly as for white sauce, above, but double the quantities of butter or margarine and flour used.

CHEESE SAUCE
Makes ½ pint or 250ml

Make up ½ pint (250ml) white sauce (see this page). After sauce has come to the boil and thickened, add 2–4oz (50–100gm) grated cheese and ½ level teaspoon mustard. Stir sauce over low heat until cheese melts.

SHORTCRUST PASTRY

Makes 8oz or 200gm pastry

8oz (200gm) plain flour
1 level teaspoon salt
2oz (50gm) lard
2oz (50gm) butter or margarine
cold water to mix

1. Sift flour and salt into a bowl.
2. Cut fats into flour with a knife.
3. Rub fats into flour with fingertips until mixture resembles fine breadcrumbs.
4. Add water little by little, stirring with a knife until mixture forms large lumps.
5. Bring mixture together with fingertips and knead lightly into a ball.
6. Roll out briskly on a floured board. Avoid stretching the pastry.

Note
Baking temperature: moderately hot, 400 deg F or gas 6 (200 deg C).

CHEESE PASTRY

Makes 8oz or 200gm pastry

Use for savoury pies, canapé bases, cheese straws and savoury flans.

8oz (200gm) self-raising flour
1 level teaspoon salt
pinch of cayenne pepper
2oz (50gm) lard
2oz (50gm) butter or margarine
5oz (125gm) cheese, grated
1–2 egg yolks
cold water to mix

1. Sift flour, salt and pepper into a bowl.
2. Cut fats into flour with a knife.
3. Rub fats into flour with fingertips until mixture resembles fine breadcrumbs. Add cheese.
4. Mix in egg, then add water little by little, stirring with a knife until mixture forms large lumps.
5. Bring mixture together with fingertips and knead lightly into a ball.
6. Roll out briskly on a floured board. Avoid stretching the pastry.

Note
Baking temperature: moderate, 350 deg F or gas 4 (180 deg C).

FLAKY PASTRY

Makes 8oz or 200gm pastry

Use for pies, vanilla slices, sausage rolls.

8oz (200gm) plain flour
1 level teaspoon salt
3oz (75gm) lard
3oz (75gm) butter or margarine
1 teaspoon lemon juice
water to mix

1. Sift flour and salt into a bowl. Blend the fats on a plate and mark into four portions.
2. Rub one portion into the flour until it resembles fine breadcrumbs.
3. Mix to a smooth dough with lemon juice and water.
4. Knead dough lightly and roll it out on a floured surface into an oblong.
5. Dot two-thirds of the pastry with second portion of fat.
6. Fold the bottom third up and the top third over into an envelope shape.
7. Allow pastry to relax for 10 minutes in a cold place. This is especially important in warm weather.
8. Repeat the whole process until all the fat is used up.
9. Fold pastry in two, roll out to $\frac{1}{4}$–$\frac{1}{2}$ inch thick and use as required.

Note
Baking temperature: hot, 425 deg F or gas 7 (220 deg C).

Note
When using metric measures for your pastry it will be necessary to increase the amount of flour to 225gm and other ingredients proportionately, as 1oz is equal to 28·35gm.

PUFF PASTRY

Makes 8oz or 200gm pastry

Use for vol au vents, bouchée cases, patties, mille feuilles, palmiers. It is essential to keep everything including hands very cold for this pastry.

8oz (200gm) plain flour
$\frac{1}{2}$ level teaspoon salt
8oz (200gm) unsalted butter in a block or 4oz (100gm) cooking fat and 4oz (100gm) margarine mashed and formed into a block
2 teaspoons lemon juice
6–8 tablespoons very cold water

1. Sift flour and salt into a bowl.
2. Chill the fat if soft. Rub $\frac{1}{2}$oz (12gm) fat into flour.
3. Mix to a dough with lemon juice and water.
4. Roll out dough to twice the length of the block of fat. Place fat on dough and fold dough down over it, sealing edges well with a rolling pin.
5. Give pastry one half turn and roll gently out into a long strip.
6. Fold dough in three, envelope style, and leave, covered, in a cold place for 30 minutes.
7. Repeat turning, rolling and folding six times.
8. Leave pastry to relax for 30 minutes between rollings and before use.

Note
Baking temperature: hot, 450 deg F or gas 8 (230 deg C).

PANCAKE BATTER

Makes $\frac{1}{2}$ pint or 250ml

4oz (100gm) plain flour
pinch of salt
1 egg
$\frac{1}{2}$ pint (250ml) cold milk
1 tablespoon oil

1. Sift flour and salt into a bowl.
2. Make a well in the centre and break egg into it.
3. Gradually beat in half the milk and continue beating until batter is smooth.
4. Fold in rest of milk with oil.

Index

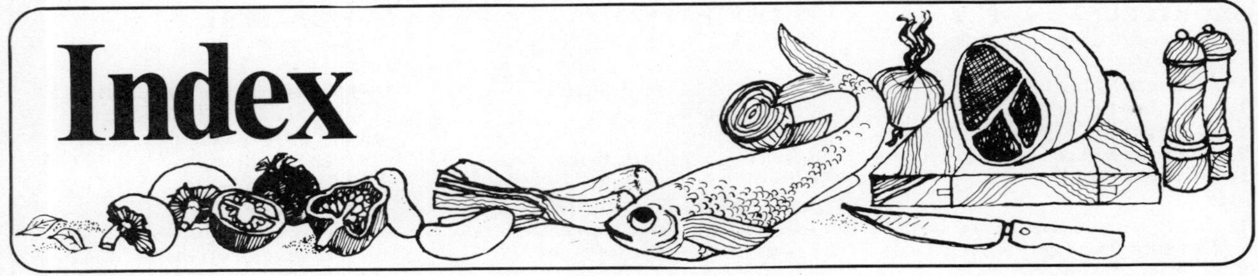